ILLUSIONS

Biography of a High Class Escort

Order this book online at www.trafford.com/08-0108
or email orders@trafford.com

Most Trafford titles are also available at major online book retailers.

Edited by Marilyn Conibear and Shirley Campbell.

Note for Librarians: A cataloguing record for this book is available from Library
and Archives Canada at www.collectionscanada.ca/amicus/index-e.html

Printed in Victoria, BC, Canada.

ISBN: 978-1-4251-6966-4

*We at Trafford believe that it is the responsibility of us all, as both individuals
and corporations, to make choices that are environmentally and socially sound.
You, in turn, are supporting this responsible conduct each time you purchase a
Trafford book, or make use of our publishing services. To find out how you are
helping, please visit www.trafford.com/responsiblepublishing.html*

*Our mission is to efficiently provide the world's finest, most comprehensive
book publishing service, enabling every author to experience success.
To find out how to publish your book, your way, and have it available
worldwide, visit us online at www.trafford.com/10510*

 www.trafford.com

North America & international
toll-free: 1 888 232 4444 (USA & Canada)
phone: 250 383 6864 ♦ fax: 250 383 6804 ♦ email: info@trafford.com

The United Kingdom & Europe
phone: +44 (0)1865 722 113 ♦ local rate: 0845 230 9601
facsimile: +44 (0)1865 722 868 ♦ email: info.uk@trafford.com

10 9 8 7 6 5 4 3

To Melissa,

Hope you won't !!
be shocked..!

Ellen Thomsen

ILLUSIONS

Biography of a High Class Escort

As told to and written by

Ellen Thomsen

Disclaimer

All the e-mails, personal narratives, descriptions and explanations throughout this biography are authentic. In order to protect the privacy and anonymity of all persons mentioned, not only are all personal names changed, but also occupations, cities, geographical sites and sometimes even countries. On rare occasions the narrative of the e-mails were changed somewhat to protect an individual's identity, but the content remains true.

Front and back cover photos are courtesy of Elysia's modeling shoes and lingerie given to her by clients

Author's Notes

I first met Elysia through a mutual friend and knew her casually for about two years before I realized she was an escort working in the sex trade. There was no reason to suspect her. On the occasional times I saw her, we chatted informally as all women do. She was always the most stunningly beautiful woman present, but that was the only noticeable difference. Eventually over time as our conversations developed, I realized she maintained a closely guarded secret life. I mentioned to my friend that Elysia's story would be interesting to record. A week later Elysia asked me to write her biography.

To maintain her privacy for the purposes of this biography, she chose the name Elysia. She patterned it from the word for the mythical Greek paradise, Elysium. Elysia understands how to take a man to paradise. She was equally scrupulous in keeping private the identities of the men who bought her services. As a result she could be completely open with me, even about being dishonest when she was a 'service provider," an 'escort,' or a 'working girl,' as most prostitutes call themselves. In our three years of conversations, she freely discussed all aspects of both her private and professional life.

I learned there are levels of prostitutes and Elysia was at the top. Her high class level is very different from a street hooker. I was aware of the usual stereotypes when it came to prostitutes, but one of the most important things I learned was that they do not want to be pitied. They do not all feel they have to be 'saved' either. At Elysia's level at least, they have chosen prostitution as their vocation. They view sex as a basic human function where a man's insatiable biological desire provides working girls with a living. As an escort Elysia treated sex as professional granting of sexual pleasure that had nothing to do with romantic love, her own womanhood, nor her personal sexuality. She fulfilled a need and made a lot of money at it. In fact, the moral judgement of others bothered Elysia more than the sex she performed for hire. Indeed, we discussed how some very respectable women marry, and stay married solely for financial gain. As Elysia said, "Women pick and choose their pressures."

Most of our conversations took place in her apartment, which was immaculately clean and organized. She had tastefully decorated it, and her clients had bought much of the furniture as presents. She picked it out and they bought it. She had an expensive stereo, plush couches and chairs, high end ornately carved wooden tables, a computer, ski equipment, a guitar, a car, and even a fully decorated live Christmas tree delivered to her by a client. As far as I could tell, the men were so in love with her, or the idea of her, that they would do anything to please her.

After many months of conversations with her, I became curious to gain more insight into the psychology of the men (clients, johns, or tricks as she interchangeably called them) who hired her. When I suggested interviewing some of them, Elysia was confident they would cooperate provided we guaranteed their anonymity and privacy. When I expressed my amazement, especially when they learned it was for a biography to be published, she said, "Oh, I can get them to do that." She was right! She simply made the request during one of the their sessions. Their high regard and trust in Elysia certainly played a role, but she has a sixth sense about men and she knew whom and when to ask.

E-mail:
From: Tom
To: Elysia
Subject: Blissful, blissful
Dear Elysia,
After I left you on Friday, I was flying home reflecting back on the last hour, almost subconsciously, gradually, noticing the sky was at a beautiful stage of twilight. I realized I hadn't even turned on the music yet. So, I put on some jazz on the CD changer and just enjoyed the feeling. Yes, my Elysia, you worked your extraordinary magic again.
You mentioned you might give "Ellen" my e-mail address in case I might be able to offer something that might help in the book she is writing about you, Hey, how many people can really say they saved someone's life? This might be an angle! I feel 'saving a life' means saving someone from a premature death. While not as immediately noticeable as say, saving someone from drowning, my major weight loss did the same for me I am sure. As I told you before, you were the catalyst for this. Don't get me wrong, even before I wasn't in immediate danger of a heart attack or something, but,

down the road, who knows what may have happened. I would be glad to
talk to Ellen (e-mail or otherwise) if desired.
Well, I am eagerly anticipating our next meeting.
Love, Tom

My interviews with her clients revealed that, for the most part, they ignored the reality that Elysia was performing a job. She was so good at making their fantasies reality that they 'forgot' they had hired a prostitute. They certainly didn't want to think of themselves as a 'trick' in her business. If the men felt she was conning them, she made them feel so good that they didn't care. Over time many of her clients blurred the distinction between the escort they were paying for and the woman they wanted to relate to. They were basically unaware of who she was in her daily 'real' life.

Elysia's personal life was equally paradoxical. She went to great lengths to try to keep her working life a secret from her family. She also found difficulty in managing her personal social relationships in tandem with her working relationships. Dating a man she liked while making a living selling sex was an uncomfortable scenario, whether he knew about her profession or not. During one period Elysia found happiness in a ménage à trois, which she did not keep secret from family and friends. Although at times overwhelmed by negative reactions, she said, "Well, I suppose it is fascinating to see the obvious affection in a threesome relationship. But lots of men accommodate two women: a wife and a lover. They don't usually know each other. We happened to know each other very well."

* * *

My appreciation and special thanks to my children, to editor Marilyn Conibear and author/editor Shirley Campbell for their help and support, and a special hug to Bill Cady for his kindness, laughter, and insight for living life well. If these people could be cloned, the world would be a much better place.

One

LADY OF THE NIGHT

I am a prostitute, though I never call myself that. People usually associate the word prostitute with sleazy, dysfunctional women who stand on street corners trying to earn money for drugs. I am a high-class professional escort. It's a service profession that some very respectable men enjoy. I give men what they need ... for money. I'm very good at it.

North Americans, and most of the world, may accept prostitution as the world's oldest profession, but generally won't recognize it as a legal, respected profession. More typically it is viewed as some kind of perversion or sexual deviance. Sometimes that bothers me. People's respect for me and my profession is a juggling of judgment with varying standards as perceived from person to person. I take full responsibility for the flow of events that led me to being a professional escort. I have not lost my soul or my honorable spirit. Through this book you will learn just how human I am, and that my professional life is just one side of me. Perhaps in sharing my life with you, we will both learn something.

I will begin by telling about the 'me' who is a professional escort. The journey through my private life comes later. People have a fascination with the details of 'hookerdom' and how escorts handle intimacy with so many men. It's all about earning a living. I suppose some escorts do what I do with rich men for a slim hope of marriage, for paid vacations, or occasionally for a good fuck. I do it for the cash. It's much more realistic. And if that's the draw, being a high-class escort pays better. I decided early that if I was going to do it, I wasn't going to work for a hooker's minimum wage.

Do I enjoy hooking? **Absolutely.** Well, let me confess there are parts I'd rather skip. The truth is I'm addicted to the money, the power and the total control. From start to finish, I say when, how much, and what's going to happen. From the first contact until he walks out the door, I'm the boss. It's amazing how much power I command because men desire me. To me, it's all about the money. To them, the experience is more important than the money. They will give me whatever I want. I totally enjoy that power. And the money makes me appear to be somebody who is powerful because I can buy whatever I want to make me look and feel like a million bucks. I have expensive jewelry with every kind of stone you can think of; a sporty car, a nice place to live and expensive furniture. I know all this stuff doesn't make me who I am. It's layers on top of who I really am. Being a high-class escort is what I do, but this job doesn't define who Elysia really is.

I am well aware of the stereotype out there that all hookers, escorts, or working girls (as most prefer to be called) are drug addicts. A lot of them are. I was in the beginning but not now. Certainly not working at this high-class level, and that's the reason I am so expensive. If a man can afford $500 - $1,000 ++ bucks an hour, then that's the kind of guy I want to see. At that price, they don't want a drug addict ... they want a real dream. If they can only afford $50 to $150, then they will get the hookers working the street corners who are on drugs or have pimps or other problems.

How do I find my clients? Easy. Everyone uses the Internet these days, even escorts looking for johns. It all starts long before I ever see a client. I advertise on an Internet site in an escort listing. Anyone in the world can find this site if they know where to look. I post pictures of me in various poses to entice them and information about contacting me. Basically this is it:

Hello Gentlemen! My name is Elysia. I hope you have enjoyed my pictures and that you are sufficiently excited and intrigued. I am an independent gentlemen's companion and I provide an exclusive level of companionship to discerning gentlemen.

Allow me to introduce myself. I am proud to say that I am an authentic Canadian girl with an appetite for the fun and naughty! During our time together I will provide an hour of erotic entertainment in a relaxed, non-rushed and sensual environment. I come complete with luxurious long blonde hair, bright green eyes and soft sun-kissed skin. My body is tightly toned and my curves are totally touchable. I am sure that you will enjoy the delicious lingerie I wear, but you will love it even more as it slips to the floor before you. If only the best will do and you require a companion second to none, you have found who you are looking for! I am the perfect blonde

2

playmate just for you!

My rate is $500 (U.S.) cash an hour and it is non-negotiable. I don't take credit cards. If you are interested in getting to know me more intimately, I will require a reference from you to verify that you are a gentleman and not law enforcement. To confirm your appointment, please forward to me your name and a work number that I can call and VERY DISCREETLY ask for you. If you are not comfortable with this, I will accept a referral from another advertising provider. All my appointments are pre-arranged and I do not book appointments once I have arrived at my destination, so if you would like to make an appointment, please let me know what day and time works best for you.
Hugs and tickles, Elysia xoxo

Of course, I entice my regular clients with a more personal message about when I am working. I have many regulars who want to know when I am coming to their city.

E-mail:
To: Mr. Trick
From: Miss Elysia xoxo
Subject: Elysia here! :o)
Hello there again!
This is your favorite blonde sex kitten with some end of summer details! I will be coming into Atlanta for a couple of days for some fun and I would love to see you again. I thought we could enjoy some naked entertainment! I will be there in the late afternoon Wed. Sept. 19 until sometime on Friday afternoon Sept. 21. If you have some time and need to release some stress and enjoy yourself for awhile, please drop me a line and let me know what day and time works for you. I hope all is well with you!
Forever yours,
Elysia xoxo
P.S. Enjoy the pictures.

On my Internet advertisement, I list which cities I will be visiting and when, and I give my e-mail address. If a man is interested, he contacts me and introduces himself and is typically very friendly. Most men give me their real first and last name because they know I will be checking their references. A phony name won't check out, especially since I use 411 reverse look-up to verify their information. Then I start the seduction. I e-mail them sexy pictures. Sometimes they send me pictures of themselves. Sometimes I go into detail about a session. It usually depends on their response, my mood, and if I am in need of extra money.

E-mail:

From: A first timer
To: Elysia
Subject: meeting you!
Hi Sweetheart,
I would love to meet you in Victoria sometime. I live on an island but will come there to spend the night at the Hermosea Inn, which is my favorite place to stay. Is it possible that you could meet me there and spend a couple of hours with me? I would like that very much. What should I expect? Are you a GFE; Girlfriend Experience as in kissing and oral sex allowed, and FS, full sex? Because I would be interested in both. I would like to hear from you. Love, F.

From: Elysia xoxo
To: A first timer
Subject: re: meeting you!
Great to hear from you. Seems the rain has eased up and I can slow down production on my ark! :0) My rate per hour is $500, in cash of course. I usually provide the hotel room, but if you are going to take care of that I could lower my rate. Initially, I will be wearing something extremely hot and sexy for you so that when we sit and chat, perhaps with a drink, you can undress me with your eyes and imagine what all the curves I am concealing feel like! After some conversation and an adequate amount of teasing and torture, I will change into some lingerie. I have quite the collection of delicious gear! I love corsets and how my boobs pop out the top. I love garters and stockings and how they feel on my long legs, but I will wear whatever you like. I would love it if you slowly undress me, revealing my soft burning skin …. I will give you an awesome deep, sensual relaxing massage stimulating you with soft moaning and whispers in your ear while you throb to be inside of me. I am going to hungrily look into your eyes when I am going down on you, you will want to watch me because I love what I do! I like to start out on top, this hits all of my buttons! I will take you to the edge and make you look down. I like to have fun! I am definitely FS but not GFE, so if this is a must for you, perhaps I am not the girl for you. I hope that this helps you out in your search for the perfect O … yum!
Warmly, Elysia xoxo

From: A first timer
To: Elysia
Subject: Your Internet Ad
Hi Elysia,
Again, I am more than interested. If you could take a personal check or credit card, I would book 100%; otherwise, I would still be interested and look forward to hearing your thoughts? You are the most beautiful blonde I

have ever seen on these boards and websites. Love, F.

From: Elysia
To: A first timer
Subject: Hi Loverboy!
There you are again! :o) You're always so full of compliments and love ... It seems we are destined to be Internet lovers for a while longer. At this point I am unable to take credit cards. I would consider a personal cheque from you if we had some kind of history, but since I have never met you, I am sorry to say that it has to be cash. Let me know when you have some spare change :o). Have you ever considered a paper route, any spare pop bottles around, mowing the neighbor's lawn, do you own a squeegee? LOL :o) Keep in touch!
Love, Elysia

They will either reject me because of the price or because I am not GFE or they will write back and suggest a time to get together. GFE means girlfriend experience: includes kissing, oral sex with the escort allowing the man to go down on her and basically doing whatever he would do sexually with a girlfriend. For me, kissing is outlawed during work. It isn't with all girls. Most men who hire escorts know the women have boundaries. For me personally, it's about intimacy. Frankly, it would be gross. These men are clients. Some men pay the girls so they can go down on them. They want the GFE with nothing barred and everything permissible. On the web site where I advertise, I don't offer GFE. Who knows how many women he has been with or if he is bisexual, or has gum disease or cold sores? Who knows their health issues or where their mouths have been. Just think of the things an escort could pick up if she's kissing all her clients. The clients are stupid about it too. They've hired an escort! Does he think she's exclusive to him? Where has her mouth been while she's working?

E-mail:
From: James
To: Elysia
Subject: kissing?
Do you have any rules about kissing? I've run into a few gals who do and a few who don't.... I apologize if this intrudes into any subject matter that might offend but it WOULD help me make a decision about which provider I might choose at a given moment. Thanks Elysia for keeping me in your "loop" knowing when you'll be in town. I really appreciate that about you. Liking that a lot,
James

From: Elysia XOXO
To: James
Subject: Re: Kissing?
Hi there James,
Great to hear back from you, thanks for the e-mail. I thank you for asking for what you would like during your appointment. It is always good to talk about the things that we require from our lovers, that way no one gets hurt or disappointed. Kissing is an extremely intimate and important aspect to some people and really can make the difference in an experience. Now that I know you are one of these wonderful people, I must regretfully decline your invitation to get together. Perhaps if we had met under more personal circumstances and we hit it off things could have been different. Unfortunately, I do not share that part of myself while I am with my friends of this nature.
Sorry if I have disappointed you.
Take care, Elysia xoxo

Some would ask why I charge so much if I won't do everything? Well, because I'm worth it. Men can go to what I call the 'buffet' and eat where every guy has had lunch, but not with me. The guys that come to me feel the same way. They get it, either subconsciously or consciously, that I make my living as an escort and they don't want to put their mouths everywhere either. I only allow my clients to touch my breasts, arms, back, butt, legs and feet. They can't touch my pussy. If they try to, I usually just move around or move their hand to a different spot, and I try to treat it with humor. I sometimes say, "Oh, no, cookie monster, no cookie for you." Most men are fine with a girl's limits and treat an escort exactly the same as they would other women. If a woman says, "Don't do that," men usually know they're not supposed to and they stop.

Occasionally, they try to kiss me anyway. It depends on the person but sometimes I will either give them a sweet, sexy, soft kiss on the mouth if I feel there's no other way out of it without offending them or jeopardizing the situation. I never open my mouth because that would give them an opportunity for a French kiss. I absolutely don't allow that possibility. Usually I do something to distract them. I'll take their hand and put it somewhere to get their mind off a kiss. Whatever. It's just part of the game.

In my love relationships in my personal life, it's another matter. If a guy can't kiss well, he doesn't have a chance with me. Kissing is a dancing rhythm to me. I like a man to kiss me firmly, but not aggressively. I'm not easy to please in bed either. I know how to please myself and some guys catch on quickly and some don't. Those that don't are given the boot.

When a client writes back and wants to make an appointment I require their phone number at work or a referral. I see no one without a reference or referral. Then I phone their work number and ask to speak to them because I have to know they work somewhere that isn't a police department. The business has to have a receptionist, voice mail; a business I can look up in the phone book. It can't be just an answering machine. By requiring the confirmation of the client's name, work, and phone number or by getting a referral, I think potentially violent men would probably not contact an escort. Fortunately, I have never experienced a single incident of violence. As for the law, of course a cop could still rig something and girls do get busted. I don't know how the cops go about doing it or what kind of girls they look for or why they would do so at my level. At any rate, there are only so many precautions I can take to protect myself. If 'Joe Client' is working at Microsoft, chances are he's not a cop. Chances are the cops are not going to be busting me. Touch wood. Who knows? It's a risk. It's a risk I take.

The one time I did get ripped off in Calgary. The guy didn't give me the regular information because he said he worked for himself and didn't have an office. He gave me his phone number and e-mail address. He said it was his first time and so he didn't have a reference from another working girl. He obviously convinced me and I took a chance. He showed up and was very well dressed, well mannered, wasn't aggressive and we had a regular basic session. When we finished, I went into the bathroom and he basically ran out the door. He left his expensive suspenders behind but not a dime. The truth was he was well known for ripping off working girls. I found out I got off easy. He had spent twenty-four hours with an escort and tried to hand her a credit card at the end. He left her when she told him she wouldn't take it. Just imagine the scumbag type of guy that would rip off an escort! I learned the lesson to never take a chance. If the trick can't provide the information necessary, chances are he's going to rip you off.

Of course, other escorts co-operate in trying to keep each other safe. We check a man's reference by asking each other and that's a reference I would most trust.

E-mail:
From: Lynne
To: Elysia
Subject: Reference please...

Hi Elysia, I hope things are going well for you up that way! I don't know if you remember me, but I am Lynne from Seattle. A gentleman by the name of Jim – e-mail is …..@hotmail.com sent me you as his reference. If you can get back to me when you have a free moment, that would be wonderful. Hugs, Lynne :o) phone # ……..

From: Elysia
To: Lynne
Subject: Re. Reference supplied
Hello Miss Beautiful Lynne, :o)
Yes, Mr. Jim is a nice young strapping fellow! You should have no problems with him at all. He was a little shy and nervous at first, is new at enjoying the company of us fine ladies and he tends to arrive early. I am glad to hear that we share another client! You have a great reputation and I am more than happy to recommend you to my clients when I am not in town. Take care and be safe.
Warmest regards, Elysia

From: Lynne
To: Elysia
Subject: Reference received
Thanks Elysia,
It is nice to know there are many ladies out here with good qualities as yourself. I appreciate your kind ways and if I can ever be of any assistance please be sure to let me know. I will also do my best to send anyone looking up North your way.
Hugs ~ Lynne

What might surprise you is there is also a site where men evaluate and rate their sexual experiences with an escort and post their reviews for other men to read. I also get lots of business from referrals from the reviews. The following is an authentic review of me, well, the part of me that is the escort.

Internet Review Board of Hookers
Review of: Elysia
Posted by: John
"I had to do it. I had to find out for myself. I made the appointment. We talked about a half an hour on the phone and got along incredibly well. She was fun, smart and very positive. Great conversationalist. I made an appointment for 1:30 PM on Tues. She called and said I could come over to her hotel early so I did. Knock, knock …… she opened the door. There stood a vision. What a gorgeous lady. The room was dimly lit and she had candles burning. She ushered me right into the room. There was a spread of

delicious food and a romantic setting in the living room. She made me feel comfortable right away. We sat down and talked, laughed and ate wonderful food. After a very comfortable amount of time, we retired to the bedroom. She proceeded to give me a professional yet very intimate massage. It felt like I had known her for years. When it came to the more intimate portion of our encounter, there was nothing I was left wanting. I can tell you it was one of the most stupendous, thrilling and fulfilling encounters I have had with a service provider. She is a lady and very feminine. She is also in unbelievable physical condition, which made things even more entertaining. All I can say is you're missing out on a wonderful experience if you don't give this lady a call. Feel free to e-mail me, but I won't get into a detailed discussion at Elysia's request. Do's and don'ts I will be glad to share. Believe me, it not because she has anything to hide. She just cherishes her privacy. Thanks for the dream, Elysia. You're a sweetheart!"

As I said, I advertise which city I will be visiting and make the appointments. I choose a classy hotel, usually with a sitting room adjoining the bedroom. The rooms usually include a fridge and microwave, which comes in handy for the snacks I provide. Everything must be really clean and nice. In the winter I like the rooms to have a fireplace. Some of the rooms have jacuzzi tubs. I don't normally encourage guys to get into the same water as me. I suppose I might if I ran out of ideas on how to entertain them. I pay for the room and generously tip the cleaning staff because they must know what is going on, since they clean up the candles and probably see the condom wrappers in the garbage. In one city, one of my regulars, who works for a university, takes care of my hotel bill in addition to paying me. He writes it off through work. I guess he has a budget that he can blow and hide things. Sometimes he also flies me to him, also part of the university budget for higher education. Well, he's learned some things from me!

At precisely the time of our appointment, which is a must since I need time to prepare between clients, he knocks on the door. I invite him in. I'm usually in a dress and heels but always in something really sexy. It is typically tight fitting, soft, slinky and low cut to show off my investments. Men love breasts and I have no problem showing them to their best advantage. If I know a man's favorite color, I'll wear something in it. If he prefers a certain look, I'll dress in that too. It's about pleasing him.

I make sure I gently hug him right away. It relaxes him. He feels my warm body pressed against him, my breasts pushing into him, responding to him and welcoming him. I'm never the first one to let go

9

of a hug. Shhhh! A secret, to ladies of the world, when you're hugging, let the man always be the first one to let go. Even when they do, sometimes, if they feel rigid, I will say, "Nope, I'm not done," because it makes them think I want to hug them, which is about as intimate as you can get, holding a person, without having to kiss them. They think, 'She's not letting go. Yeah.' All men want to feel desired and enjoy being touched and hugged. It almost always softens all their initial nervousness. I can sense a lot from that hug. I know if he's nervous, relaxed, feeling an urgent need, or tired from whatever pressures brought him to me.

When a client comes in, I don't ask for money up front. You're supposed to. It's like the golden rule: *Always get paid first because he can run.* But I was also told never to ask for money because that's how the cops bust you. At least in the U.S. However, at my level of escorting, the clients normally do lay the money on the table right away because they know the rule. If they don't, generally, I give them a hint. I will say to them after our beginning conversation, "O.K., I'm going to go get dressed in my lingerie. You take care of business out here and I'll be right back." Of course when I come out of the bathroom, I'm looking for the money on the table. If I see it, I can be happy about it and further my seduction. If not, I coyly give them another hint such as, "Did you forget to take care of me? I'm not seeing it here. Did you hide it in something?" I never call it 'money' and I never count it in front of them. That would be rude. I've never been ripped off by someone stacking bills so it looked like more than it was. In fact, more often than not, they give me more. It's about respect. By not asking directly it becomes a matter of trust that I think impresses most of these wealthy men. I'm not sure.

When it sometimes happens that they pay me at the end, I tell them, "Just so you know, you should always pay the girl up front. I knew you were going to be okay, but just so you know, with the other girls, this is what you have to do." I teach them if they don't know otherwise. Pay the girl up front. You can't go shopping and take the clothes home before paying. They pay first, and then I give them their dream.

I take his coat, hang it up, take him by the hand and show him to the couch where we sit down and I begin a conversation. I ask him, "What can I get you to drink?" The coffee table is covered with goodies such as gourmet crackers and cheeses, fresh shrimp or prawns with a cocktail sauce, fresh fruit sliced into bite-size pieces, candies and drinks: alcohol, juices and bottled water. They often bring me presents, such as chocolates and bouquets of fresh flowers or a single red rose. Sometimes they amuse me with their creativity. I have received a piece of cheese cake in a regular plastic container as well as all kinds of other desserts, bottles of perfume, shoes, dresses, and of course lots of vampy lingerie. Sometimes they bring me a bottle of champagne or wine. I offer to open it for them to drink, but usually they say, "Oh no, it's for you." Most of them sneak away from work to see me because that is the easiest time for them to get away without their wives' knowing, and therefore they usually drink only water. Once I know what they enjoy to eat and drink, I write it down later to make sure I have it for their next visit. I never forget the details. After all, this is their fantasy. I try to make it right. The key is to make them feel comfortable and relaxed and that I care. It's also about making them feel like they're not paying me. I want them to feel like I'm their girlfriend.

While on the couch, we talk about little things. I might start the conversation with the weather, something about sports, certainly something non-threatening. You'd be amazed what that leads to. Of course they all talk about their lives. I never tell anyone the confidences they share with me. They tell me yada, yada, yada. Sometimes I listen and sometimes I don't. They might talk about their pets, their houses, their jobs, taxes, or cutting wood for their fireplace. Most of the time there is no discussion of the girlfriend or wife. I would never ask either. It makes no difference to me and I really don't want to know. Sometimes they'll talk about fantasies. I remember one where he dreamed of his ex-wife sitting alone at a table in a restaurant while he sat nearby at a table with pretty women who were flirting with him. Sometimes they talk about their lovers, which their wives don't know about. I realize that probably his wife or girlfriend is just a normal person who enjoys sex when the time and energy allows. Maybe they've been together for twenty years and it's not exciting for her and it's not exciting for him and we all know how exciting it is to be with somebody new. Whatever. It can be interesting, though mostly not, and I don't keep it in my head. Too much information. This isn't my boyfriend, this is my job and I'm there to make him feel like a king.

So we talk and get to know each other. I make him comfortable. I project a sense of desirability. Sexy women know what I'm talking about: a flirtatious confidence, ever-so-slightly disinterested, titillating with body language, a shy smile, arching the back to press the breasts forward, or a hand flip of the hair. I discovered, even in high school, that the development of my sexuality to the fine-tuned art it is now, is my 'show.' When I use it, I always turn men on.

First-timers are generally very nervous. They're afraid they're going to get arrested. They're afraid I'm going to rip them off and take advantage of them. They're nervous they've paid me $500 bucks and that two seconds later I'm going to ask them for more money. Often, they are very shy. Yes, shy.

A lot of the time my looks intimidate men but usually it excites them because I'm their impossible dream. Tall, blonde, tanned, slender, long legs, and big boobs and an easy smile. Relaxing a man is very important to his sexual function so part of my job is to make them feel relaxed and to feel like a normal man enjoying a woman's company. I make them comfortable enough so they can trust me, so they can reveal to me whatever is in their heart, their soul, whatever is on their mind. I do whatever I sense is needed to enable them to reveal themselves to me, so that I have an understanding of how best to give them pleasure.

It takes an incredible amount of energy to appear interested and pretend I sincerely care. That is **the** hardest part of the game. Sex is sex. Men can get that on any street corner. Most men who come to me enjoy part 'nature-nurture.' By that I mean they want to be with somebody who will fulfill their ultimate sexual fantasy, but who also appeals to their personal emotional side. I try to make them feel wanted, desired, valued and a worthwhile person and not just there to get laid. Mostly, it's all about the brain. Their dick will always work. Don't worry about the dick. Of course some part of sex is technique, giving a blow job is technique, but I believe they become my regulars because I also offer them my devoted attention. It makes it more pleasurable. I must be right. I have never been without lots of clients.

I can make my voice sound very sexy. It's all in my tone of voice and also in how I look at them while I'm saying it. I soften my voice and I always keep eye contact. Sometimes I smile slightly shyly and look them in the eyes with as much innocence as I can pretend. Sometimes I ooze femininity with slow body arches, or bending forward to show them my boobs. All the time their eyes are on me, devouring me. It's all acting and the act depends on the guy and what he wants. The reason I'm there is to make money, but I'm not with him to 'rip him off.' It's a fair exchange and a 'win-win' situation. I fulfill his dream and make money for doing it.

After our conversation on the couch, usually fifteen to thirty minutes, I'll say, "Okay, I'm going to go change into my lingerie." Then I prepare the bed by turning back the covers. I take his hand and lead him to the bed. "You get undressed and relax and lie down." I usually say something like that. Then I go into the bathroom to change. When I come out of the bathroom in my lingerie, most men will be lying on their tummies, face down. Very rarely will they get on the bed naked, face up. Most of the time they'll start on their tummy and I like it that way. I don't want to come in and see their dick. I don't want to see them lying there like a starfish with a hard-on. You can roll over later, buddy! Anyway, most of these men know that they're going to get a massage first. Some tricks have a hard-on right away and some don't. It depends on what's happened prior to getting to bed. Each client is different. If we're sitting there and my point is to get them aroused before we get to the bed, then yeah, they will have one. They will do whatever I want.

First, I gently run my hands over his body so he gets used to me touching him. Then I start the massage. I use a very expensive fragrance-free, non-staining massage oil and typically start massaging his back. It's all about arousal, seduction and foreplay. Men respond to my touch, and I can intuitively tell what they most enjoy having massaged. It's a long drawn-out seduction. Usually I bring them to the edge of a climax several times with a hand job, just to excite and tease them. I make them ride the roller coaster. I take them to the edge and challenge them. I'm very careful to make sure they don't come during a hand job or before the final sex, and they love that because then they know I'm not there just to get them off. I'll say to them, "Now, you let me know if it's getting too close," so I can stop it. Sometimes I lie over the top of them without even touching them. It's too easy to get them off. Any escort can do that. I like to excite by teasing a bit.

When I'm ready for undressing, I have the man on the bed, lying face up and I am on top of him. Since my 'costume' usually has a garter belt, stockings and high heels, I stretch out a leg and begin to undo a stocking. I try to take my time with that. Sometimes I make them roll it down and take if off. The longer the time spent on undressing, the less time they are inside me. When the timing is perfect, I reach under the pillow where I have previously placed a condom in a tissue. I put it in my mouth and slide it down with my lips and tongue while I begin to give them a blow job. Most of the time they are totally unaware I have put the condom on. Women of the world, you should know by doing it this way men are less likely to object to wearing one. All the while, I'm smiling, making eye contact, making sure they think I am enjoying their bodies, as I constantly touch them, tease them by not making it too easy and twisting and stretching my body to excite them. It's so important that they think they are turning **me** on. Sometimes I'll take his hand and put it somewhere on my body. When they touch me, I say something like, "Oh, your hands feel so nice," and "Oh, you're arms are so strong."

I try to massage them and play with them so that they are so turned on that they're inside me for as little amount of time as possible. They're ready to 'blow' by the time I'm ready for his dick to be inside me. Men are completely predictable.

When they actually enter me, I close my eyes and go somewhere else. I can blank my mind out. It doesn't take long. I just don't think about it. It takes a very, very short amount of time. I try to make it the least amount of time possible. Maximum ten minutes. I could get an Oscar for mentally being blank while at the same time expressing how much they are turning me on. It's all an act. It's their fantasy and my acting. Imagine fucking ten guys in two days. It is truly disgusting! But I will come home with $5,000 U.S. and a sore cervix and bored from men's bullshit talk! The best part is when I can count my money.

Internet Review Board of Hookers;
Review of: "Elysia"
Posted by: David:
Subject: The Juicy Details:
She met me in a see-through red lacey teddy and offered me a drink. She's really pretty with a fabulous body. We talked a bit and she was sexy, sweet and intelligent. We proceeded to get comfortable with an awesome massage and then she flipped me over. She has a nice implant job with beautiful thick attentive nips. She proceeded to a great covered blow-job and then onto the usual positions. She let me rub her pussy on the outside and she was quite responsive. I don't know if she was really into it, but I didn't really care. If she faked it, she did it convincing enough for me to enjoy. Overall, a great attitude and I will definitely see her again.

Review of: "Elysia"
Posted by: Joe Happy
I was trying to decide what to post and the comment "You pay for what you get" keeps coming to the front of my mind. There have been a lot of posts regarding Elysia and her higher price. All I know for a "fact" is it was probably the best experience I have ever had the pleasure to pay for. (and I DO MEAN PLEASURE!) I've done a couple of drugs in my past that I liked a lot and managed not to become addicted but Elysia is unquestionably addicting. I'm sure we connected and everyone else will have varied results but WOW......LUCKY ME

Two

LADY OF THE NIGHT - part two

It's not the norm, but not all men have orgasms. Believe it or not, some choose not to. Some don't come to have sex. Some guys don't want to cheat. They might be lonely even if they are married. They crave some attention. Sometimes they don't have an orgasm because they are too shy or too worked up. Whatever, sometimes they just can't and so they don't. I never say anything when it happens. I try my best to get them to the point where they're aroused enough to have one. If they can't, I stop and I slow down and I backtrack and try again. They get a couple of tries. They get a little bit of everything. I pleasure them everywhere with my hands. Maybe they'll get a boobies rub, where I pour oil slowly over my breasts and let them massage them or rub their penis between them. Sometimes I give them more of a blow job. Sometime they can't orgasm with a condom on, so I take it off so they can come on me while I work them with my hands. Whatever it takes.

I treat them all like respectable human beings. I am honest in my caring for them and being attentive to them and pampering them. That's what they pay me for, to make them feel like the king, like they are desirable. That's what it's about for that hour; so they walk away feeling more confident, more powerful, more - whatever they want. My job is to make their egos bigger. It's not about me liking them. They're not paying me to actually like them and enjoy it. They're paying me to fake whatever makes them feel great. It's the game. It's going to burst a lot of egos when men read this book.

Some men like it when I cup their testicles in my hand and wiggle them while slightly pushing on them just as they have an orgasm. By doing this, the balls will sometimes slip back into their body cavity which heightens the orgasm. It doesn't work on some men; their balls won't go there. It takes quite the technique and I have to really know the man and he has to be totally relaxed. To do this, it's important to play with their balls, to stimulate them the whole time during fore-play. First, lightly touching them, holding them and lightly squeezing them. The cavity is just above the balls and I push them closer and closer and, when everything is tense, they pop right up in there just as he comes. It's not for every man, but some like it. Ladies of the world: use caution when trying this at home.

I've seen a lot of dicks. Of course, no two are the same and some are circumcised and some not. Each man smells differently. I usually account for it to different cultural diets. Some men just smell and they can't help it. When I worked in the massage parlor, odour was more noticeable. When I became more exclusive, the men had a different sense about clothing, cleanliness, and cologne. As a result, body odour has rarely been a problem, but if it was a problem, I'd say, "You know what? I'll do a really nice hot towel treatment and you'll really like it." Then I'd get the towels and clean them. Better yet, if it was really bad, I would ask them to take a shower, though not with me unless it was a regular. Somehow, they would never know it's because they smell because I present it as a treat.

So, you probably want to ask, do I enjoy any of it? I would enjoy it if they just slipped the money under the door and went away. I'm not talking about my private life here. This is a job. I don't care about their dogs or jobs or homes or girlfriends or wives or lives. Escorts who say they are into it for reasons other than money are definitely rare or, more likely, liars.

So that you really understand about how much it is only a job to hookers, some will try a technique called the 'fake fuck.' (I describe it in my massage parlor section) One night, when two other escorts and I spent a relaxing evening together, we tried to come up with a new 'fake fuck.' Anything to get out of actually having to turn the guy. We were in my hotel room lying on the beds like girls do, smoking a little recreational weed, chatting and laughing and sharing stories. One of them, in all her innocence if one can describe her this way, piped up and said, "I wonder how I could do a fake hand job?" Well, we burst out laughing with the thought. I mean really, how could one possibly fake that? "Well," she piped up again, "we could just get him to do it himself." With gales of laughter we worked it out. First, the idea is to tell said 'fake-victim' that you have a secret fantasy that really turns you on. The escort must appear slightly embarrassed for even thinking of such a thing and, even more so, for sharing such a 'fantasy' where she is a voyeur and would LOVE to watch/catch him jerking off! Then we came up with several different versions of making this happen. I said that I would pretend to be the maid and I wanted to walk in on him. One of the other girls said she wanted to stand behind the curtain and watch and move the curtain while pretending to be jerking off too. Well, we laughed our heads off! What guy wouldn't fulfill a fantasy for their girl? The thing is, we decided it would work. If a client just wanted a hand job, which is rare with this caliber of working girl, then chances are he is just gullible enough to fall for it. It's all in the presentation of the idea: a little coyness, slight embarrassment while revealing 'such a thing' for the first time and of course horniness, because that is really all they care about. They like us 'horny' while they focus on their dicks, pussy, sex and orgasms.

Having said that, occasionally I do enjoy some clients. Sometimes booze or pot makes it better for me because being able to escape and 'not really being there' is good. I like men who are nice, respectful and funny and I usually enjoy them. A sense of fun and adventure makes it good, instead of just fucking. I like it when they are shy or new or young. I find it more attractive and I have more patience with them. They seem more real and less like a jaded 'know-it-all-impress-me' trick. Real communication takes less effort.

When I know a man is painfully shy, I try to be even more affectionate, more understanding and more coddling. One man was so shy that it took him a long time to look me in the eye. It is hard because I then have to do all the talking when we're on the couch. Typically I will reach out and take his hand. I might sit on his lap. I get as close to him as I physically can. I try to look him in the eye, all the while being very tender. I move very slowly with a shy man. It's not about getting him aroused while we're on the couch. It's about getting him relaxed enough that he stops shaking so he can enjoy sex. When I come out of the bathroom in my lingerie I know, for certain, a shy man will be lying on his tummy, face down. Once, one of my painfully bashful tricks thanked me. He said, "You know, you've made things better with my girlfriend and me. I'm more able to relax." I smiled. I'm happy this guy has better sex with his girlfriend for having seen me. You might say, 'a job well done.' That matters to me.

I won't tolerate much in the way of 'kinky' sex. One trick liked to spank me, but paid for each spank on my bum in addition to my hourly fee, and for the hotel. He really was gentle but got off on spanking. During our conversation time, he often would bring pictures to show me. Some were of his dog, sometimes photos of his house renovations, or his cabin on a lake, but never any pictures of his wife. Go figure! For all outward appearances, he was a normal guy. However, he liked me to play a game where I was the bad girl and it was all about my acting again. He'd say something like, "Oh, you've been a bad girl. You're going to get a spanking." He was a bit like a chess player, conniving, and always thinking about the next step. He liked to play mind games. He'd say, "I'm going to pay you for every spank." Then he would start to negotiate by saying something like, "How much are you going to charge me?" I would say, "100 bucks per spank." He'd say, "Oh no, no, no. Two bucks." I'd say something like, "How hard are you going to spank me?" He'd say, "Well, you haven't been that bad, so not too hard, but I might have to get my belt." And we'd go on like that, which kept it exciting. I had to remember not to laugh. He had a hard on the whole time. *Talking* about it was *the* most important part of the seduction for him. He knew how much he had in his wallet and how much he was willing to spend. I eventually would come down to 50 bucks per spank. So if he spanked me four times with his hand, he paid me 200 dollars extra. When he spanked me, I'd yell, "Ow, no, that hurts." Things like that. He never hurt me, because he spanked me very lightly. It was his fantasy, his game. Then I would roll over and he'd have sex with me but in a very controlled way. He liked me to pretend to have an orgasm. He'd say "Oh, are you done, baby? Have you had enough?" I'd have to say "no" and then "yes" and then he'd come.

E-mail:
From: Mr. Trick
To: Elysia xoxo
Subject: Birthday Girl.
So how old is my favorite blonde? And when is the big day? I have a secret friend who just turned 34 this month. Can you guess what happened to her 34 times? Do you know what Miss Elysia will be doing with me this Wednesday? And do you understand what happens to naughty girls who don't pay for their own hotel rooms? Unless you get a better offer, maybe you should pencil me in for Thursday morning too. Then if business is too slow on Friday, and if your little bare bottom doesn't chicken out and you can beg me to give you all that you deserve, maybe you could see me then too. Your call, but I promise there is adequate green paper if you're so inclined three days in a row.

From: Elysia
To: Mr. Trick
Subject: Birthday Bumps
You naughty, naughty boy!!!
I am all yours! My tender pink bottom awaits you....

Love, E. xoxo

Another trick had a mild rape fantasy, if one could call it that. It's more like taking advantage and it wasn't aggressive or violent. He never hurt me and I saw him for years. He had a wife who was frigid, or so he said. Their marriage was a marriage of convenience and shared money. He was frustrated because he couldn't have sex with his wife, so while he was having sex with me, he talked a lot about taking her against her will. He pretended that she was sleeping and he'd have sex with her anyway. He's not someone that thinks or even pretends that he is going to go out and rape some chick, it's not like that at all. His fantasy was overcoming his frustration that he couldn't have sex with his wife and had to visit escorts. I don't think it was a vengeful act either. I think it was just his finding a way to have sex with his wife and it just so happened he needed to pretend it was against her will, but he was not doing it to get back at her. If he told her about what he does with escorts, then that would be vengeful.

Then there was the trick that I never had sex with. He was young too. We just hung out in his apartment. I knew him for some time before I trusted going to his apartment. I got the impression he had a lot of money. He was a night owl, so I would arrive late, usually around ten o'clock and he was usually just stepping out of the shower or just getting dressed. He liked me to wear sexy lingerie, so, of course I did. He loved music, so I would get him involved in playing music for me because I knew that would take up a good hour. But I also enjoyed the music, even though it was just my way of using up time. He really liked to cuddle and, basically, only cuddle. The very first time I saw him, I think he mentioned his mom eight times. Every time afterwards, he'd mention her too. He was obviously close to her. Perhaps he was a 'mama's boy.' It didn't matter to me. He paid me well. He did mention other women in his life, other than his mother, so I guess he had girlfriends.

He was a high class kind of guy. He was definitely not into just hiring $150 dollar girls and having them come and do their thing and leave. He said something to the effect that he really liked to get to know a girl first and feel comfortable in a girlfriend type experience. It certainly wasn't about sex. Finally, after many visits I said, "You know, I need to talk to you about this. This is not what usually happens. It would help me if you told me what you expect or want for the time I'm here. You're paying me $500 bucks an hour. What do you want?" After hemming and hawing, he finally said, "Oh, you want to know what I want?" I said, "Well, yeah, basically." He said, "I just want to have a good time and get to know you." He told me he was into intimacy with integrity and honesty. I think he wanted to make a connection, a real friendship and not just pay me to come to have sex and leave. He told me he had trouble meeting quality-type girls. He said he wanted somebody who's really good looking, sexy and smart and "all those things." Don't they all! I thought it interesting that he had no problem with my being an escort. Not long after that, while we were fooling around on his bed, he was almost naked and I put my hand on his dick. He was very shy and embarrassed about the size. He might have had what I call 'small-dick syndrome.' I certainly didn't care. The money he paid me was not an issue with him. And I liked him. But we never had sex.

Most of my tricks are over forty years old. It's rare to have one in their twenties or thirties because they can go to a bar and get it for free, but certainly it does happen. There was one young man, who was painfully shy, and who was a real jock. He sold his skateboard to get enough funds to come see me. Money was an issue for him. He was so adorable that I lowered my fee!

E-mail:
From: 'The kid'
To: Elysia
Subject: you
Hi Elysia,
I would love to see you except to be honest I just can't afford it. Don't get me wrong. I think you are worth the price you ask but the most I can afford is 2 bills. You are one fine piece of air-time. Hope things are well with you. Take care, the kid

To: 'The Kid'
From: Elysia
Subject: you
Hi there, Great to hear from you again. Thanks for the e-mail. So sorry to take so long getting back to you. I have actually had to cancel my visit this week because I have come down with some kind of flu :o(I thank you for your honesty regarding your situation. I know my rate can be a little steep and I am more than willing to work something out in the future if need be. Be well, be happy! :o) Love, Elysia xoxo

From: 'The Kid'
To: Elysia
Subject: Thoughts of intertwine leave me feeling so divine;
I whispered to you when we were lying on warm soft sand under a bright moon. We listened to waves crash passionately on the beach just below our sandy, bare, naked bodies. I confess I was dreaming but I felt the warmth of

the sand and saw your sexy smile while staring at the stars ..... yep, I'm a dork. It felt so real until my kitty attacked my hand and woke me up. Have an awesome day! And thanks, 'The Kid'

I do not allow pictures to be taken during a session, though many men have requested it. Fat chance! They have to pay to come and see me.

E-mail:
From: Finny of film
To: Elysia
Subject: Photos
Finny here .... From Ferndale, North Carolina. May 11 would be great. For fun, let's make a movie with my camcorder starring Elysia and Finny....... and of course the tripod. Let me know.

From: Elysia xoxo
To: Finny of film
FINNY! You are so naughty!! Sorry, hon, no movies. Not a chance. If you still want to meet up on Friday let me know what time works for you. Cheers baby!

Some men fantazise about how a woman's panties smell. Amazing to a woman but nevertheless true.

E-mail:
From: Lingerie Man
To Elysia
Subject: Erotica
Hi,
I unfortunately will miss your trip to New York by a few days. (I travel there on business every three weeks.) I would like to know if you might be interested in selling me a pair of your panties? Let me know and hopefully we could work something out. Thank you.

From: Elysia
To: Lingerie Man
Subject: Panties
Dear Sweet Lingerie Lover,
I am so sorry to miss you in NYC, LM. I would love for you to have a pair of my sweet delicious panties! I am certain you will know how to enjoy them both in touch and smell and you will be one happy man. Send me $200 cash and your address and I will mail them off immediately. Do you have a color preference?
Enjoy, Elysia

When the cash arrived, I pulled a bright pink lacy g-string from my bulging panty drawer and mailed them to him in a clear bag via the post. He thanked me later for the extra embarrassment. I laughed, it was a bonus.

There are men who just want to have sex with a 'babe.' I know I'm very lucky to have the body I do. I'm also blessed because I remain slim and fit no matter what I do. I use my gym membership sporadically. I tell my customers, "This body is a gift that I abuse on a regular basis!" Sometimes I really am into working out but it's hard work to be dedicated. I do not need to go to lose weight but to improve my general health and to remain firm. I feel better when I work out, but sometimes I am too lazy. I do love to go to yoga, though I can be lazy there too. As for food, since I occasionally smoke pot, I do get the uncontrollable munchies. I love chocolate but only around my period. I love chips and salty stuff. I try to only eat one fat group at a time: i.e. no butter if I am using mayo. I am not really a big red meat eater, although I eat at fast food places sometimes. I have come to a point where I rarely cook for myself. Cooking to me is making toast. Hey, there's heat involved. Somehow, I stay thin, thank you very much.

These men, who just want to hire the slim, blond, gorgeous 'babe,' sometimes feel that in their personal lives beautiful women might not look at them and, let's face it, some men probably would never get to be with one. So they come to me and not only does he get to be with a 'dream' but she cares about him. The 'babe' is a person and a woman he can care about, so the experience becomes even bigger.

E-mail:
From: Wishful thinking Ron
To: Elysia
Subject: Excited by YOU!
Hi, my name is Ron. I saw your Internet ad and wanted to compliment you on your beauty. Great body and I'm sure that you are gorgeous. One of your pictures has a guitar in it. I play guitar, I kind of taught myself. Keeps me sane. You are coming to Detroit on the 16th? I know there will be a lot of guys to take you out. I just want to say I have never gone out with a blond before. I'm not interested in any services, but if I were, I'd definitely choose you. I just wanted to drop you a line and give you a compliment. Take care and have a great holiday! Ron

From: Elysia
To: Ron
Subject: Hello

Thanks for the love! Peace and Happy Holidays!
Santa is going to be good to you!
Love, E. xoxo

Of course, single men come to me too. Sometimes they don't have anyone and they want physical contact. They're lonely. They want to be with somebody. Sometimes they're brainy geeks. I get lots of computer geeks from a major West Coast computer company, who've got pockets full of money and no one to share it with, no one to spend it on, so my fee is nothing to them. Mind you, some of them come to just get laid and that's their focus and that's fine too.

Men from around the world respond to my Internet seduction too. Here is a response from a man from Syria. I wrote him that I would not meet with him because I do not travel out of North America for working purposes.

E-mail:
From: man in Middle East
To: Elysia
Subject: Safe
My Queen, you don't have to feel surprised for my attention in you because you deserve it. i like so much and i think that you are the woman of my dreams. The woman of any human dream. you deserve to be a queen .... really .... and you don't have to feel any bad feelings about my country because its very safe country. you have a very wrong idea about my people ...believe its more safe than your country and its not a jock. i am a civil engineer and i own a design company...single. i have so many reasons to be a happy man ...i have a lovely family...great friends ...good business ...a good future ...i'm very romantic person ...i love sports and reading and cinema. all that i need is to find a princess like you...a lady can give my the good feelings ...to make me feel like heaven... Look ...i don't know anything about you ...but i feel that you are a very good person inside ...from your picture i can see that ...please answer my question. can you accept me like a friend? that will be a lot to me. And what's your real name ...please tell me.. lady...i'm totally honest with you ...i like you and i want to make anything to make you happy or make you accept to see me...maybe i can meet you in united kingdom...is that good for you ..please just tell me your rate...and i will be more than happy to pay it...but i think that you worth more than money. Thank you. K.

Sometimes men want to share me with their girlfriends:

E-mail:
From: Bert
To: Elysia
Subject: Wish List….
I will be in Hawaii on the dates you will be in here. I am finally taking a vacation – hurray! Please let me know when you are visiting again. Do you ever do anything with couples? I have just started dating a very attractive young lady who has never been with another woman and she is completely turned on by the thought of being with another woman but wouldn't want to risk anything with a long-time friend. I thought I might surprise her some time. Is this outside your comfort zone? Bert

From: Elysia
To: Bert
Subject: :o)
Hi there Bert,
I hope you have an awesome vacation and I am way past green with envy! I am sorry to say that I am not the girl for your new friend to try out. My experience(s) with women are personal and private and not available for an hourly rate. If I can think of someone who would be suitable, I will let you know. It may be a tricky situation. Working girls may not be the best experience for a first time with women, if you know what I mean. It's not really real and you might want to try to find a girl who is really into being with your girlfriend and you, rather than a financial arrangement. I would hate for her first time to be bad … that would really suck! It should be great! As to not give her the wrong impression of what it is like to be with a woman. Just my two cents worth. Women out there these days are quite open to being with other women. It has become quite trendy! And you can find someone who is willing. Take care on your travels, Elysia xoxo

From: Bert
To: Elysia
Subject: RE: :o)
Your message is well taken and very kind. I will do as you suggest and stay away from working girls for this particular need. Shouldn't be too hard (I hope). Thanks for being so sweet. Please keep me on your wish list. I will let you know how Hawaii is. Best regards, Bert

Some men just don't want any 'hassles' in their lives, which a girlfriend or wife might bring. They usually are married to their jobs and have plenty of money and often beautiful homes and cars. I'm a hassle-free diversion they can afford, who expects no commitment. One man comes to mind who was always tense, stressed, really cocky and up tight. I knew he sometimes smoked weed, so I usually made sure I had a little bit of weed to help him relax. He was big and very strong and had a sense of powerfulness about him. He brought a sense of power-control that made him tense into the room. At first, he would be absolutely rigid. I would sit down on his lap and be very affectionate, moving my hands slowly, touching him gently. By sitting on his lap, I made him soften; I was a soft playful sweet little thing, who he could pick up like a loaf of bread and toss away if he wanted. I was so non-threatening that gradually he would relax. Sometimes I would say outright, "Oh, come on, loosen up." It worked with him, but I can do that with someone else and it won't work. Some men find it to be too aggressive. Instinctively I know.

I get it. I get the game. I know what it's about. I make that human connection. Those that want that become my regulars, and I have favorites who I treat particularly well. Women of the world should remember: it's about his ego, and everybody wants to feel special sometimes. Men of the world should remember too: it's about her ego and she wants to feel special too. Every person wants to be passionately and tenderly touched by a human that desires them. And men are more than willing to pay my fee to get it.

Some people have said to me that I provide a valuable service to wives who aren't 'into' sex. I guess. I don't know. I suppose so. It's better their husbands come and see me than to get a girlfriend because then they could lose their husbands. A girlfriend or lover usually wants him, an escort never does. If a husband is going to a prostitute, a woman can usually keep him around the house that way.

Men can be so blind about getting sex from their wives. There was this married guy at work, at my 'square' job. A conversation came up when someone said to him, "Oh, Awni, I hear you've cheated on your wife." He was from somewhere like Iran, very chauvinistic, and we all started to talk about marriage. He said something about his wife being cold and implying it was her responsibility to turn him on and take care of things. I said flat out and in a loud voice, "If you're not getting laid by your wife, it's YOUR fault. YOU are doing something wrong." Everyone turned around and looked at me. The room was silent. Someone took their glasses off and laid them on a table. I continued, "If you're not getting laid, if your woman isn't putting out, YOU are doing something wrong. You're either bad in bed, you've pissed her off, you've ignored her, or you're not romantic. You name it. There's a reason she's not putting out for you."

He seemed to think about it. Maybe. Certainly he kept his mouth shut. But it's true, because I believe most women enjoy sex just as much as most men. We just don't want to bed any man we can lay. And women are just as horny as men. I told him, "If you had a good sex life in the beginning of a relationship and now she's not interested, obviously you're doing something wrong. It's all in a man's technique and romance and approach. If a man treats his woman like the mother of his child, or his wife like a comfortable old slipper, then she will lose interest. Maybe she thinks *he's* lost the ability." Bet he never thought of that. All those guys who think their women aren't putting out should know there's a reason. He needs to find out what that reason is and to understand it's not always the woman's fault. Men should take responsibility. Maybe they just need to be kind to their woman instead of intolerant and take some books out of the library on romance. Maybe they need to hire a babysitter for the kids, and take their wives out to dinner. Maybe their wives have low self-esteem, whatever. But why do they have low self-esteem? Maybe because men think of a 'wife' as a servant, like their moms. I don't pretend to know it all. But sex is a two-way street. Going to an escort is not giving your wife the attention she needs. Going to an escort instead of your wife is a dead-end for turning your woman back to the tigress she has sleeping inside. Men of the world, you like being treated like a king? *Well, treat your woman like a Goddess and you'll both get what you want. Remember, if she's happy, you'll be happy.*

And women of the world, remember TSB or toxic sperm build-up makes men retarded and irrational. Who knows why men get married? I know even men who are married or in a committed relationship still have that need to get rid of their sperm, even if they're getting laid every day. Of course, the majority of men who come to me are not getting sex, for whatever reason. I've learned some men are 'into' fucking just about any woman they can, married or not. It's like in nature, where the male animals have a need to propagate and get their seed to as many females as they can, to make sure that their genetic material continues. I think men can compartmentalize sex differently than women do. Some men can just go out and get laid. It's just their dick. It's about sex. It's about testosterone. No emotional commitment attachment required. With women it's usually different, though some women can also do that. Yes, we like to think we're higher beings and can control our needs and desires, but most men can't. That's why they have prostitutes and girl-friends and lovers on the side because they need to jack off and get rid of that sperm.

* * *

Things can go wrong in any business. It's no different in the escort business. You fix the problem or learn to live with it.

Crossing the border into the States was not usually a problem, though one time it turned into a nightmare. My car broke down and I had booked appointments for the next day in a U.S. city which I usually drove to. My girlfriend's U.S. sugar-daddy was in town and offered to loan me his car, which had New York licence plates. He also loaned me his apartment which was in the same city I would be working. At 6:30 the next morning, I arrived at the U.S. truck border crossing. There were pylons in front of all the gated lanes where one would normally drive to get through Customs and into the States. I somehow missed the sign that pointed to where cars should go, and drove into a truck lane. Anyone who is not familiar with border crossings should know that a car enters the U.S. 'ground' before actually going through customs. Cars form lines that feed into the lanes where a custom's agent has the power to let you in (or not). When I saw the pylons, I thought Customs was closed. Well I obviously wasn't thinking because I thought I had to turn around and go back into Canada. I got out of the car and moved a pylon so I could loop around. I got back into the car and realized I was now driving to Canadian Customs.

I thought, 'this is a huge mistake' because now I had to explain to Canadian Customs why I was copping a U-turn at the U.S. border. I told the agent, "I was on my way to the States and the border's closed." He said, "What do you mean, it's closed? It's open 24 hours." I said, "There's pylons there. You can't go. I don't know what's going….." He demanded to know, "Whose car is this?" Then he got a little piece of paper and started writing. At first I didn't know I was in trouble. Then he looked at me and said, "Do you know that it's illegal to be driving an American-plated vehicle in Canada without the registered owner in the car?" I was like, "No, I had no idea." I didn't either. He ordered me to pull over, park my car and go inside the building with my suitcases to be questioned. Customs agents began searching the inside of the car.

Meanwhile, inside, they were checking my passport and driver's licence against the car's registry. "Who's Dick? Who's this guy? Phone numbers?" He began to search my purse. I had a nursing book on 'Child Abuse and Treatment' along with some research papers in my purse. I told him I was an RN. I said, "This is my friend's boyfriend's car. He loaned me the car. I'm going to visit his place and do some studying on child abuse. This is his phone number and address. You phone and check."

The Customs man was a fucking prick, like you wouldn't believe.

Thank God I didn't have any weed on me or in my stuff, like I occasionally did. "So," he said, "do you smoke?" I said "No." He said, "Then what do you have a lighter for?" I didn't even answer that question because it was just so stupid. I thought about saying 'Well, I have six panels in my luggage that you haven't found yet....' but I kept my mouth shut. He began to go through my luggage. I had my escort lingerie, escort stilettoes shoes, lots of g-string panties, lacy bras, bras with nipple holes, thigh-high nylons, lots of condoms, candles, a feather shawl, my computer, ropes, the works in the suitcases. He saw it all. He said, "Well, there seems to be a lot of green flaky lint in the bottom of your bag." He was harassing me over purse lint!

It was 6:45 in the morning and I had clients starting at 10. I was standing there with this agent looking me in the eye, eight inches from my face, demanding to know, over and over, "Now this is it. I'm only going to ask you one more time. Where are you going? Why are you going there?" What could I say? He pushed aside the lingerie and found more green lint in the bottom of the bag. He said "This could be illegal. I could impound your car for possession, smuggling of narcotics, and there's enough evidence here for me to charge you and impound everything." What could I say? I was sitting there watching him go through my escort stuff as if it was his wife's flannel underwear. Maybe, around his house, his wife wore a negligee as a bathrobe and stilettos for slippers. He didn't notice anything unusual other than green lint.

I'm sure I looked petrified because I was. I thought, "Oh fuck, there goes his car." I thought for sure they were going to impound the car. I stuck to my story. I knew not to say anything unless asked a specific question and to stick to the story. That's exactly what I did.

They actually didn't keep me long. He finally said, " Now this is what you're going to do. Get back in the car. You're going to go over to the U.S. Customs and you're going to tell the agent there the exact same story you told me. You take this car across the border and you leave it there and find another way home." I said, "Okay." Then I burst into tears. Boo hoo. It was like the good guy-bad guy sort of thing. His 'good guy' handed me my driver's licence and said, "It's okay, relax. Just go over there and tell the guy what you're doing. Don't even worry about it." I looked at him and said, "What? Are you sending me to the hounds now? Am I going to get in just as much trouble trying to cross the US border with this car as you're giving me here or what?" He said, "No, no. It'll be all right." Another agent said, "You're going to have to take your chances."

So sure enough, I drove to the U.S. border and the guy looked at my licence and looked at the car's registration and I repeated, "A friend of mine loaned me his car. I'm just taking it to his place." He said, "Okay, whatever." And he waved me through.

I drove the car to the closest U.S. airport and left it there. I had planned to use Dick's apartment to see my clients. He didn't know that, of course. But since I had given the agents the address, phone numbers, etc. I took a cab to the Hilton. I arrived with just enough time to call my clients about the new location. I said to each client during their appointments, "You're not going to believe what happened to me this morning." I told them the story and all five clients were very sympathetic and wanted to rescue me if it ever happened again.

E-mail:
From: Elysia
To: Gene
Subject: Broken Condom
Dear Gene, Hello again. This is your favorite Canadian Blonde here! I just wanted to drop you a note and let you know that you have been on my mind as well as our unfortunate incident where the condom broke. Now that the shock has worn off, I am planning to make a visit to the doctor on Monday just to be sure that everything is okay for us. You know how nature and the universe can throw a curve ball when you least expect it, so I think it's best not to take anything for granted. Please do not take anything personal because it is not intended that way, but I want you to be confident as well. I'll be in touch honey bear!

From: Gene
To: Elysia
Subject: Broken condom
Elysia, Thank you. I hope you are in good health. On my end, I have not had unprotected contact with anyone other than my wife in about 10 years. She has had tests done recently because of pregnancy – all negative. I'm sure you're aware that the tests you have done will tell us about your HIV status six months ago so I am more concerned about any test you take six months from now. All the talk of tests and such aside, I did enjoy our encounter a lot and will be fantasizing about you for a long time. Would you please send me more pictures? Also, I would like to stay on your "wish list."
Thank you! Gene

I was not taking birth control pills. I took them for ten years and there came a time I wanted to stop because I didn't want to be on chemicals any more. I just wanted to have my own natural hormones and so I quit. Obviously a broken condom was serious for more than health reasons. Fortunately, I never got pregnant from a client but I know working girls that did.

I make considerable effort to meet with my clients not only in flying or driving to meet them but in the preparation of a room, food, candles, etc. As any doctor or lawyer will tell you, missed appointments are rude. I usually e-mail my clients who have done so and give them a piece of my mind, as I did to 'Michael' who had missed more than one appointment. I told him to not contact me again but a year later he did.

E-mail:
From: Michael
To: Elysia:
Subject: Las Vegas Nov. 3
Dear Elysia,
It has been about a year since we last exchanged e-mails. My missing an appointment and not cancelling ahead of time was unforgivable. I apologize for all the inconvenience I cost you. I thought it was worth one more attempt to make it up to you. I am going to Las Vegas for the first time on Nov. 3 and thought you would be an ideal partner to seek out the best of the city. I would be more than willing to cover your plane tickets, hotel room and time in advance if you are interested. Just provide me an address and I will send you funds to cover the trip. You would certainly have the option of keeping the money as a repayment for the inconsiderate way I treated you last year. I am willing to take that risk. I look forward to hearing your response. With best regards, Michael

From: Elysia
To: Michael
Subject: Re: Las Vegas Nov. 3
Hello Michael,
I am currently in New York and should be here until the end of Oct. I would be willing to consider your offer but I must be honest with you and say that I do not trust you. You have made plans and cancelled with me so many times that I am afraid to make plans. If you are truly interested, then I will need more details from you in regard to our arrangement including how long you would like me to spend with you and how much you are willing to pay for my companionship. Vegas is an exciting and very fun place with lots of great things to do! Is this a business trip or personal for you? Looking forward to hearing back from you.. E. xoxo

From: Michael
To: Elysia

Subject: Re: Las Vegas Nov. 3
Dear Elysia,
Thank you for your prompt reply. It was nice to hear from you again. I understand your lack of trust in me. It is certainly well founded. However, in my business, my plans change frequently. I had no idea you had gone to such trouble to meet me in San Francisco. I wanted to offer to cover your costs last time, but your e-mail to me suggested I should not bother corresponding with you again. I would, however, still like to make that up to you. If you let me know the extent of your inconvenience, I would be delighted to reimburse you.

Now to the future. I will be in Las Vegas on business. As a result, my plans could change, again. I propose we start off slowly. I need to prove my reliability and having you come all the way to Vegas may be too risky. Why don't I come to Toronto sometime soon and take you to dinner? If you are willing to travel with me after that, then we can plan the next trip. How does that sound? I look forward to seeing you again soon. With warm regards, Michael

To: Michael
Subject: Re: Las Vegas Nov. 3
Dear Michael,
Thank you very much for your heartfelt e-mail. I accept your apology and your invitation to make things right between us. I would really like to join you for dinner and have a fresh start. I realize that work and life can get hectic and I do understand the need to change plans. So where do we go from here? I am willing to make plans with you and willing to accept the fact that you may cancel at any time. I know now not to hold you to your appointments, that they are in pencil and not pen. That is OK with me so long as you are willing to compensate me for my time and inconvenience, which you seem willing to do. I hope you understand that I have a 'straight' life at home. I have a semi-full time job and for me to make plans to travel and meet you requires me to take time off work and come up with a 'story' for my family as to my absence. I know you are reasonable and were not being disrespectful to me or my time, although at the time it felt like it. Please feel free to call me later this week. Yesterday I found out that my grandmother is going to pass away any time now and I must return to Toronto earlier than I had planned. I look forward to hearing from you and working things out.
Sincerely,
Elysia

From: Michael
Subject: Re: Las Vegas Dec. 3
Dear Elysia,

I appreciate your understanding. I have not "seen" anyone since our time in San Francisco and I am glad to have the chance to try and make it up to you. I am sorry to hear about your grandmother. Mine passed away this year and I miss her very much. I will check in with you at the end of the week. The best time for me is Thursday evening, Pacific Time. I'll call you then. With warm regards, Michael

I never heard from him again.

* * *

I also have a few warnings for men that use prostitutes. They should know it's buyer beware. Not everyone is respectable. There are huge misrepresentations out there. Some girls use a different picture on their Internet site. Some will take the money and run. Some do an 'up sell,' as in 'Oh, well, $200 is only for this, and if you want that it will cost you more.' Of course, safe sex is an issue, big time, both for the provider and her client. A lot of guys want 'BBBJ' (bareback-blow-job), meaning no condom or to go down on the provider, and, if they can get away with it, condomless sex. Then there's the deep French kissing which exposes them to all sorts of other germs. If the escort is willing to do it for a price, then they will do it with anyone. Girls like this are extremely high risk for STD's and HIV and let's not forget the disgusting factor! For me, when I'm working, it's 'no glove, no love' and there are no exceptions ever. Some of these bozos are very protective of this type of behavior and they do not see anything wrong with it. Well, if a trick just ate out some scanky ho and then comes and thinks he can kiss me or put his dirty mouth on my pussy, well, EEEUUUUU!!!! Not a chance. I think guys need to be warned that there is a full spectrum of girls and activities, and all involved need to be aware of safe practice and have respect for individual boundaries and limitations.

Three

Clothes to Entice

I dress to entice men and my body language suggests that I am willing to satisfy them. I know I'm desirable and men want the satisfaction a sexually confident woman can bring. Believe me ladies, they all want it sexual. If you're good at it, in fact even if you aren't very good at it, they'll happily pay for it one way or another.

It's important for wives and lovers to remember that men don't want to see everyday bras and panties all the time. They certainly don't want to see me in what their wives wear. They want me in the clothes from my seduction drawer. I have an array of soft sexy clothing and sheer lingerie from gentle pastel colors to leopard prints to seduce and please them. Lace, bows, buttons and ribbons to untie to waste time to slow them down and excite them. Some are fur lined with the right amount of see-through sheer fabric and some are the cotton sporty look that a cheerleader would wear. I have feathered lingerie and soft velvet velour bras and panties. I wear bratty sheers with sequins and shimmering fake jewels and all sorts of teddies. I have negligees with the nipple holes cut out, bras that unbutton in the front and lots of frilly skimpy things that expose my soft skin for their fingers to touch. I've got handfuls of stay-up nylons with elastic at the top to hold them up.

What they really want to see is my body. They want to touch me. I encourage them to participate in undressing me and sometimes I let them do it quickly and sometimes I turn it into a slow tease. Oh, but they all do enjoy taking it off. 'Dumb' would be the woman that undresses herself. Women of the world, buy lingerie and make your man take it off you. Make them work for that orgasm.

I mostly shop for my working clothes from catalogues and sex stores with escort style apparel. I wear g-string panties, for sure, all the time. I've been wearing them for as long as I can remember, everywhere. I prefer cotton g-strings that have, what I call, full coverage. You may laugh at what I call 'full coverage' but some are so tiny there is no coverage. I like the ones with a small panel in front. As for bras, I like to have a little bit of padding for my everyday styles. These are what hold my 'investments' up and keep them looking alert and perky. Sometimes they have the wire around the cups but they have to be soft and comfortable. I have all colors, but mostly wear black and white under my everyday clothes.

E-mail:
From: Michael
To: Elysia
Subject: Enchanced
Well thanks for the picture!!!! You wear them well!!!! I am all for the natural but yours look so nice so I'll pay them a visit soon. I am out until mid April but I will come up then...
Hugs to the twins!!!!
Michael

From: The twins
To: Michael
"Enchanced????" Do you mean enchanting? Well, then yes I am! :o) If you meant am I enhanced?! Then I'd have to say yes, as in 390 cc saline in each! Here's a pic of the twins. Love, Elysia

My breasts show in all my dresses and I wear bras to push them up. Black, red, white bras, whatever. One favorite is a green-turquoise frilly little thing, which I call my 'bratty sheer.' It has bows to untie in the front and I make the men do that. I'll wiggle it at them and I'll make them put the bows in their teeth to pull it open. I say things like, "Oh, look inside." It's just like opening a present. They pull it open, feel my warm inviting nipples, and get really turned on. I have corsets too, bright deep purple corsets to traditional black with red, which I encourage them to untie. I once bought a pink feather boa from a children's dress-up store and just sewed it onto one of my favorite negligees! I have worn all these clothes to death.

My favorite dress is black satin and long, with ties that lace up the sides but show plenty of skin between the ties. It's very glamorous and silky to the touch and very feminine. I call it my 'Vanna White dress' and I've worn it to death. I think it cost me thirty bucks. I've made thousands in that dress.

Women may think they have to buy expensive clothes; really, I never do for working. The suggestion of what clothes expose underneath turns men on and then it's all about taking them off. Once I know a client, I will sometimes answer the door in nothing more than a white bra, white panties, white nylons and white high heels to surprise them. I like being unpredictable. They love it.

I wear stiletto shoes, mostly six-inch heels. Women, don't kid yourselves that men do not prefer high heels. The higher the better. Guys are turned on by shoes, feet, legs and stockings. I often buy slip-on shoes, because I can easily slip them off and then hop on the bed. If I'm wearing black to greet my client, I have a favorite pair, which is black and white with turquoise bows over a clear plastic top that covers yet exposes my feet and toes. They're kind of like glass slippers. I also buy shoes with laces, so I can entice my clients to untie them and take them off. Leather boots that go up to my thighs are a fantasy to some. Having them unzip them can be fun. I don't wear my 'working' shoes outside because they scream escort. But, you know, nowadays even square girls are wearing exaggerated high heels everywhere. To me, the stilettos are my props and since I'm a *real* escort, I don't need to advertise my sexuality out there. Unless I want to.

Sometimes clients buy me shoes and bring them as presents. One man brought me several pairs of $200 Kenneth Cole's shoes. He said something about his wife wearing clip clop plastic thongs at home. Sometimes men will just give me extra money to go and buy shoes. The next time they visit, I put them on. They take them off.

Taking care of my feet is important to me. I have a pedicure at least twice a month and use bright red polish on my toenails, as well as other bold colors. Whatever strikes my mood. I wear a toe ring and a favorite one is silver with tiny hearts. My feet are soft and sexy, with no calluses. I wash and cream them almost nightly to keep them that way. I use a pumice board, if necessary. Women who don't take care of their feet usually don't take care of their bodies either. I was lucky when I was given tiny ankles and nice feet and toes. Have you ever gone up an escalator and noticed a woman in front of you wearing sandals and her heels look like a dry cracked desert? Men notice. They don't want to kiss or suck toes that sandpaper their tongues. I have masturbated men with my feet. It's called a foot job. (But that's a different chapter.) Ladies, keep them soft.

I don't usually wear jewelry, unless they are taking me to dinner, a play, or out somewhere. I usually take it off when I have sex because I know it can get in the way and I don't want it to get broken or scratch my client. I also don't wear perfume. The woman in his life might smell it on him later.

It's all about the show, tantalizing and enticing men with an image of how most men fantasize a sexual goddess would seduce them. I become an actress. I have amazing intuition about what they want. They don't have to work to let me know. I know. Some are shy and need me to draw them out. Some are aggressive and like things to happen fast. Some just want to look and talk for a while. I know how to please them all.

Internet Review Board of Hookers
Review of: Elysia
Posted by: Luster
She is absolutely unbelievable. Just left her in Manhattan at her hotel and it was one of the top 2 or 3 ever. She is beautiful and well worth what she is asking…DON'T MISS HER. You guys are lucky to have her locally. I have to wait for her to come to town again.

Four

SAM'S CONFIDENTIAL SLICE OF HEAVEN

All right. I guess I can provide some info on a composite experience with Elysia. I will do that but would prefer not to give my personal history, except to say I am not married and am in the production of movies.

Why would I visit an escort? Well, I'm a hard-driven, workaholic man with a schedule and pace that leaves no time for a personal life. An evening with Elysia is an extra-special treat to reward myself and ease my tension. Hiring an escort is easier and more direct and less time consuming than searching for a partner at a singles bar or through a classified personal dating service.

I 'found' Elysia on her Internet site. I think of Elysia as a separate person unto herself in the world of prostitution. There's a surprise element to her. She actually makes me feel she's into my needs and that she cares about pleasing me and easing my tension. She presents a bit of a challenge, in a positive way, because she is different. I don't feel the same with Elysia like I have with others, like I was with a prostitute. She's high class, sophisticated, confident and beautiful. I have tipped Elysia thousands for the difference. She's my little slice of heaven that I treat myself to as often as she's in town, which is not often enough.

Perhaps first I should tell you, since I have been seeing prostitutes for years, that I am in the position to judge a 'good' one from a 'bad' one. Hiring a hooker from the Internet or from a newspaper 'escort' advertisement can have its surprises. In some cases, after the initial introduction, I have actually said, "Well, thank you very much," and given them some money to compensate for their travel but declined their business. Some turn out to be not quite as wholesome as one had expected from their description on the Internet. Some appear to be drug users and I stay away from that situation because they can be somewhat 'zoned out.' I suppose they do that intentionally just to put themselves in a different place while they do their prostitution. Some have an unkempt physical appearance, which I don't buy into either. I've had cases where I've hired girls to come to my hotel room, they call it 'outcall,' and they're not what I asked for. It's not uncommon to get a woman that's completely different. Sometimes they are late for the agreed appointment time, so I will call to see what's happened and they will say something like, "I'm almost there." Then, another half hour later it's, "Honey, I'm almost there, really." They may show up hours later. Sometimes you're sitting there in your hotel room waiting, worried, wondering if you're going to get stung by the police. Sometimes you get a woman who wants the money right up front, then once you get started, they say they only do a certain aspect of sex, even though that was what you were led to believe would happen when you hired them. Then they either want a lot more money to do the other part or they just don't do it at all. Of course, one would be hesitant to go to the police and complain. But for the most part, one usually gets what one expects.

Prostitution is all about the fantasies of a man and his pursuit of an escort's sexual secrets and her finesse at taking him to the heights of sexual climax. In the days when I was still looking for someone like Elysia, I had experiences with two women at the same time. It's kind of a fantasy for most men, at least to try it once. Since I could buy it, well, I decided to do it and it wasn't as exciting as I thought it would be. Now maybe it was the particular participants but I really can't blame it on them. They were pretty good. And it's not like I felt any pressure because I was the only man there. When you boil it down to the cold mechanical aspects, you're paying for it. If you're not good, that's not a problem. You still pay the money and they go through the motions and give you their show, so it's not my problem if I'm not good. Since I am paying her for my pleasure, I also can go to bed with an escort with no guilt and no strings. I mean it's not like sex in the back seat of your car with your high school sweetheart or a college date with a woman you feel the need to impress. At any rate, the two women both worked my body over at the same time, which was nice, but it was just too mechanical.

Okay, as for an hour with Elysia, it begins when I receive an e-mail from her confirming an appointment. It's two weeks out. Amazingly, I look forward to our getting together with almost unbelievable anticipation, yet at the same time I don't want it to get here because then it will be over again. Got to remember, nothing in life is for sure. I had provided her with my preferred date and time, and that is what she confirmed. I check my calendar again. I look to make sure nothing else is happening that day that could conceivably interfere with the appointment. I wonder to myself, what would it take to make me miss an appointment with Elysia? It would have to be some emergency. Does "life or death" qualify?

She is usually in town for two days. I always wonder whether to book the first night or the second? Common sense would say the first night. But she usually travels during the day and I remember one time when she was running late. It was a lousy weather day, raining the proverbial "cats and dogs." She said she had to cancel her first appointment, I was the second. I would hate to be the guy with the first appointment and receive the cancellation call from Elysia.

Her e-mail note says she will be staying at the "usual" place. Good, I know exactly where that is, so there won't be a chance to get lost on the way. She makes excellent choices in lodging. As usual, she will call me when she gets in to let me know the room number. After reading her note, I feel like I have taken some wonder drug. Maybe this is the feeling runners get when they talk about the endorphin high, except this feeling comes back several times during the next two weeks, at no extra charge!

I need to write in my agenda to pull out the funds a day or two in advance. My luck, I would rush up to meet Elysia and have forgotten the money. That would be really embarrassing. I remember one time with her when my appointment time was running out and we were both trying to get me out of there so she would have time to freshen up before the next appointment. I was in a hurry and started to leave without attending to the financial aspects with her. I think she gently said, "Aren't you forgetting something?" I actually felt embarrassed.

Well, it's finally here, the day for my appointment with Elysia. It's still dark outside, 5:30 AM, and time for me to hit the shower. With that special incentive waiting for me later today, I can't wait to get out of bed and get started. After the shower, I throw on some clean clothes and hit the road. As usual, my mind shifts to work issues and before I know it, I am entering the office parking garage. As usual, here I am back at the office ready for another workday. Time to go through the first daily ritual. Check the voice mail, check the e-mail, and then check my appointment calendar. Yep, it's right there, the code word for my Elysia appointment. Unconsciously my hand moves to pat my wallet pocket on my slacks. Yes, I did remember to bring my wallet. Time for the first phone call and I am launched into my workday's fun and games. Later, back from what seems like endless meetings, I check my voice mail. There are eleven unheard messages. I put it on fast speed and listen to them. I skip to the next one. There it is! Elysia's voice whose charisma reaches out and grabs me even in a voice mail. She says she has made it into town and confirms the location details. I'm set!

Later in the day I'm in a meeting and I glance at my watch. Where did the day go, it's going to be time to leave soon to meet Elysia. I make sure we get back on track and get the meeting closed almost on schedule. I attend to a few more e-mails and then impatiently wait for the laptop to shut down. I grab the papers I will need later tonight to finish up for tomorrow and stuff them in my briefcase. I'm running a little behind schedule and hope there are no traffic slow-downs. I make it on time. It's always tricky. I would like to hit the timing just right. I certainly don't want to get there late. I have heard horror stories of guys getting to appointments such as this before the appointed time and thinking it would be okay to just knock on the door early. That has proven awkward if the previous appointment has run a little long. I'm right on schedule as I park.

As I head up the elevator, I enter that calm period that is such a contrast to my feelings earlier in the day and to what I will feel in a few minutes. I don't know why this happens, but I guess that is one of life's little mysteries. My senses become alert, as I find the room.

I knock on the door. It swings open and there she is again. I step inside and we hug and exchange greetings. She leads me to the couch and offers me something to drink. I have water. I hear soothing music. Candlelight warms the room. She snuggles up to me and tells me how good it is to see me again. I catch a hint of the fragrance of her blond hair; it smells so fresh and exotic. I caress her shoulders and I am surprised how delicate they feel. She has an athletic, extremely feminine frame. We talk for awhile, then she stands up and heads to the bathroom. She turns and says, "Let's get comfortable." What a walk – bouncy, extremely sexy, very natural, not exaggerated in the old "Marilyn Monroe" way I have seen in the movies. She says she doesn't always work out regularly. Must be one of those genetically blessed thin bodies. Her skin is smooth and unblemished and always lightly tanned even in the dead of winter. She says she doesn't sunburn easily and the hotter the better for temperature.

I discreetly put the money on the coffee table while she is in the bathroom. I shed my clothes and lie on the bed. She will return attired in her choice of suitably skimpy and wild lingerie. Very shortly she comes out of the bathroom. I feel awed. Watching her coming close, I think that the best 'Victoria's Secret' models would be second-rate. Elysia puts them to shame. She maintains eye contact with me and makes me feel like she is focused only on me. She gently sits down next to me and asks me to turn over and lie on my stomach. Oohhh, time for the back and shoulder massage. She puts oil on her hands and begins. This feels so good. I turn my head to get a glance of her.

We talk a bit as she relaxes my muscles. She tells me about an encounter with a well-known actor and singer, though she didn't give his name. She said she was at the airport returning from a trip. This person noticed her, probably along with all the adult and adolescent males in the area, and he struck up a conversation with her. He was in town for a few days and she showed him around her city. They went out to a club and he went up on stage and joined the musicians. He called out her name several times from the stage. I can imagine what an experience that was for her. She pointed out that there was no sex involved, he was a married man, apparently, with children. I have to confess, I felt envious of him, even jealous. I don't necessarily believe he didn't have sex with her.

The massage part feels great; her hands are strong but very soothing. I typically wait for her to tell me to turn over. I do so, and bang – there is that eye contact again. She moves her body over me while swaying as if in a little dance movement. Little black laces that hold her lingerie around her breasts fall on my lips. She smiles. I bite the laces and pull them open. She slowly slips off her lingerie. Then, there it is, that look! When I looked at the photos on her Web-site, at least three images of Elysia are invoked for me. First, the freshly-scrubbed cheerleader type, second a playful, youthful, wildly exuberant grin showing the gums which reinforces a youthful aspect, and finally the sophisticated, sultry, unobtainable woman. The last image includes a smile with a slight upward curl on one side of her upper lip, almost like a sneer but totally sexy. That is what I am seeing right now, live and in person. The unobtainable may become obtainable, if only for a short while.

41

As we continue, I notice a glint from her belly-button area. I get up the courage to ask if she has a piercing there. It is so small I worry that maybe I am seeing a piece of lint or something. That would be just great to have noticed that! But, she confirms that she does.

She slowly moves downward on the bed between my legs. Still maintaining eye contact, she reaches for a condom from under the pillow and gracefully puts it in place so discreetly with her mouth that it is a pleasure. She slowly takes all of me in her mouth and begins. I am fully at attention and enjoying the sensation. After a short while she gently takes me from her mouth and climbs upward on me, straddling me in the waist area. She leans forward, offering a breast to me. I take the hint and caress one nipple with my tongue. Amazing, I think that even this part of her is what I envision when I think of what type of perfection in physical form I dream of in a woman. I lean my head back. She says, "We need equal treatment here!" and I perform the same for the other nipple.

After a while I stop, then without words she moves backward and she maneuvers us together, firmly sliding me inside her, and begins to slowly rock back and forth. At this point, words always fail me. The silence sometimes seems awkward, but I don't know what to say other than the tired "wow." She always reassures me that I don't need to say anything, or one-word expressions are just fine.

She moves off and to the side. It is cool that we have now been together enough and are familiar enough with each other that no words are necessary to explain the next move. Subtle body language movement is enough. She moves on her hands and knees. I stand immediately behind her off the bed where she guides me. She leans her shoulders down so the front part of her is down on the bed almost in a sleeping position. Her waist looks so small from this view from behind. On her web ad, she listed her measurements as 36, 26, 35. If this is a 26-inch waist, I can't imagine what a 24- or 23-inch waist would look like! Not as well, I conclude. I guide my penis into perfection.

After a few strokes, I withdraw and again no words are necessary as she turns over and lies on her back. The tried and true missionary style is always a pleasant way to conclude. The condom does cut down noticeably on the sensation, but is.a necessary evil. The upside is that it probably helps prolong the overall experience, particularly with someone as sexy as Elysia. There is always an upside to every-thing!

She begins to speak to me in a soft but very erotic manner. She uses my name and her nickname for me, while graphically asking me to continue doing what I am doing, in a variety of ways. I find the verbal action to be very stimulating and enjoy it. Elysia being Elysia has noticed this, I am sure. It is probably one of those actions she is able to take to subtly help guide the pacing of the session to a conclusion. I am amazed how I never notice her looking at a watch or clock, but she has an excellent sense of timing. I move closer and upward and increase my pace. She increases her encouragement. I feel climax approaching and …. it is more intense than I can remember before in my life. She arches her back upward to briefly keep us together. She's perfect. She definitely motivates me to want to repeat it!

She removes and disposes of the condom and returns with a hot wet towel and gently cleans me. She hops into bed and we snuggle and make small talk. I really appreciate this phase. So many of the other escorts don't do it. The old stereotype is that this part is what the woman is supposed to like, to chat instead of the male just turning over and going to sleep, but the stereotypical escort wants you to leave at this point.

Finally and sadly, I suggest that I probably should be leaving and she concurs wistfully. She is so good at knowing how to communicate things. I begin getting dressed and ask her when she will be back again. She says she typically doesn't plan these out, but that I am definitely on the notification list. We hug again at the door. I tell her to have a safe trip home and to come back soon. She gives me a small kiss on the cheek and I head out the door.

Five

GROWING UP

Not so long ago, driving home from work after smoking a joint, I decided to go to Alaska. I was going to drive there. And not come back. Ever. I had had enough. I am trying to remember what drove me to such hopelessness and exhaustion. I just wanted to leave my life and not be me anymore because I was so unhappy. I remember feeling like such a failure and like I had wasted my life with such bad decisions. Giving up. I gave up. I didn't think/care about my apartment, my friends, my family or myself. I remember listening to a CD. It was loud, the sun was shining and it wasn't until later that I realized the CD was on repeat and I was listening to the same song over and over. I remember flying by Horseshoe Lake and then I was in Rainbow Cove and I pulled over. How was I going to get through Centerville without seeing my brother? Seemed a weird revelation. I didn't even have a coat and only a little weed. My head was reeling and I knew I was in trouble. I wasn't sure what to do. I was so scared.

I was still a hooker and I felt shame. Yet sometimes I have no problem whatsoever with what I do. I wonder why? I mean, it's okay with me and not the rest of the world? Yet I have a problem with what people would think if they found out.

I was born in Toronto, Ontario. My parents are both Canadian. My grandparents are from Western Europe. I'm second generation Canadian. I have a sister and a brother and I'm the middle child. Everything you've read or heard that pertains to the middle child syndrome, I'm it. And I would have to say I'm like the black sheep. I remember my brother once saying that I was the one that always got picked on. It's funny that I remember that. We were at my cousin's place at Christmas and all the cousins were gathered in the basement and all the parents were upstairs. My brother and sister were laughing with my cousins because they thought it was a joke that I was the one always getting in trouble all the time. If someone was caught misbehaving while we were goofing off, I was the one who would get blamed. I was the one that would be the example, as in someone who always messed up. I always took the heat. It seemed whenever we couldn't remember whose turn it was to wash the dishes or whatever, well, it would always turn out to be my turn. Seemed like it was always my turn. Little things like that. My cousins, brother and sister acknowledged all that with laughter. I remember being really upset that they thought it was a joke. Well, that's how I felt as a kid anyway. It's funny that I remember that; well, on second thought, maybe it's not.

Sometimes, when I was upset, I'd go into the bathroom and lock the door. I could get away from everyone in there. I remember one time getting really upset and I went into the bathroom, slammed the door and locked it. I remember leaning against the sink, which was attached to the wall, and the sink fell down and smashed, with water blasting every-where. That was how they got me out of the bathroom. I don't recall if they were very angry about the sink, but what I clearly remember is being really sad and embarrassed because my family was laughing. They thought it was so funny. I clearly remember the laughter.

Now when I look back as an adult, it's clear that, probably, both my brother and sister had their turns at getting into trouble. Of course, as a kid, I was involved in my own world and it was always me, me, me getting into trouble. Basically, though, I guess I never felt like anyone defended me. I never felt special, one way or another.

I guess most people think that prostitutes must have horrible, abusive memories of their childhood. Well, no one memory stands out as horrific. I thought of it then, and still do, as just a regular way of grow- ing up. Not good, not bad, just the way it was. We attended church most Sundays and I attended Sunday school regularly. I went through the whole confirmation thing too. We were the model family. I was never physically abused. I got spanked when I was in trouble, but I figured everyone got spanked or grounded. One memory pops up that was about as bad as it got. In grade eight I went to one of my girlfriend's birthday parties. We had previously planned to sneak liquor from our parents, which we did, and so we all went into the bush drinking and necking and messing around. Without anyone paying much attention, it became dark and we all had to leave. Well, the birthday girl's parents were freaking out and had called the cops. There was a big hullabaloo about where the alcohol came from and, eventually, my parents realized that I had lied about taking their alcohol. The next day when I was walking home from school, my Dad came to pick me up. His car pulled up and I knew I was in trouble. I started talking and he hit me in the mouth hard and said something about lying. He said, "Don't lie to me," and it all came out. I was grounded for two months. That's about my worse memory of those early years.

Basically, when I think back on how my whole family handled problems, I'd say through denial. If you don't talk about it, you don't see it. Then everything is nice and rosy. Since the cops were called and there were other parents involved, my Dad felt it necessary to confront me about the party. Otherwise, unpleasant things were basically ignored. *I* felt ignored, especially by my father, although to ignore somebody takes some energy and basically my parents didn't even have the energy for that. I felt like I was there, nothing more and nothing less.

I remember my first kiss. I was in grade 8 and attending a school dance. We did this full-on French kissing thing. I was ready to go. That's when it started. That's when I learned I could use my sexuality to get attention and acceptance. Like any other teenager I really wanted acceptance. Somewhere in there, I decided it was okay to be sexual, though the first time I had sex was in grade 11. By then, it was definitely okay to sleep with guys and it was okay for me to mess around. I didn't feel I had to wait any longer. I was most comfortable hanging out with the crowd that was smoking, doing drugs, being sexy or having sex. And I was good at socializing. I got attention, that's for sure. Instead of finding it in a sports club, or the computer club, I found it in the rowdy club. I was the one in the smoking section, skipping school. My friends and I were smoking pot, going to parties and having sex. That's just the way I went about getting acceptance. I got what I wanted. The truth is, while I was doing it, I did feel remorse, sometimes. Even then. The truth is I even struggle with guilt today, being an escort. I'm okay with it most of the time, but sometimes I'm not. My early experience was a progression to who I am now. I accept that it happened. Whatever.

In my last year of high school, I remember wanting to leave home. It really bothered me that I never seemed to get my parent's approval. I was tired of being criticized. I had had enough. I was tired of getting shit all the time. Didn't matter what I did, it just wasn't good enough and I thought, 'Fine, I'm out of here.' I remember standing in my parent's front room and looking out the window and my dad came in and said, "So what's going on?" He could tell something was up. I said, "I'm leaving." He said indifferently, "Well, okay, the door's always open." I clearly remember him saying that. I ended up running out the door when my friend came to pick me up. I stayed at her house for one night. The next day my brother came to get me. Mom had sent him. So I went back to finish high school. I went back home. I was pregnant by that time too.

I became pregnant in April but I was about to graduate when I realized it. I figured I was about three months into it. Nobody knew. It was a big fat secret. Obviously I didn't want to face it right at graduation, with the exams and finals. When I had finished all the graduation stuff and *finally* acknowledged the fact that I *was* pregnant, it was too late to get an abortion. I had already had one, secretly, at sixteen. What I remember well about it is the fear that my parents would find out. I thought I would be disowned and that would be it. I went to the doctor and found out that to have an abortion at that age, I needed a permission slip from my parents. So I went out into the hallway and signed it myself. I went back in and handed it to the receptionist and nobody knew. My girlfriend and I skipped school the day it was to happen. She took me to the hospital. I went in and had it done. She came back and picked me up, dropped me off at home and nobody knew. Nobody knows to this day.

When I became pregnant again and realized it was too late to terminate the pregnancy, I was confused and not so sure that I wanted an abortion this time. So I just kept it a big fat secret. I was doing our family denial thing. I actually never told my parents. I tried to but could never find the words. I remember once walking into the living room, looking at my parents, sitting down and taking a deep breath, and then getting up again and walking out without even exhaling. I distinctly remember not exhaling. I'm not sure they even knew I was in the room. I was ripped with guilt and seriously stressed. Eventually they found out at a family event. I thought I wasn't showing but I must have been because a relative asked my mom when I had gotten married. My mom said, "What are you talking about? She's not married." The relative said, "Well, she's pregnant isn't she?" My mom looked at me and she knew. I was about five months and I was hiding it. Can you believe? I was still living at home hiding it. The next day Mom asked, "So how far along are you?" I can still see her sitting across the table from me as we drank tea in the kitchen. Well, I almost fucking died. I had been waiting for the right moment or the courage …the courage…the courage to tell them. I was just so afraid of my Dad finding out.

No one told me about sex. My mother never told me about my period, getting pregnant, birth control or anything. I remember my girlfriend told me girls have eggs and I imagined them like chicken eggs. Later I saw the little sex movie in elementary school, and my class had the usual short embarrassed non-discussion afterwards. As I got older, I just figured everything else out. There was never talk about stuff that's important in my family. Lots of families were like that back then. We went to school. We came home. We watched TV. We had Shake'N Bake chicken for dinner. We did our homework and we watched "Happy Days" on TV and we went to bed.

I told the man who was the father. He was twenty-three. The first thing he asked was how did I know it was his? I thought I loved him and when I heard that, I was devastated. There was no one else. I didn't blame him then and I don't blame him now for getting me pregnant. I've thought plenty about the choices I've made to get me to where I am now. I accept my responsibility for where I am today. I chose to be with whoever. I chose to have sex. I chose to give myself. Based on where I was at the time, I still made those decisions to do whatever. I take responsibility for all my actions.

At the time, I was so confused and scared. It was like I was living in some kind of altered reality. I decided I should give my baby up for adoption. I went to the adoption agency and arranged it. What else could I do? I felt so bad about myself and what I had done. The agency told me to go to Lamaze birthing classes so I went alone. I thought a lot about the baby and the wonder of pregnancy. I felt like my baby would never forgive me for abandoning it. I was so young and I felt like such a hopeless failure.

My mom helped me through the delivery. I had the option of either going home that day or staying four days in the hospital. I decided to stay. I was afraid to go home and I was afraid to make a final decision and I was afraid to walk away. At some point I asked to have the baby brought to me. In those four days I bonded with her. The social worker kept coming in and asking me what I wanted to do. On the fourth morning, I left my baby in the hospital to be adopted. That same afternoon I decided to keep her and I went back to get her the same night. And then I tried to be her mom. I spent three months at it. I was a kid with a real live baby. I didn't know what to do. I had just graduated from high school. I had her with me in my bedroom at home but, even in the middle of the night, my mom would come and help me. She would take her and feed her and I realized, after awhile, I couldn't be a single parent. I thought my baby deserved better than *me*. I was mature enough to know my child was a treasure but not mature enough to raise her well, and I didn't think it was right to exhaust my mother with my choice either. I felt I had burdened her. I agonized and eventually decided to put her up for adoption again. I loved her but she needed two loving parents with a home and the maturity to raise her. I knew I was right but my guilt rose to an unbearable level. Anyway, I really didn't know what else to do.

While that was the best decision, I was terribly traumatized. I felt irresponsible and horrible and I couldn't handle it. My self-esteem was non-existent, and I felt such a huge sense of failure for having brought a child into a less than perfect situation.

I had no choice but to move out of my parents' house after her adoption. I mean I felt that way, but I actually did have a choice, though I didn't feel like I did at the time. At seventeen, you think getting pregnant is a mistake, and I felt too guilty and ashamed to stay home with my parents. I was so wretched about it all. I couldn't run away fast enough. I was so miserable I wanted to feel nothing, to just hang out and party. I didn't want to think. I felt like I had no future. That was basically the end of me for a long time.

When I left home for good, at age eighteen, I was working part-time for a modelling agency. I had actually started going there when I was in high school. My school had a program where they chose two girls from the sewing class to attend the agency. It was a way for the agency to promote itself and teach two girls to be models. I learned how to model and became involved in promoting the beauty business. I took all the courses and eventually they offered me a part-time job teaching people how to use cosmetic products.

I moved into a tight, small community in the hooker area of Toronto. It was a low-rent, affordable housing area, though it was still in a nice part of town. I was in a physical and mental transition, moving from my parents' home to getting a new group of friends. It was mostly a community of drag queens, hookers, transvestites, transsexuals and gays. They became my friends and most of them did drugs. They are the ones who supported me, took me in, and gave me a place to stay. When I was poor and needed money, they gave me money. They gave me everything I needed.

The man who introduced me to the area was named Peter. He was teaching a cosmetic course at the modelling agency. We became friends. One night we decided to go out and we went to a gay bar. Peter was dressed up as a woman. That was the first time I had ever seen a drag queen. I was like, 'Oh my God,' but then, in the same second, I thought, 'Okay, I don't care. Whatever.' He was beautiful and probably one of the best in town. We became fast friends and started hanging out. We had fun. Then one night Peter said he had met a bunch of people who were doing drugs. I asked him what he meant by 'doing drugs' and he said, 'using needles.' I told him I had never done that before but, because I was game for anything, I ended up meeting those people as well. And ended up at a party where they were doing it. And ended up trying it. I started smoking pot occasionally in my last year of high school, but this was moving to cocaine and MDA. We called it the love drug and it was the party drug of choice. It came before ecstasy. Mostly I did MDA because it was only ten bucks a hit. Then we would drink our faces off. I became fast friends with all these people and some of them are still my friends. Many are now dead from AIDS.

There was lots of bar hopping, drinking and partying at clubs where we were all dressed up in exotic-type, sexy costume clothes and wearing lots of make-up. We were not using needles every single day, nor every weekend. It wasn't like that at all. Every once in awhile, we'd have this little binge. I don't even know how much. Oh, it's gross just thinking about it, what I was doing to myself. I got high. I got really high. It was just an escape. It was just another way to party. Everyone was doing it. That is what we did. I used drugs quite heavily during that time as a way to not feel anything. I also wanted to fit in with the new crowd I was hanging with. For at least a year or two, I did IV drugs, shooting heroin and stuff into my veins. I have hepatitis 'C' and I probably caught it at that time, though I didn't know for years. I either caught it from using drugs or from getting a tattoo. At the time the sanitary regulations for tattoo establishments weren't like they are today.

During this time, my only purpose for living was to escape, to party and to laugh. I had quit the cosmetic's job, since I could not earn a living, and I tried to get another job. I tried to work as a waitress and that didn't work. Somewhere in there I turned my first trick.

I became friends with another tranny drag queen person, whose name was Eric. He was part of the downtown crowd, the wanna-be crowd hanging out, and I hooked up with him. Eric ended up becoming Roxanne. She was working the streets, in the neighborhood I lived, where the prostitutes worked. I wouldn't say he turned me out, per se, but that's the person I was closest to at the time. I asked him how it worked. He told me how and what to do and what to charge and stuff like that.

I knew all the street hookers in the area. I'd walk around and say hi to them, using their names. You know, like, "Hi, Momma Kate." She was one of the oldest trannies, oldest hookers, of Toronto, who became a very good friend of mine and still is. So I was around it. It was familiar. I thought, 'Okay, I can do that.' When I walked out my door, that's the people I ran into and saw. I didn't start hooking right away. But I lived there. They knew me. I knew them. They were my peers at the time. Well, I needed money so I said to myself, 'I'll just go out and get some money' and that's how it happened. I did what they did to earn money. I started hooking when I was eighteen because I had no money, and I needed to pay rent and buy food and drugs for my partying so I would not feel anything and yet be a part of something.

That first time, I remember standing on the sidewalk in front of the building where Momma Kate had an apartment when a guy walked by and asked Momma Kate if she was real. Momma said no, but pointed to me and said, "She is." She asked me if I wanted to go with him and I said, "Sure." That was how it started. I went with him to her apartment. Momma stood outside the door because she knew it was my first time. We had regular sex. I only recall vague little clips of information about those first times. I've spent years burying it. I don't want to remember it. You know, that's kind of just where I was for awhile.

I've never had a pimp and have never even been approached by one. I was lucky. Really lucky. I could have easily gone into a different road with the working girls who were down that route. I mean, how did I not end up dead? I was lucky enough that I ended up with a bunch of people who were not in that pimp group. Just plain lucky. I worked the streets for a very short time.

I made other friends. Jim became a very good friend of mine. I lived with him. He was gay and he had a lover. The one thing I still remember about Jim was the time he came home from somewhere and he walked in and saw my friends and me bingeing on drugs. He looked at us and I saw what he saw. Oh my God, it was so gross. We were sitting there, stupefied, around the fucking spoons. People were just sitting there stoned, sweaty, and dirty. Really disgusting. We hadn't eaten. We hadn't seen the light of day. We were freakin' high. It was an escape. It was just gross what I was doing to myself. I saw that and I thought, 'Oh my God, forget it.' I thought, 'That's it, I'm not going to do this anymore.' So I just stopped. I never touched it again.

During this time, when I was hanging out with my gay and tranny friends, no one knew about HIV. I was around nineteen at the time and messed around with several guys. A few of those lovers eventually died of HIV. I can't remember if we even practised safe sex. Years down the road, when it finally hit me that I could have HIV, I freaked. I realized I had to get tested but it was a tough thing to do. My anxiety level was maxed. I went into the gay and lesbian center as a number, instead of using my name, because I was sure it was going to come up positive. It took two torturous weeks to get the results. It was negative. Well, I fell apart probably just as much as I would have if I had found out it was positive. I cried with relief. Luck again, just plain gifted luck.

I decided to go back to school. I enrolled in a cosmetology college and became an esthetician. I got a diploma. The problem was it cost me around $10,000. Again I needed money. All that time I never moved back home and I never asked for money from my parents. I've always had to pay rent. I did various things along the way. I came in and out of straight careers, in and out of school, doing different things, but I would always slip back into prostitution. I kept trying to survive in a straight life but prostitution was always there to fall back on. One way or another, I needed to pay my bills and the money was good. When money issues didn't work out in my straight life, I thought, 'Well, okay, I'll be a prostitute for awhile.'

The area Jim and I were living in also had a lesbian community where drug use just wasn't as prevalent. Since I had quit drugs, I started hanging out with a whole new group of people who happened to be lesbians. Low and behold, one came into the picture who was attracted to me. I went for it. I started dating just women because that's who I was around. I loved them and they were good to me and I had good relationships and bad ones.

I'm trying to remember the first time I slept with a woman, like, how did that happen? My twenties are such a blur of survival. I know I was trying to cover up the pain of giving up my child and of feeling like such a failure and such a fuck-up. When I left home, I thought my life couldn't get any worse, I felt like I had no future. How did I get there? How did I become a lesbian? Well, the women of the gay community were my friends and I felt accepted and desired. When I told my mother about my girlfriend, I'll never forget my mother saying to me, "You weren't born that way." She was right. I didn't desire girls growing up. I think it was just learned behavior. That's what the people around me were doing. They were lesbians. They were still alive. It was no big deal. Looked like fun. I'm an open kind of person. I'm always going to be that kind of person that says, "Yeah, okay, I'll give that a try." You know, even now, if a person says, "Let's go rock climbing," okay, sure,

I'll give it a try. I'm open to new things. Starting from the first time I turned out and worked, or the first time I did drugs, or the first time I was with a woman, or the first time I went scuba diving, or the first time I did anything that was different or risky, it never occurred to me to not do it. I never said, "Oh, I better not do that." There was never that thought. It was just, 'GO.' I'm in there. I'm gone. I'm the first one in line. I'm a risk taker, always looking for a thrill and maybe a way out of the box. There's a part of me that thinks, 'Maybe if I do this, I will feel better.' Well, maybe if I loved a woman, I'll feel loved. Well, maybe if I go scuba diving, I'll feel more exciting. Or maybe if I'm an esthetician, I'll feel like I have a career.

One of my most significant relationships was with Trudy. We lived together for three years. I was twenty-three years old when it started. We loved each other. We were a couple in every way. We both had straight jobs. I worked as an esthetician. There were lots of parties going on, and I remember big parties at a local swanky club with the drag queens. All the dykes went there too. We dressed up into crazy things. Really, the clothes were costumes: star wars, emperors and empresses, showing our boobs, wearing sexy revealing clothing and spiked shoes and tons of makeup. Eventually Trudy and I broke up, though to this day I'm not sure why. I guess we just grew apart or the love just didn't last or we were young or I didn't know what the hell was going on. The breakup was hard, really hard for me. It was heart-wrenching.

I decided to move on from lesbians to straight friends and eventually I started hanging out with a straight girl friend, who I met at a party. We started doing cocaine and MDA but just snorting, no IV drug using or anything like that. That's when I met a drag queen named Dan. He was a master of ceremonies for 'Ladies' Night' at a local club. He would hire a group of guys to strip and then he'd do the introductions. He and his business partner hired girls to strip as well and to travel to clubs in other cities. They called the girls' act *Hardly Legal*. Well, I said, "hey, I can dance. I can strip," so I hooked up with *Hardly Legal* and off I went on the road. Five girls, a band, and a driver.

We bebopped around the States for six months, doing the stripper shows in bars. We would drive and drive and hit all the town clubs where the local horn dogs (as we called them) would drool. We each had a solo dance and five costume numbers. We dressed up as cowgirls, cheerleaders or harem girls or whatever, but all the costumes were outrageous.

For my personal act I danced to George Michael's "I Want Your

Sex," while wearing a studded black leather outfit which I slowly took off down to a basic black g-string. It was all choreographed, titty dancing, no total nudity, no floor shows or anything like that. All g-strings. We'd dance around the tables topless, wearing just a g-string. Or we would start with a costume and go down to topless. I had small flatish boobs, but I was blond and I was sexy and lean. Lots of guys liked me but most of the time they liked the other chicks with the big knockers. The big tips often depended on the size of the knockers. Fine. I didn't care. I didn't care at all. I didn't get jealous or insecure or feel weird. The men were young and old and everything in between; just regular guys who had a good time drooling over us. They all had the same lusty smile and a look they would all get as if mesmerized by our boobs. I didn't find them disgusting. It was more about having fun tempting them. Their pockets were full of money and I made tons of money dancing for them and had such a good time. I remember having stacks of dollar bills wrapped in elastic bands that were six inches high in my suitcase. Sometimes we each made $300 dollars a show.

Eventually, back in Toronto, I met Jennifer, who introduced me to massage parlors. Jennifer was a full-fledged dyke lesbian who became a good friend. She worked at the "Rub & Tug." She'd give a really good massage or a hand job, and she'd give blow jobs but she wouldn't fuck the men. She told me that if a guy really wanted to get laid, she would go get one of the other girls. So one day I went down and applied at "Rub & Tug." The owner wouldn't hire me because he said I hated men. I don't hate men. He was just an idiot. Jennifer told me about another massage parlor called Anita's Palace, so I went and applied there. That's when I started working in a massage parlor.

Six

MASSAGE PARLORS

We all need money. Some women marry for money, some women work in offices for money and some women hook for it. A common misconception is that prostitutes/escorts do what they do because they were molested. Many children are fondled or molested and do not become escorts. Some very famous public personalities have admitted to being molested but didn't become escorts. The primary reason women become escorts is for the money. I suppose psychologists might need to label a reason for it and maybe for some prostitutes there is a thread to that assumption. However, in my opinion and knowing prostitutes, it's all about survival and the unbelievable amount of money in the business. I've done many different things but none as financially rewarding as being an escort.

A massage parlor is a place where guys pay for time at the 'club' and get to use the facilities. Each club is somewhat different and each club has different rates and different girls. Working in a massage parlor as an escort is not as freaky as a lot of people think, depending on how you work. You may laugh at this, but a massage parlor can be a safer place for one's health than sleeping around with lots of lovers. All the massage parlor escorts I know always use condoms for blow jobs, do not kiss on the lips, do not let men have oral sex with them, and don't allow the clients to touch their pussy at all. Recreational sex isn't always so healthy. Working in a massage parlor is safer than street prostitution too because a massage parlor has rules, which are enforced either by the escorts or the madam.

A man, called a trick, john, or client, will come in the front door. The escorts, or working girls, will come out of their staff room and sit on a sofa, or stand and pose, looking pretty and smiling. They are always dressed in slinky sexy clothes, usually showing lots of skin and bulging boobs, and wearing stiletto heels. The idea is to titillate men into choosing them. There are usually about eight to ten girls on each shift at Anita's Palace and usually, depending on which girl enters the parlor first, any one of us will act as the hostess when a man comes in. The other girls don't say a word to him, other than maybe a hello. The hostess greets the client, and finds out if he has been there before, if he knows the routine and, if not, she will give him a 'door speech' about how the club works. There is a point system at Anita's Palace that is important to the girls because it determines the weekly scheduling. The hostess asks the client who he saw last time, or if he wishes to request a particular girl, and as long as he mentions her name, she will get a point whether or not she is there. Each girl is given a point if she is picked. If he extends his time, which he is expected to pay for, she will also get more points. Each week the girls request the days and time they wish to work, and whoever has the most points gets the first scheduling choice. If he doesn't request a girl, the hostess introduces him to each of the girls and, at that point, he has to pick one.

There are parts of being an escort that take some serious under-standing like how you can walk into a room with eight other women all dressed up, all competing to allure a man's sexual attention. You think you know what he wants. Then you wonder why he picked the girl next to you that looks like a dog. You think,'Why did he pick the girl who is butt ugly?' There are other girls standing there that have an average look, some are pretty and some are gorgeous. So how does it work the man picked the dog? I have seen some ugly women make good money. They go upstairs with their client and come down with lots of money in their purses. Why didn't he pick the classic beauty with big boobs, long slinky hair and Tina Turner thighs? Most men do, but not all the time. As they walk up the stairs, we hear the men say things like "You are so beautiful, so sexy, I've never seen anything like you" to the ugly ones and pretty ones alike. And you know very well that you're standing next to a woman that could do the same thing to a different man, no matter what she looks like. An escort's tummy may have been bulging, or her boobs aren't as big as the girl sitting next to her, but she will be picked anyway. Turns out, all women are beautiful. You don't have to be pretty to be an escort. If a woman feels sexy, if she thinks she's sexy, if she knows she's sexy, she will drive a man nuts. Men can sense it, plain and simple. We have the boobs, the hourglass figures, the round butts, athletic or skinny legs, soft skin, pussies, everything a guy wants. For every woman there's a guy out there who will find her his goddess.

I guess I should have been nervous when I first started working at Anita's Palace. To be honest, I was more worried I wouldn't get picked than I was worried about the possibility of sex. If I was going to be there, I wanted to make money. I wanted to be picked. As it turned out, I never had a problem.

Madam Anita charged the clients $50 for the basic room and massage. For that they got to use the facilities and have a massage. That's it. The only money Madam Anita took was for the rental of the room. The girls didn't get a dime of that. The Madam trained me how to give a massage. There was no mention of sex. I didn't know what the other girls were doing; we seldom talked about it. Since I was trained to do massage and since 'hand jobs' were mentioned, I just assumed that was what everybody else was doing because that's the kind of club it was. It wasn't really, really hard core. But who knows? Maybe I was just so green and naive I didn't know.

Once a man was in the room I would solicit him and negotiate a price. Back then, all I did was hand jobs. A hand job, where I kept my clothes on, was $50, topless was $75, and for me to take off all my clothes while doing a hand job was $100. Sex was $200 but the place was really all about hand jobs. I remember my first trick at the massage parlor. I thought I was going to get arrested. I didn't care who walked in the door; I thought it would be a cop. I would say, "So, do you want something extra?" Then he would say, "What?" and I'd say, "Well, I can give you whatever for whatever." Then I would be arrested. That was my biggest fear. Huge fear. I got really tricky about what I would say, though eventually I basically came out and just said it. "Hand job?" Most guys went for the full nudity hand job.

Once the client chooses a girl, she is allowed to talk to him all she wants. She takes him upstairs to show him the fantasy rooms and the basic rooms, which are priced differently. The fantasy Jungle Room is a favorite, but there is also a Mirror Room and a Chinese Room. Most men pick a cheaper basic room, which has, you guessed it – basically just a bed in it. She settles him into the room where he is left to change into a clean bathrobe provided by the parlor. She then goes back downstairs to pay the supervisor the money the client has given her for the room. She gets him change, if needed, and registers the room they are in, for how long, and what time they went in. Then she goes back to the room.

In the meantime, the client is supposed to have changed into the bathrobe, and she then takes him down to the shower area. Most men are quite clean but we don't give them a choice. They must shower. In

Anita's Palace, the girl doesn't get into the shower with the client but in some establishments they do. Some have larger, more elaborate rooms with showers and hot tubs in them. Anita's has a big common bathroom with two large showers. The hallways have dividers to keep it private for the men walking to and from the showers, and if the shower room door is shut, the girl doesn't open it until it is free. The showers have pump soap dispensers instead of bars of soap so germs are not transferred through hard soap. The supervisor, or the girls that are not busy, will freshen and clean the shower facility. Doors are wiped dry, the shower is dried out, fresh mats are put down, fresh towels and face cloths are laid out. Anita's Palace is not a five-star hotel, it's a massage parlor, but the Madam that runs it does keep it impeccably clean.

While he's in the shower, the girl puts on her lingerie or a special dress, shoes, stockings or whatever she wants to seduce him. She does this in a changing room set up just for the girls where she will also choose a CD to play, and a drink for her client and get the massage oil. All this is done in record time as she waits for him to come out of the shower. She does not wait in the room he has chosen because the girls are not allowed to be there without the man present, since most men leave their wallets and clothes there while they shower. She waits outside the shower to take him back to the room.

When he comes out and sees her standing there with her lingerie on, lots of men will get an instant 'hard-on' because he typically hasn't seen a real woman in real life in lingerie for twenty-five years. To the wives of the world I'd like to say, "PUT IT ON." It's all about getting what you want by giving him what *he* wants. You know that fur coat you want? Ask for that about mid-blow job. If *any* man tells you it's okay that you don't want to have oral sex with him, you've got a problem on your hands. Forget the fur coat.

To get an indication of what the man wants, the girl will say things like "what sort of fun do you like" or "when was the last time you had a really good blow job?" and see how they respond. It depends on the person. Basically, we already know what the men want because, mostly, they simply want to get screwed by someone that seems to want to screw them. Simple as that. Very direct. They may say, "Come on, little girl, let's get in here. Let's do it." It's so funny sometimes; you can't help but laugh. Some girls ask what the man would like and then tell him how much it costs. Some girls will ask him how much he'd like to spend. It can be a bit of a discussion, but the vast majority of men are far too intimidated, in the presence of a woman that's turning them on, to want to negotiate, and they don't want to degrade the girls. They want to enjoy her. A sales technique I used when a man was hesitating about the price: "Well, I normally charge $400, but I'll give it to you for $350." It worked well too. The client might say that he has a couple of hundred bucks, whereupon the girl tells him not to worry, she'll make him happy with that.

I remember one 'regular' who came in twice a month and who had a fetish about belly dancers. First he liked to chit-chat with the girl and then he would ask her to do a little dance for him with her belly button showing because he would always place a jewel in it. Every girl in the parlor ended up at some point with a jewel in her belly button. Then he liked the girl to do a hand job. He lived with a girlfriend, but going to Anita's Palace was a little thing he did on the side. Lots of men come for a little extra entertainment in their sex lives. In the summer, Anita's Palace often averaged 30 sessions a day. The record was 69 men in one day. A lot of Americans would come up to Canada, partly due to their economy and their dollar being worth more than the Canadian dollar. By the way, Canadian men are a little cheap compared to American men.

All kinds of men would come in, everything from underage, to old, to good looking, to big fat ugly bald guys who were disgusting hairy monsters. Whatever— every type; rich, poor, students, and seniors who had just cashed their retirement checks. When they wanted more services but didn't have the cash on them, I'd keep their wallet or car keys for collateral while they walked to a bank machine. I found a way to get the coins and the lint out of their pockets, man. We took it, we took it all. That's the name of the game. I earned it, of course.

The money that's given to the girl in the room is all hers. She gets nothing if the man doesn't give her cash. So whatever money she can convince him to spend, he gets that service. He would be lucky to get the massage that's supposed to be included with the room rate if he doesn't come up with some cash. Madam Anita provides the room, bathroom supplies, and sheets, and the girls provide the condoms, the lubrication, and their lingerie/clothes. The establishment wouldn't provide condoms for legal reasons. If the girl decides to have a dozen condoms in her purse, that's her business. Sometimes the girls would forget to bring them. I had no patience for that and so I charged them $10 for one of mine. When the girl finishes a session, she removes the man's condom with a tissue and then flushes it down the toilet. The evidence is gone. The wrapper does not go in the garbage either but leaves with the girl when she finishes her shift.

In a massage parlor, there's a fixed minimum and maximum amount that the girls are allowed to charge. There has to be consistency or it really could turn the cat house into a cat fight. They are not supposed to ask more than the house standard. There are lots of ways of getting around that, but it's not the kind of business where it really means much except to set some limits. If a man is willing to give you more money, well, does a waiter turn down a generous tip for excellent service? And you can bet the girl wants to keep the man coming back, so she works for that and a generous tip. Obviously a man that treats a girl generously is usually going to get better service, especially if he comes back a second time.

The house maximum is set so the girls won't gouge anyone or take advantage of the men that are loose with their cash. After all, the Madam's establishment has a certain reputation to keep. If full on sex is $300 minimum, a girl might ask for the maximum of $500 and then see what the man will pay. Of course, if a man is not prepared to pay for sex, the girl doesn't do it. A lot of the men know there's a minimum, mostly because some stupid hooker told them. They know the game well enough that they know the girls will give it up for the minimum price, so they won't pay more because if she isn't willing to come down to the minimum price, then he can complain to the management and the girl will get into trouble. These jerks also know that the girls are supposed to spend the entire time that he has booked for the room with him. A girl needs a good reason to finish a session early or the Madam will get angry with her. Remember these girls need to make money. He can make it uncomfortable enough for her so that she gives it up for the minimum price. Of course, we have our ways of dealing with cheap men. One of them is called the 'fake fuck.' The assholes get it for sure. Men of the world, never be cheap with a prostitute.

To be honest, escorts would prefer that the clients never enter their vagina. Of course the man has a condom on, but it's still her body. We're not talking love here. We're talking making money. So sometimes the 'fake fuck' is ideal. Women of the world are going to laugh. We pretend we are fucking them. It's not always easy to do. It is important for the room to be dark so the client can't see as well, and it works best on men with small dicks. They think they're inside the girl and they're not. The man is lying on his back and the girl is on top of him. She takes his condom-covered hard erection and puts it behind her and covers it with lots of lube as she enticingly strokes it. Then while making a strategic shift in her pelvic position, she pretends to move it inside of her. Really, all she does is press it firmly between her hand and the crack of her butt, forming a fake vagina. She slides it back and forth and he

60

thinks he's inside her. And he's not. There are a couple of positions girls can do that one. Doggie style is another one. It may seem like he could see that one, but he's hanging onto her back. They're hardly ever looking down at their dick. The girl holds the penis tightly in their hand, again rubbing it against her body. It's surprising how many guys don't know. We're giving them pleasure all the same. They still enjoy it. They still get their money's worth.

Most men don't come to us after they have been drinking, and seldom when they are drunk. Alcohol has very little to do with it. In the evenings, occasionally a group of guys would come in fairly drunk from partying and those were usually nightmares. We don't encourage men to drink alcohol and we certainly don't like them drunk. First of all, because of the alcohol, it's harder for them to have an orgasm. Sometimes they're more generous with tips, sometimes not. With alcohol you never know what might happen.

Everyone likes a bargain and Anita's Palace had morning specials. The Madam would publish a coupon offering half price in the local newspaper. Seriously! Men would clip them out and bring them in. They would come at 9 or 10 o'clock in the morning. They'd be standing there waiting for us to unlock the door.

God made prostitutes for two reasons: so that really, really stupid women can make good money too, and really, really intelligent women can make a killing. There are all kinds of girls that work at massage parlors. There are hard-core types, really stupid girls, emotionally messed-up girls and women like you or your neighbor next door. Not all the girls that work at Madam Anita's have a brain. There are lots of girls that were 'turned out' by boyfriends who have them work at massage parlors. They all make money. But really, I think that some of the madams shouldn't use some of the girls because they're so messed up, for whatever reason, and the madams are adding to their injury. Madams are often hardened ex-hookers. They've been around and have their limits and are not going to be taken advantage of by anyone. Life has taught them to not give anyone a break. I think it's wrong to hire these girls so the Madam can have ten beautiful girls sitting on their sofa because that's what she advertises. She has about thirty to forty girls on staff, sharing two shifts a day. There are only six rooms in Madam Anita's, yet she insists on having eight to ten girls on staff per shift and the girls get fired for not showing up.

Escorts can handle what they do when they count their money. When you go home at night and throw $1,500 to $2,000 on your bed and you remember that at 10:00 that morning you didn't have a dime and were in debt with the rent due and now you have $2,000 - you can feel pretty good about what you're doing. The only reason women do it is for the money. And the only reason men go to prostitutes is for sex. It's really quite straight forward. Money, sex. That being said, sometimes in meeting each other's needs, it can't help but develop into other things for both participants, such as more self-esteem or more confidence for some men in their personal sex lives.

One of my funniest memories about working at the massage parlor happened when six of us were lounging around on the parlor's back porch one sunny afternoon. The porch is behind the massage parlor and overlooks a side street that slants downhill. We are not allowed to smoke inside the parlor, so some of us were smoking and some were just enjoying the sunshine while waiting for tricks. Of course we were in sexy, tight dresses, boobs overflowing and legs exposed. You can imagine the typical cleavage, short skirts, net stockings or bare legs, and high heels all over the place. Most of us were leaning on the railing facing the street when we heard the noise of roller-blades on the opposite sidewalk. A boy, probably around eighteen, was whipping along because it was just steep enough to really get going on a pair of roller-blades. He looked over and noticed us and his mind must have gone 'bong,' as his eyes riveted on us. Well, it's the magnetic power of prostitutes and heads always turn to see us. We had his complete attention. I remember this as if it happened in slow motion. He streaked along with his eyes locked on us, right up until he hit the back of a parked car and bounced back on his ass to the ground. We could see the stars and tweety birds flying around his head. It was terrible, but funny, like out of a movie. Thank goodness he wasn't hurt, — well, except for his ego, no doubt. We were falling apart with laughter. We yelled, "Are you all right?" He yelled back, "I'm fine." He got up and roller-bladed away and while he couldn't look at us, we could read the 'Oh shit' of his body language.

* * *

Women of the world, you should know how easy it is for a man to go and visit a massage parlor. It wasn't unusual for men to come in on Saturday, from late morning to late afternoon. They were often in a hurry. We figured they had dropped the wife at the mall, at her hair salon, or to visit their mother-in-law, and promised to be back in an hour or two. They were always in a hurry. Honey, just make sure you know where your 'ole man' is when you go to do your thing and he tells you he has some things to do and promises to pick you up in a few hours. He may have driven six blocks down the road to us, entertained

62

himself for an hour, freshened up in a shower and picked the wife up on time. She may have assumed he'd gone to watch a football game in a bar. We don't take very long. Men can get a forty-five minute session at a massage parlor. We have him in and out of the room in forty-five minutes, including his shower. Easy come, easy go.

Seven

LOVE, JAPAN, AND THE STOCK MARKET

I was working at Anita's Palace when I met Ian. We were both in our late twenties. He was a doorman at a local nightclub where I hung out. We hit it off right away. Ian's the only boyfriend that knew I was a prostitute. I don't think I ever told the others. He found out because one day I was outside on a back terrace at Anita's in a skimpy dress with stiletto heels, in plain view from the street. I was talking on my cell phone and a truck went by slowly. I could see it out of the corner of my eye. I knew it was him and I hung up the phone. My phone rang and it was Ian asking, "Is that you?" When I told him yes, he put his truck in reverse to check me out one more time. I remember I smiled at him. He smiled back and flashed me a sexy look before he drove slowly away. He was with his girlfriend at the time.

Within three months we started living together. He knew everything about me, which was wonderful 'cause I didn't have to hide 'the secret.' He accepted that I did massages and only hand jobs. We were really in love. We were happy for about two years and lived together for three. I wasn't using drugs then, though Ian was a habitual pot smoker. I used to ride him about how much money his pot smoking was costing, but he didn't care. He'd do it anyway. I'd just bug him and I probably had a smoke every once in awhile, though rarely.

Eventually, he didn't like the fact that I worked at a massage parlor. I'd come home and he'd say, "So how much money did you make today?" And I'd unload pockets full of money. He knew what I had done for that money. But I wasn't having sex. And if I did, it was rarely. It was hand jobs. So I quit for Ian and he started supporting me.

I went back to school to learn computerized accounting. Ian and I were together and doing just fine. He supported me through school and I made him take a job at a local warehouse. I thought a guy should do whatever it took to ensure I didn't have to be an escort. That was a requirement of whatever guy I was seeing personally. And we struggled, man, for cash. I always took control of the money. I'd say, "Just give it here. Here's your $40 dollars for pot and that's it." Sometimes he would ask to pay the bills and take charge of the money but I couldn't stand it. I had to know what was going on and make sure we had money. I don't want men to have that kind of control. I don't know why.

I loved Ian, I really did. I thought I'd be with him forever. I felt inner peace with him. But he had an affair. I suspected it, questioned him, and he didn't have the integrity to tell me about it. I fully realized it when one day we had lunch together and had fucked, and eventually ended up going back to his work place together. 'She' was walking towards us and I knew. Instantly. There was that energy between them. I knew. I asked him and he said no. Later I found a credit card receipt. That's how I figured it out. I looked in his stuff and saw the receipt. I snapped. I got a huge steak knife, like some steak house restaurants have, and I took the bill and drilled the knife right through it into a huge beam in our apartment until the blade was buried up to the fucking wooden handle. I lost control. It scared me, to know I could snap like that with such boiling anger. So we broke up - bing, bang, boom. It really hurt.

I knew a couple of nurses back then and they said, "Ya know, you'd be an excellent nurse. Why don't you go and be a nurse?" I said, "You know, I can do that. Sure." I figured that if I got sick of nursing babies, I'd nurse old people. If I became bored with that I could be a teacher. I figured there'd be room for growth, the future, whatever, if I got bored. When I was accepted into nursing school, I got a student loan for $10,000. I lived on that for a while, but I wasn't finished school and I was flat broke. Life was tough. I was just surviving, living by myself. I had broken up with Ian, moved to an apartment in another part of town, and started school all within a month. And I had only me to support me.

After awhile, I was overwhelmed and needed more money. I thought, okay, I need to pay the fucking bills and I can't stand it anymore. When I get my nursing job, I'll quit escorting. Someone I knew from Anita's Palace was working at another massage place, Madam Clem's, and told me I should work there. I applied and got the job right away. This massage parlor was different than Anita's Palace in that it was definitely about having sex. Here again the client paid for the room but this

Madam had the girls pay a $10.00 manager's fee, which she claimed was for cleaning. The Madam ran a tight shop, as she would take the $10.00 and then get us to clean up the room after our session. She didn't have a shower for the girls so we used baby wipes that we supplied ourselves. She had lingerie for rent, and before the girl left she had to wash it herself in a certain way the Madam taught us and then hang it up to dry. She controlled the music, made the coffee, and supplied pop or juice for clients but no food. She had a strict rule that if we ordered food delivered or brought it in, it couldn't smell. All the while she made us think she was doing us some kind of favor and that we would fail if we tried to work anywhere else. In retrospect, she was an unkind, tough, hard-nosed business woman and we hated her.

What we made in the room, we kept. It was $100 for a hand job (I keep my clothes on), $150 for a nude hand job (I take all my clothes off), $200 for a blow job, and $300 for full service. Full service means a little bit of everything and they get to fuck you at the end. Anything weird or kinky was $500, but few of them had $500. By weird or kinky I mean they would have a foot fetish, or were into bondage or peeing, stuff like that. The rage at that time was peeing. It had been talked about in *Penthouse* for a year. Guys would want me to pee on them. It's because there's something fascinating about the female body to guys. Some want to see it, especially to see women peeing. Some want to see those things. They wanted to see me. So I peed on them or in a bucket or whatever. It just depended on the guy. Yeah, I'd pee on their bodies for another hundred bucks. Anyway, nothing shocks me or scares me.

I was given the nickname Ice Princess at that massage parlor. That's what a few of the girls called me. It suits me sometimes, even now. Sometimes I'm just ice. I don't give a shit. I'm cold. It's a protection thing I do; a controlled part of my personality to cope and close things off. I mastered it at Madam Clem's. I reminded myself, 'Okay, I'm in school and when I get my nursing job I'll quit the massage parlor.' I never thought of escorting as a permanent occupation. I justified it to myself believing it would get me through until the perfect job came along. Nursing school gave me that hope again. I told the other prostitutes, "If I am still working here after graduation, you can kill me or you better kick me out of here." Eventually I graduated from nursing school. I had sailed through. I was thirty-three years old.

I was so happy I threw a graduation party for myself at an Italian restaurant. I invited my parents, my siblings and some close friends. We all drank a little too much and at the end of the evening I noticed one of my close friends was crying. As we were leaving, my dad had

66

apparently made some negative comment about her huge faux-fur coat. The next morning I phoned her and learned that my dad had also said, sarcastically, to each of my friends, something to the effect, "Now that she's gotten an education to become a nurse, she expects to be forgiven for the life she's been leading and thinks everything is all right now." My friend was upset about his unkind comment about her coat, but she was crying because he was mean with his negative insinuations about me, and she couldn't say anything back to him out of respect for my party and me. Sometime later my dad said to me that he guessed he owed my friend an apology, but then he immediately said, "No, no, I take that back." I never learned exactly what was said but I do clearly remember thinking, 'So I graduated from school, paid for it myself, become something he thought I should be, and he still thinks I am not good enough.' It really bothered me a lot that I still didn't get his approval.

The great satisfying nursing job never came. I tried working at various hospitals but hated it. I worked for a nursing agency for a while, where I was sent to various places as a temporary nurse and that was even worse. I began to wonder what I had got myself into. I decided if I was going to continue escorting, until I found another job I liked, then I would take it a step higher and make some real money!

* * *

I decided to work in Japan. A friend, who also worked at the massage parlor and who had worked in Japan before, arranged it. She was my connection. We were both going. Two weeks before we were to leave, she found out she was pregnant and couldn't go. I had just spent $1,200 dollars on a plane ticket. She said, "Well, you just go," and I thought about it for a second and said, "Sure, why not?" It was that easy. She had made all the arrangements and all I had to do was go. I didn't even know if I was going to make tons of money. I got on the plane and fourteen hours later I arrived in Japan.

The Mama-san from the club where I was supposed to work picked me up at the airport. I had already sent pictures of myself so she knew what I looked like. She drove me to an apartment in downtown Osaka, which was about four blocks walking distance from the club. I was to pay her rent for the apartment, which was expensive. Two roommates greeted me, two girls from Australia, so I knew I was going to be all right. They'd been there for months. They knew everything. The Japanese woman told me that I had to go to work that day despite the fact I was seriously jet-lagged.

She took me to a private club, or what they call a Hostess Club or Hostess Bar. Men pay a lot of money to become members and then they also have to pay to come in and they have to buy their liquor. Sometimes they'd pay $200 U.S. a bottle. I was to be a hostess. My job was to sit at the table, smile, look pretty, pour their drinks and light their cigarettes. I got a commission on champagne, so part of the job was to get them to buy it instead of other drinks. Mama-san wanted us to encourage them to drink because she would make more money, so I ended up drinking every night because I was supposed to encourage them to buy me drinks too. If they spoke English, I would talk to them. Mostly they would ask me where I was from, chit-chat about the weather, what I did in Canada or what Canada was like, because they wanted to practice English and talk to a pretty white girl.

Clothes were a problem because just about everything I owned at that time was black and we weren't allowed to wear black. Mama-san explained that the place would be like a funeral club. So I had to buy clothes and put together a wardrobe of anything that wasn't black. I bought dresses slit up the side and they also had to show cleavage. Nightclub clothes.

As my days progressed, I realized there were no dancers or strippers at the club and, most of the time, the men were carrying a lot of money. It was an expensive club and the Japanese men would bring their business associates there to impress them. They'd come in wearing Versace and I could smell the money. They all wore the current haute couture with gold necklaces and bracelets and leather Italian shoes; all of them looking expensive but classy, and like what I imagined Japanese gangsters would look like. Their leather brief cases and leather wallets were full of money. Some had personal assistants and limos with drivers. I concluded a little entrepreneurialism was in order.

I decided to throw on a foxy CD and put on a costume and dance. The Mama-san approved. But I wouldn't do it for less than $100 a song so, first, I'd look around the club and count how many men were there. I knew the smallest denomination, as I recall it was a bill worth approximately $10, and if there were enough people in the club that would cough up enough tips to make my hundred bucks, then I'd begin to dance. You see, if one Japanese man tipped, which was always the case, then all the men tipped because it was embarrassing not to. It was all about the Japanese 'saving face.' It was all part of my game. I would read the crowd and pick out the men in the audience with the fattest wallets, which were easy to spot. Then I'd dance especially close to them because they would typically tip generously. I would dance in front of them and strip to my g-string. Then I'd dance around the club for all the men to put money in my g-string. I did a few songs a night and I would usually go home with an extra $500.

I didn't have to share my tips with the Mama-san. I was paid a wage, around $4,000 a month, for showing up five nights a week. I started work at 10 o'clock at night and didn't get back to the apartment until the morning. Sometimes I partied with the Australian girls on our nights off. I decided Australians were fun and we became good friends. I really had a blast. I was in Japan! I went for sight-seeing rides on the subway, sometimes alone, sometimes with the Australians. We visited tourist sights and we would go to nightclubs to party and dance and meet men. They were always square and they knew I was a working girl but they didn't care.

The Mama-san was a Madam as well and she knew I was a working girl. Most of the hostesses were not escorts. They were getting paid to be a waitress and didn't want to be a sex object. I was the only one in this club that was an escort. The men knew too because I presented myself differently. I flirted. I touched their arms or legs or played footsie with them. It's more about how you look at them and how you say things. I'd look them in the eye and say something like; "We should get together" or "Do you want to go out?" I'd smile and be seductive. They'd know what I was talking about. I tried to get them to tip me because they could tip you while you were sitting at the table.

If any of the clients wanted to nookie, Mama-san would set it up. To my knowledge she didn't take a percentage; certainly I kept what the men gave me. Japan has hotels called 'Love Hotels' that you can rent by the hour. They are made specifically for sex. Some of them are very bizarre. The lobby is black, with pictures on the walls of the different rooms one can rent. They'd have a mirrored room, the American room, and the heart-shaped room — all different kinds of theme rooms. When you decided on the one you wanted to rent, there was a tiny dark window with a slot, making it completely private, and that is where you paid. Someone would slide a key out and you would go into your room. The rooms were funky. I mean they had little boxes of condoms and they had hot tubs and they had fully tiled Japanese baths where you basically just hose yourself. Most of the bathing rooms had glass walls so the men could see in. Some would have a little tub, some a shower stall, but most of the time there was just a basket with a towel, shelves, a hose or a bucket, and a bench you could sit on if you wanted to scrub your toes. Guys like to see the girls bath themselves, so I basically went in and soaped up and hosed off while they watched. The bed headboards had buttons that controlled the lighting, music and vibrated the bed. I'd put on a little show pushing the buttons, especially if they didn't speak English, and the men would laugh. A trick's a trick. I would charge $500 US. The men always had lots of money and had no trouble spending it and they paid me a lot. It was a step up from the massage parlor, for sure. Overnight was around $2,000 US and they paid for the hotel. Back then, that was a lot to me. Overnight meant I would just stay the night and get up and leave in the morning. Japanese men are very square; very normal, respectful 'missionary' men. They were gentlemanly and I never had any problems.

There was one big-time player. He owned the club and oozed money. All the hostesses wanted to date him. He took really, really good care of some of the girls, meaning he gave them lots of money. Mama-san had a gambling problem and he used to support her gambling habit too because I saw him give her lots of money. I personally saw him hand one girl $20,000 US and I later learned he had bought her a house in Canada. She was 'his' girl from Canada. He constantly handed her money. I was waiting and waiting to date him because he was the one big mark in that club. Once she returned to Canada, he asked for me. He called Mama-san and told her to bring me to a Japanese casino where he played baccarat, or whatever they call it.

The casino was very small and underground, probably illegal. There were no windows and it was filled with cigarette smoke. When he saw us, he handed her an envelope with a stack of money, approximately $12,000 US. She took out a grand for herself and when she handed me the rest of it, all $11,000, she gave me a wink and patted my hand as if to say, 'You go, girl.' I didn't know how to play baccarat, so I sat at the table with Mama-san while he was gambling with his friends. Mama-san told me to gamble $500 and put the rest in my purse and to pretend I had lost it gambling. "Hide it, hide it," she said. That's what she did. She told me how to make him think that we had no money because he would always give us more. So basically I had to learn to play baccarat. I sat down with him and watched him and he watched me while I flirted with him the whole time. He encouraged me to bet money. "Come on, put some money," and I'd put down $100. I'd often win and he said, "See," and then he gave me the winnings. I put the money in my bra or purse. I was playing but trying to stay awake. Six o'clock in the morning and there I was, still in the casino, breathing stale cigarette smoke.

Eventually his driver drove us to his apartment. We called it his 'trick' apartment. He had a wife and kids somewhere outside of Osaka where he lived and the apartment was where he played with his women.

He gave me a stack of money, all new crisp bills from the bank with the little white paper strip still holding it together. Then I had to have sex and it was really gross. He couldn't get hard. I tried everything I could think of and nothing worked. Eventually he got up and went to watch TV in another room. I got up and had a shower and dressed. I really didn't feel comfortable and I couldn't fall asleep so I thought, 'Well, I'll just go and grab a taxi.' I asked him to call me one. He said, "Okay, if you want to leave." In hindsight, I probably should have stayed. I would have earned a lot more money.

He said he had called me a taxi. I was standing out on the street in a tight fire-cobalt blue dress up to my ass and in high heels and it was seven o'clock Sunday morning. There were no taxis anywhere. There was nobody around. I stood there and waited and waited and, by the way, waited. Finally a little man in a little truck, which looked like a North American meter maid runt-of-a-truck-without-doors, drove up and stopped in front of me. "Oh, hi, hi, hi," he said to me. "Taxi?" I said back. "No, no, no, no taxi. Come on, come on, get in, get in." So I hauled my ass into his little fish truck. What else could I do? I said, "Sony Tower." He said, "Oh yeah, oh yeah, yeah." He took me to the Sony Tower, which wasn't far from my apartment. He kept laughing as he drove saying, "Pretty girl, pretty girl, pretty girl." I'll never forget it. There he was in his black gumboots and fishy-smelling rubberized clothes and me in my tight, short hooker dress with my blonde hair blowing in the wind in a fish truck on a deserted street at 7 in the morning in Japan.

*　*　*

I didn't stay much longer after that. I saw the owner once again towards the end and he handed me more money, and I think I came home with about $20,000 US, just from him. The truth was he was cheap with me, believe me, because I knew he had given his other 'Canadian girl' between $20,000 and $30,000 and had bought her a house. For him to dish me $20,000 or so was nothing to him.

While I was still there, I was asked to make a commercial, which was fun. There was another club, owned by a different man, that would trade girls with the club where I worked. If our club was 'slow' and his club was busy, then we would go there and vice versa. I became friends with him too. One day he phoned and asked if I wanted to do a commercial. Of course I agreed. It was for a restaurant. It was very funny because I had to speak Japanese and because I'm not an actress. I guess my Canadian accent mixed with Japanese caught everyone's attention.

Within a couple of weeks, people would come up to me and tell me they had seen me on TV. I signed autographs. In the club I'd hear, "You're that girl!" I made a few thousand dollars for doing it and they asked me to do another one, but I had already made plans to leave.

That money helped pay for nursing school student loans. It paid for my boob job too. The best thing that came out of Japan was that I knew I didn't need the massage parlor anymore. Basically, the Madam that owned it had brainwashed the girls working there into thinking that was the only place to work. I decided to leave Madam Clem's and use a little more entrepreneurialism.

* * *

As luck would have it, a friend who used to be an escort at the massage parlor offered me a job at World Trading Finance. Two years earlier Jill had squared up. Squared up means she was no longer an escort. I loved the fact that she had got out of prostitution and that she was successful. I sort of mentally always held onto her skirt hem, hoping that one day I would too. I looked up to her. I used to phone her and say, "How'd you do it? How'd you get out?" She was always supportive in encouraging me to come to work for her. This time she meant it.

She had met a man I'll call Ted. When they first got together, they had very little money but he supported her emotionally to quit escorting, which is the key. The only other person I know who got out did it with the help of a boyfriend as well. Jill and Ted started a company called World Trading Finance which means they presented themselves as technology brokers. It should have been called Waste Your Money Management Company but that's when hindsight set in sometime later. Let's say if some country somewhere in the world needed to build a bridge, Ted and Jill promoted their company as the supplier of technology and as having the capability to build it, arranged the financing and put the deal together. A stock market whiz bang. That was the company in a nutshell.

She offered me a job which started as a 'girl Friday' but quickly turned into an executive assistant. I spent three months listening and learning. They had such confidence in me that we discussed my moving to Costa Rica to open an office, but the funding ran out. The long and the short of that job was they couldn't pay me after a few months because they said the technology market crashed and the funding ran out. I'd invested some money in some of their seed stock and when the stock didn't sell, I lost about $20,000. I felt no ill will towards them. We tried, it just didn't work out.

Around this time they offered me a job as a hotel/bar manager in South America run by a close friend of theirs, until their company sorted itself out. Jill said, "You know, you should go there. There's a job there. If you want to get out of town, get out of prostitution and get paid while you're there, then take this job for awhile." The whole time she was explaining the job offer, the only thing I kept thinking was that I had to go by myself and that was the one thing that was hanging me up. I kept thinking, 'You can't pluck me from my home and friends of thirty-four years and throw me into a different country and think I'm going to survive. I'd be all alone. I'd be there by myself, crying myself to sleep at night out of loneliness.' It was just too far away to commute so I turned the job down. I needed to pay my rent and I became a working girl again.

Of course I was getting older. All those years as an escort was about the money. I'm a freak with worry when I don't have money in the bank. I start to panic. My sense of security is based on having money. Being an escort is what I did to alleviate that but, in my mind, it was always temporary. It was always about 'when I get this job' or 'until I get the nursing job' or until I get 'the whatever' that comes along. I made a lot of money too. I asked myself how I was going to support myself if I stopped. I was used to living on a lot of money. Of course I continued escorting, but also opened a foot fetish internet site. But that's the next story.

Eight

FOOT FETISH WEB SITE

Even escorts can have an adventurous entrepreneurial spirit. So with lots of energy, a friend and I decided to set up an Internet Foot Fetish site. Cecilia was a working girl as well and we were looking for new ways to make money. It seemed like just about everyone thought they could get rich on the Internet, one way or another, and we enthusiastically decided to give it a try. Well, it's easier to masturbate a man with your feet than it is to become fabulously financially successful with a web site but, at the very least, we had a lot of fun trying.

Certainly in our work we had both experienced men who liked feet. I do not have a foot fetish. This does not come from personal experience. That's for the record. Why do men lust after feet? There is no understanding it. Why do people like roses? Why do people like mashed potatoes? Why do people like boobs instead of butts? Why do they prefer blonde instead of black hair? There is no reason. It's just what one desires. Some people just like feet.

When Cecilia and I were working at the massage parlor, Cecilia met a trick named Oscar. Every now and then a prostitute meets one of those men that wants to save you, well, you know, from this horrid life they believe we live. Oscar was such a man who also happened to have a foot fetish. He instantly fell in love with Cecilia and they became friends and started spending time together outside of the parlor. He was a regular who basically just played with feet, but Cecilia was the first girl he ever asked for full service. He was a computer programmer geek type and he suggested we should have a Web site. He had been involved with the foot fetish internet scene for years. Prostitution is a game, a business and a profession that is open to any opportunities offered by men. Well, he was born with a foot fetish and the thought of helping two women develop a foot fetish web site must have turned him on because he offered to help us create such a business opportunity. He told us we were prettier, funnier, and had more personality than any of the Internet sites he had visited, and that we had the prettiest feet he had ever seen. Cecilia and I looked at each other, light bulbs flashed on, and we realized '*We can do that.*' No problem! It especially appealed to us because it meant if anyone found out about the site, well, we wouldn't be judged as harshly as we would be for prostitution. We both had family and at that point we were more protective of our reputations. We jumped at the chance. He helped us set it up and then we continued from there.

It was really only a site for nude feet, where people paid money to see erotic poses of our feet. It was all about pictures. Of course the pictures often showed all of us, including our faces and us wearing seductive clothing, but the focus was always on our feet. We included a little bit of nudity, just a little bit of boobs, but no tits and clits. We didn't want a big spread of nasty, dirty, rotten stuff because we're not like that. We wanted it to be soft core. Oscar told us that we could make lots of money because he knew the market and he claimed foot sites were big business.

We started by surfing the Web to see what was already out there. We decided to make different kinds of categories or galleries to make it interesting. We used titles like *Bare Foot Nakedness, Bondage and Lace Ups, Bare Bottom Soles, Tickling Toes, Sexy Socks* and *Silky Stockings, Stilettos, Sandals and Slippers, Suntanned Toes au Natural.* We were trying to be serious; to foot fetishers it's serious stuff, but humor definitely defined our work at times. We bought a digital camera and then we just started taking pictures. We asked a fag friend of ours to help us by taking pictures of us alone and together. We had pictures playing with each other's feet, in water, in grass, surrounded by rocks, feet in high-heeled shoes, in sandals, barefoot, by camp fires, in bubble baths, feet in socks and feet tied up with ropes. Really, just let your imagination fly and we probably had a picture of our feet in it! Of course, we wore seductive clothes along with showing our feet and legs.

We charged $15 a month or three months for $40, and for that they could access our Web site to see the pictures and read the short story lines that accompanied each set of pictures. Here are some examples of feedback.

75

E-mails:

From: Jack
To: footfetish.com
Subject: Picture Perfect
Hi! This is Jack from Seattle and I would like to request some pictures of
Elysia and Cecilia both wearing tie-front tops and denim shorts and barefoot
(of course!). I'm willing to purchase 35mm photos of the above request, if
that option is available. Peace... Jack (a.k.a. "Elysiafan")

From: Jeffrey
To: Footfetish.com
Subject: suggestion
I would like to see more flats and loafers.

From: Art
Subject: sock request
I would love some pics of you beautiful women playing with each other's
socks, preferably ARGYLES. I'd like there to be a hole in one sock so a pretty
little toe can be peeking out. Thanks.

From: Eldon
Subject: sneakers
Please, I would love to see some new white canvas Ked's sneakers right out
of the box, put on and slowly dangled with the laces loosened and some
dipping and dangling, also walking around with the heel part crushed down.
Wow. Thank you.

From: Lucas
Hi Staff, Some hot buttons for me: soft foods (smashed) on feet, bubble bath
pictures, swimming pool, foot worship and sole shots. Something I do not
personally like to see: shoes, nylons, socks, dirty feet (all hide your lovely feet)
foot jobs and cum-feet (if it cannot be me, I do not like to see it) Nude or
clean is your call!

From: Peter
Subject: Request
Hi Ladies,
Last week I bought a 3 month membership with your site. And I must say
it was the best $40.00 I ever spent. I have a request or two. I like female to
female foot-tickling so please maybe more photos in that subject. And maybe
some female to female foot-tickling stories. Thank you for your time in this
matter. My e-mail address is ... Thank you.

From my experience, considering the sexuality in men, usually it's the guys that have a fetish. I suppose it's been going on for centuries because Chinese girls had their feet bound so they would be more appealing to men. The women who do have a foot fetish are certainly not mainstream. Maybe it's underground with women or maybe they have never explored that side of their sexuality. I AM certain lots of women have been on the receiving end of it. It's always nice, when you're passionate and making love, to have somebody suck your toes and slide their tongue between them. It feels good. And some men get off in giving themselves pleasure by playing with a woman's feet.

E-mails:
From: Travis
To: Footfetish.com
Subject: NURSE PICTURE
Hi there. I was looking at your sample pics on shoe play. I came across this picture of a nurse in a pink uniform with a stethoscope, obviously sitting down and having unlaced her shoe, was in the process of removing it, showing her stockinged sole. This is a recurring fantasy for me... hard working, sexy woman after work....needing a foot rub.... yada, yada, yada ....LOL. It's always 'done it' for me and will continue to. I don't know if I speak for other guys, but I think that giving a woman a foot rub after work is very sensual. In fact, I believe that you don't get too much more romantic or sensual. I'm also very proud of it: some people get turned on by some pretty violent and painful things towards women. For me, making her feel good after work IS the turn on. Are there more pictures of this nurse?

From: Glen
To: Elysia
Subject: Foot web site
I am a 37 year old submissive male in Los Angeles. I am interested in scheduling a session with you when you are in town. Do you allow foot worship sessions? I love the pics of you and your commanding, pretty, sexy feet and toes. I'd love to be made to smell, lick and kiss them clean for you. Is this possible?

From: Elysia
To: Glen
It would please me if you showed up on Wed. Feb. 26 @ 10:30 am with a latte for me, not too hot! You must be ready, willing and able to stroke my ego and worship me like no other goddess you have ever known. IF all goes well, I will let you savor my luscious, lickable feet and if you are a really good boy, I would love to have you shoot your hot cum all over my delicate freshly painted toes!
Forever your foot goddess, Elysia xoxo

He never made the appointment!

When I'm working, my clients with foot fetishes are definitely a minority but I do have a few. Part of the charm of the foot is that it is ticklish and sensitive. They touch my feet. I laugh. They like that. When I know a man likes my feet and wants to play with them, I respond. My feet play with him. If it's not openly discussed, if I don't already know ahead of time that they have this foot fetish, then it will come into play through massage or touching each other. Sometimes the client will ask for my foot. Occasionally, once I have made him comfortable, the man will grab my foot and start sucking on it. They will just do it! It becomes part of the play and I can tell when they want more. Sometimes I put my foot up on his chest or wherever and if he starts touching or kissing my foot, then I know that he likes it.

Foot obsession can have a range, from mild and just being a normal part of the eroticism, to being a full-blown fetish. I can sense if it is what they really need to 'get off.' I know when they want a foot job, which is where I jerk them off with my feet. It's what a foot fetish man really likes. I get them to sit up with their backs leaning against the couch or the backboard of the bed so they can watch me. I sit facing them with their legs on the outside of mine and their feet on either side of my bum. I oil their dick with my hands and then I lean back slightly and I stretch my legs out to fondle and rub their cock with my oiled feet. I don't use my hands at all to jerk them off, only my feet. It's really hard on my abdominals because I have to lean back to lift my legs slightly so that I can maneuver his cock between my two feet. It's also all about the way I look at them, what I say to them and how I touch myself while I'm doing it. It's a whole seduction. It's not easy because it takes awhile.

Sometimes, having a fetish is shameful or embarrassing for men and they don't know how to bring it up. They just kind of like feet. They don't know why. They know they are different. It's my job to make them feel okay about it because *it is* okay. It's just part of sexuality.

Eventually we decided to write little stories, or sometimes captions, to include along with our pictures posted in our website and placed under an appropriate category. We called them 'Tidily Tidbits.'

"Hi everyone! :o) Today I have a very sexy pile of pics for all the High Heel Dangling Lovers of the world. The luscious and talented Elysia will be showing off an incredible pair of red, like candy, high heels guaranteed to knock the zipper right out of your pants! Enjoy!
Hugs and Tickles, Cecilia xoxo"

"Hello everyone, Well, here it is … The rest of that sexy two-parter! Starring none other than the beautiful, talented and toetally sexy-footed Elysia and her sweaty, moist white socks! If you think you'd like to be there sharing her ice cream, you're right! You would love it! The luscious and sweet Elysia was having just a bit too much fun in her sassy little white dampish socks for me to only take a couple of pics. So get on your favorite easy access pants and grab a beer or two for the ride. Enjoy and stay tuned for the rest of the story, coming to your monitor soon.
Hugs and Tickles, Cecilia xoxo"

Also on the website we had 'The Club' category, which was where we posted our made-up 'Toe Tales.' It was meant to be a club for women with foot fetishes where the reader, male or female, could fantasize through a short story paragraph, along with posted pictures of Cecilia and me. Sometimes our pictures inspired our writing, sometimes we had a story line and then took pictures to portray it.

Toe Tales:
So, how about we start with some introductions and a brief tour of the Club. First to be introduced is, The Super Celeste, she is the beautiful blonde who manages Toe Tales. We usually call her "The Super," and she has the most beautiful smooth high arches ever made! She gently massages cream into them twice a day and they are soooo soft. She's good at keeping the club purring and focused on sharing our foot fantasies, and her favorite activity is wandering around the club to find someone she can pleasure by letting them massage her feet. She usually tries to find a new member for this sexual favor so they'll keep coming back.

The owner, Paula Perfect, hmmmmm, just that! Everyone in the entire club agrees that Paula has the most perfect feet ever made, which are thin with tiny toes and nails, which are always painted a delicate sweet pink color! :o) Paula's a bit shy but she loses herself the minute someone starts sucking her toes. She lets out a moan that infects the club into stroking their feet with a pressing need for a climax. Unfortunately, she only comes in the two days a week when the Super Celleste doesn't. Us girls are always playing games to see who gets to lick Paula Perfect's feet this week.

The center of activity is always in the appropriately titled "Lover's Splendor Lounge." This is a huge, oval shaped lounge with so many comfy seats and sofas designed toe-tally to relax in and put your feet up, that on a busy night it's hard to find a face through all the shoes, bare feet and socks up in the air.

The lounge has a fantastic marble bar in the middle. Candy Arches is the babe behind the Bar. This is her lounge and she makes sure everyone who comes into it feels better before leaving, all the way to the bottom of their soles and the tips of their toes! She is an amazing six-foot black beauty that walks with the legs of an angel beneath her, legs that take you all the way down to her heavenly feet embraced with gold stilettos. In the surrounding lounge walls, lots of doors open into an intriguing selection of Sensual Theme Rooms.

One of the favorite private rooms is where Alicia Amazing performs her magic. When a girl needs a pedicure there is no place like the lap of the blue eyed, 36 DD, 6 inch stiletto-wearing Alicia. Her pedicures are so sensual that often the girls are found fighting over appointment times. Believe us, there is nothing like her long red fingernails delicately tracing patterns all over your feet for a pleasurable tingling fleshy tickle.

Just yesterday after Jennifer Spice, the event coordinator, finished her pedicure and came out, still in her opened bathrobe and wearing a sexy smile, to do the crossword with us in the lounge, we heard a commotion. Sure enough, two girls were arguing about getting the next appointment with Alicia. Upon second glance we realized it was Shayla Shining, one of our favorite gals. She has this stunning, long curly blonde hair and the most panty-removing personal aroma on earth! She is this crazy party girl that travels around the world selling art, lives on old family money and stands on a pair of 7½'s that are ready to rock your inner panty world anytime, anywhere! She has a flexible double-jointed big toe that can do absolutely anything. Even thaw an incorruptible foot fetish virgin. We haven't seen her at the club for months. A big hug and a gentle foot rub (that's the official club handshake) brings her back into our midst to hear her latest tales of art and travel. Shayla's a party girl and can often be heard throughout the club yelling, "Release the hounds!" That's when her shoes are being taken off.

Part way through telling us about her trek in the hills of Chianti, where Shayla stomped some grapes with a wine maker to make her feet a rosy red, the doorbell rings and in through the foyer walks Dr. Jenni Jazz with two guests.

A half-full lounge of eyes turns to gaze upon the newcomers and, in just a few seconds, the room temperature had noticeably risen along with the raising of quite a few pairs of strategically placed feet…. This is looking like an interesting night indeed…. Savanah has a new friend with her tonight too. There is a room full of imaginations running crazy right now! And there is nothing we like more than a new selection of Tootsie Pops to lick and savour! Yum.

Dr. Jenni Jazz stops at the stereo to plug in her selection of music for the evening. That's how she got her nickname Jazz. She's a podiatrist with two tanned feet of her own to play with. The straps of her sandals have left thin sunless white lines which criss-cross the tops of her feet. Her long straight hair, amazing blue eyes and 10 long sexy slim toes with glossy sparkling gold toenails make her one of the clubs favorites. She always wears gold toe rings to match her gold polish.

Alicia Amazing comes over to tell Shayla Shining she can have the next open spot in her House of Pedicures since she will only be in town for two days. With a wiggle and a light step, Alicia is gone and the next thing anyone can see is her long pink fingernails taking hold of both the new Tootsie Pops and escorting them into her room. We all deliciously laughed. This is proving to be a busy night at Toe Tales, as a matter of fact the always nasty Bettie Ball Licker has just crawled out of her favorite hangout downstairs in the Dungeon of Domination.

Well, the two of us are in need of a bit of attention ourselves and the lovely Miss Shayla Shining is the one that will be seducing us in the pristinely clean wet steam bath upstairs.

At some point, it was so hot and steamy in the sauna that not one of us horny girls could tell whose feet we were sucking, licking and tickling. We kept Shayla Shining pinned to the top seat for quite some time, licking the little sweat droplets that flowed down her legs and into her tiny arches. After we each had a turn, we all finally collapsed in titillated toetotallated ecstasy.

The only man that we know who has ever been in 'The Club' wandered in purely by accident. We don't need to describe the look on this strikingly handsome man's face when he got his first eyeful of naked foot rubbing action. There was a notable silence in the room, which was finally broken when Diane Desperate said out loud, "Will you please come over here and lick my feet?"

He took one look at the half-naked Diane with her feet tied to the seat and her hand in her panties and almost fell over himself trying to get across the room. Everyone in the club was completely awestruck by his immediate willingness to suck and lick Diane's feet, while slowly untying the knots and sending her into an orgasmic vibrating frenzy. Bettie Ball Licker is once again crawling around on the floor trying to sneak sniffs of everyone's feet before they realize what she's up to.

Candi Arches is such a stocking nut that she actually managed to convince The Super to make one of the rooms into a Fetish Foot Store. She encourages us to try on all kinds of silky stockings, cotton socks and high heels so they will fragrantly smell like our feet. This has become one of the most popular rooms in the club. No kidding, it's like fulfilling a naked foot fantasy. Imagine going shopping for stockings without a stitch of clothes on. It's too much to take, isn't it?

Another category was 'Toe Bitz' where pictures were also included. When we were doing the website, Cecilia and I spent an incredible amount of time together. We had to do a lot of thinking and come up with a lot of different ideas, often inspired by the e-mails we were receiving. Since neither one of us had foot fetishes, sometimes it was a real struggle. Sometimes we were stressed and argued but mostly we remained in good humor. I think that is reflected in some of the crazy category paragraphs. Here's a short story from 'Toe Bitz:'

Handy Neighbor:
My car had broken down about ten blocks from home and my sexy neighbor, Randy Dandy, gave me a lift home. I invited him in for a drink. "Sure," he laughed. Inside the door he stepped directly in front of me, pinning me to the door. He smiled and told me to hold still. He slowly lowered himself to my feet. I felt breathless. I could feel the warmth from his searching fingers as he removed my shoes. He slowly peeled off my socks while softly caressing the tops of my feet and bending over to kiss each exposed toe. He slid his hand under my slightly sweaty right arch and I felt his warm fingertips nibbling. A pulsating moan escaped his lips as he lifted me up and carried me into the living room and gently set me down on the coffee table. "Perfect," he said. "Very, very sexy." He kissed me passionately on the lips while he slowly slid a finger between my toes, titillating me as an appetizer for his desire. I slipped open his fly and reached in to fondle his hot fabulous dick. As we broke our kiss, he knelt to the floor and I was anxious to feel his tongue surrender to my feet. My pussy throbbed every time his hot breath and flittering tongue touched my naked begging feet. He worshipped my feet with his rubbing, sucking, kissing and licking, with his hot saliva wetting my sensitive silky skin as he moved his flicking tongue over my soles. I was ready. So was Randy. As we neared climax, he stiffened and I purred. We came huge! Feet, tongue, sweat, moans, glory and pleasure! I must remember not to take my car to the mechanic.

E-mails:
From: Clint
To: Elysia
Subject: Re; Your foot website
I very much appreciate the pictures. I have already put them to good use (if you know what I mean). Damn, you have got some incredible legs. I can't

wait for my one hour with you. As you figured out, it is going to entail much leg, pantyhose and high heel action. I have been with girls with nice legs but not with the gorgeous face like yours and your breasts are breathtaking. You are the complete package, that's for sure! I will bring the pantyhose, if that is okay. I will bring the receipt and they will still be in the original packaging. I am kinda picky on the kind I like. If you have anymore pics I would very much appreciate it. Thanks again,

Sometimes I used the foot fetish Web site to encourage men responding to my escort Web site to visit me, or to excite them with anticipation of a coming visit.

E-Mails
From: Calvin
To: Miss Elysia
Subject: colors
I took a look at your foot Web site as you suggested. WoW, quite the cute toes! Any chance you can paint them hot pink when you come to San Francisco? Just giving you my vote for the color you look hottest in. See you next week!

From: Jon
Subject: Natural Toes
Hello Elysia. I am so much in love with your beautiful feet and succulent toes. I consider myself to be your biggest fan. Yet I have a request of you, if it is not any trouble. I would love to see your toes in their natural beauty, without toenail polish. There is something about sexy toes, like yours when they are au natural, they make me cum a river. I hope you can make this fantasy cum true for me by posting some pictures of your lovely naked toenails with nice poses and close ups, the way you know how. I think you and Cecilia should make a video with you two posing your au naturel toes.

In a massage parlor, guys with a foot fetish suck on toes and feet. It's a bit tricky to let them do it without laughing. To me it was kind of like slipping my feet into a Halloween pumpkin where you feel something dark and slippery that really tickles. As you can imagine, it's all about what's going on in their heads. Men are all about being visual and if men don't have visuals going on in front of them, then they have them in their heads.

E-mail:
From: Toadman
Subject: Custom Video
Hi Cecilia,

I would like to see a 30 to 40 minute video of you and Elysia. I'll explain exactly what I would like to see. The setting for the video would be on a bed. Outfits you wear are strictly up to you, but I would like to see you both wear sheer black stockings or pantyhose and, in the beginning of the video, high heels. To start, I would like to see you both lying together on the bed, side by side, face to face. While in this position, I want you to both put your legs together and rub/slide them together. At first the heels will be on, but then take them off so you can rub your feet together as well. What I want to see is two sexy pairs of female feet and legs in nylons entwined, rubbing and sliding together. I want to see Elysia's stockinged thighs and legs. I want to see Cecilia's stockinged feet rubbing together with Elysia's stockinged feet. I apologize for the repetition but I'm just trying to make sure that I am explaining what it is that I want to see. The part I described above would be the majority part of the video. For the last part of the video, I would like to see you both still side by side on the bed together, but this time flexing your feet and pointing and wiggling your toes. This sequence would be shot from the front so I could get a nice look at the soles of your stockinged feet.

I guess that is about it. If you think you can do a video like I described, please let me know. If you have any questions or suggestions please feel free to send them my way. Regards, Toadman

We didn't do videos, only pictures at that point. Frankly, at that time pictures and story lines were all we could handle. Everyone we hired to manage the Web site, so we could concentrate on content and not technical stuff, kept letting us down and causing no end of problems so videos weren't possible.

Some men love the scent of a foot coming out of a leather shoe. Most foot fetish men find a sweaty foot a very important turn on. I don't mean one that is rank with sweat or smell, but not a foot that has just been washed. The smell can be a huge part of it.

It's not that a foot fetish guy wants HIS foot rubbed. He doesn't give a damn about his feet and in fact they don't particularly want their feet touched. Most of these men still like the rest of the woman and are happy with all the other kinds of sex too. But to really serious foot fetishers, the foot is the pussy. It's the woman's foot they want to see and for the most part, they could care less if the foot is attached to a body. Throughout history, feet have been incredibly sexy. You know, the woman's leg showing from the bottom of her dress with her foot dangling in a high-heeled shoe. A lot of men who think they have foot fetishes really have stocking fetishes, or leg fetishes, or shoe fetishes. Perhaps 'fetishes' is a severely overused word. They just have an attraction to it. It's not really that different than being a boob man, a butt man, or leg man.

E-mails:

From: Troy
Subject: Cecilia tied & tickled
Hi Staff,
I'd like to see Cecilia tied & tickled on her feet by Elysia, with fingers and feathers, seein' her face while tickled, and her wonderful laughter!
Thank you very much.

From: Dennis
Subject: Nice site!
Hi, I just wanted to say that I joined your site last week and have enjoyed what I've seen. I'd like to see more pictures of both your feet together, perhaps playing footsie. I know there's one set like that, but I'd like to see the tops of your feet instead of your soles. I think both of you are hot and I could spend hours at your feet if given the chance. Elysia's ankles are thin and beautiful and her heels look firm and smooth like plump fresh little apples! I'd love a bite. Cecilia's big toes are like bright little light bulbs that flash for me! Keep up the good work and I'll keep coming back for more.

From: Andrew
Subject: Member comments
I am a trial member of your site. Here are some spontaneous thoughts I've noted when I browsed the pages: 1. Create a separate window for the pics. It's pesky to always use the "back" button. 2. Some stats about you two, especially Elysia, would be nice. (height, weight, age, hobbies, ambitions, favorite books, films, artist, and favorite travel locations and so on.) – not for fun, but serious. For instance: under favorite thing to do: please do not state under your picture – "Tan my skin for you" or shit like that. Be rather serious. 3. I think more intelligent people choose your site, than horny donkeys, do they? At least the kind of pics allow this conclusion. 4. To me, there also has to be something personal to get it perfect. One has to combine thoughts of pleasure with some intellectual or personal complementaries. Don't you think people that wisely choose such high quality feet Web sites are more likely to enrich a complete view of a thing than only the sexual purpose? Please let me know in which aspects you agree or disagree. Is it possible to chat or e-mail with you, Elysia, once or twice in a lifetime? Greetings from Germany. Andrew
p.s. to leave a positive statement last but not least: I think your site is one of the finest and cultivated in the whole www. Honestly, Elysia's feet and poses are of a superior quality. Keep on doing the good work. (hope you understand my english)

Unfortunately the foot fetish site wasn't profitable and we had to unplug it. We wished it had worked because we actually had a riot with it. It was very entertaining running all over town taking foot porn pictures but we were a couple of blind fools. It was a bit like going into brain surgery when you had only graduated from med-101. Building an Internet web site and then managing it takes a lot of work and technical skills. We easily handled the foot part, the pictures, the stories, but the technical part was tough. We hired a designer, an editor and a marketing director to help us set it up but it just went from bad to worse. The Web master kept letting us down and so did everyone else. Since we really didn't have a clue about Web sites and computer stuff, in general, we finally had to throw in the sock.

E-mails:
From: Night Owl
To: Footfetish.com
Subject; Please, Please read and don't leave.
To Elysia and Cecilia,
Boy, that sounds like BEGGING and I guess it is. You know I fell in love with you two the second I saw you. I will be a sad SAD man if you don't keep feeding my addiction to your feet. I do want you to stay on the Web. Please find a way. Back to begging ....PLEASEEEEEEEEEE STAY.

From: Elysia/Cecilia
To: Night Owl
Subject: Re: Please, Please read and don't leave.
Well, we certainly caught your attention. Yes, it's true, we have had nothing but troubles trying to find a webmaster and after trying five of them in two years, we are finally giving up. We can't afford anyone fancy and all the people we've tried have been a schmozzle. We are very sorry to be leaving cyber space and would love it if someone could run a web site for us and we'd provide the content. We are just not able to do all of it by ourselves :o(We love being the girls for all of you, but we just aren't the teckies. We did think of some type of partnership, but have no idea who to turn to as we have to be careful, you know, there are many wing nuts out there all very happy to help but who really just want to look at our feet. Till then, thanks for being there all along and take care. Hugs and Tickles,
Elysia and Cecilia xoxo

From: Manny
To: Footfetish.com
Subject: So sad
Sexy Ladies,
Wow, I am really sad to read that you are shutting down your website. I

wasn't really into feet, but it was great seeing the photos of you both and reading about your escapades. You teased by saying you might be in cyber-space soon, let all of us know if/when that happens. I will sign up again. Good luck to you both. It was fun.

Nine

TOM

I don't think of the nature of our relationship as a professional one. Well, I guess obviously that's the nature of our relationship, and that's what she provides, and she does do that, but I think of her more as a friend, a female friend that I just happen to have sex with. It just so happens that I leave money at the end.

Let me tell you, I never planned on becoming involved in a long-term relationship with a prostitute. Even using that word for Elysia feels improper to me. She deserves respect. She's an amazing woman. I should know, I've spent three years spending lots of money on her and have never regretted a penny. As I say that, I have to laugh, as I recently have reflected on how our lovemaking has changed over the years. It's almost like many long-time couples. It is not as "elaborate" as when we first met! One of the reasons I tell you this is my concern about this experience as reading material. If you are expecting a lot of wild sexual escapades, I may fall short on that end! However, as the person that is living it, I still feel I am living a fantasy that many men would envy. Elysia's charm is not just limited to a few minutes in bed.

How did I start down this road? Sex had not been good for me at home for some time. My wife had put on a lot of weight and I suppose she'd lost self-confidence in herself and was having a difficult time trying to get back her self-image. She didn't want to engage in sexual activity anymore. I loved her as a person, her personality, our friendship, and our interaction, so I hesitated to do anything about the sexual part. To be honest, I had put on a lot of weight too and I probably wasn't feeling that good about my self-image either. I kept thinking, 'Gee, am I going to go to my grave without having sex again?" And I thought that was a depressing and scary thought. I wasn't really inclined to have an affair, as is quite often the case, so I thought, 'Well, what could I do that would still provide sex for me but not have an affair?' So, at that point I thought, 'They used to call it prostitution in the old days' and I thought I'd check into it.

Obviously I wasn't going to drive around streets looking for prostitutes. I was over forty-five years old and had never hired a prostitute before. I was in unknown territory. Since I am familiar with the Internet, I started my search online. My first fear was that perhaps the girls on the web would be involved in some kind of sting operation where law enforcement was involved. As I came to learn, if you're looking for someone, there are websites that appear to be legitimate in an illegitimate way. From my experience, apparently, law enforcement leaves it alone. After experiencing a number of service providers, I learned about Elysia on her web site.

There's also a website that I don't use much, but it's one where men talk about the prostitutes doing business in the city. Since Elysia and her friend Saffire had just started advertising, the men were wondering 'Who are these Canadians?' There was some grumbling about the high prices these women were charging. At that point nobody had met with them before, so it was a little bit risky. For some reason I was attracted to them. I also saw they had a foot fetish web site and, although I don't have a foot fetish, I checked it out. It was very tasteful, relatively speaking. Nothing like some of that stuff you can find on the Internet.

What caught my eye in Elysia's web advertisement was not just her picture but the written text had something special that seemed to come through. There was something there, perhaps the way it was written was more creative than most, and I found it interesting and it attracted me to her. So at that point I wrote her an e-mail and we arranged a time to meet.

The first time I booked an appointment with her, I went to her hotel and knocked on the door. Of course she opened it and, oh, she was beautiful! This really was the person in the photo. You'll find sometimes in this business that they do the 'bait and switch' so the person you see in the ad is not the one you actually end up with, or she just looks different and usually older.

Elysia, standing in that doorway, knocked me out because her photos don't do her justice in terms of her physical beauty. Seeing a woman like her grabs your heart. She showed me in and then we sat down on the couch. She said we should get to know each other. She had a surprising variety of hors-d'oeuvres on the coffee table: cheeses, seafood cups, some vegetables, soft drinks and candles. She's really into candles. You can guess I wasn't in the mood to eat at the time. She also had drinks, both alcohol and fruit juices. I had orange juice.

Sometimes exceptionally beautiful women make men nervous. Her beauty is of that caliber but I wasn't nervous with her. Maybe, that first time, there was a little sense of intimidation, but in retrospect, I wasn't as nervous as I would think I could have been. Her personality diffuses that, right from the beginning. There's something about her that disarmed me, right from that first time.

We carried on a conversation for about twenty minutes. She made me feel so comfortable that I felt like I was with an old friend. It was great. I was totally charmed. To be honest, a lot of these women are not people you'd want to have a conversation with. They can be kind of callous, immature or just sometimes very unusual in terms of their personality. They probably want to distance themselves as much as they can from the activity, at least mentally, and some just have a very unusual sense of values about things. But in the case of Elysia, it was not like that at all. She seemed real.

Hiring a hooker is all about fantasy, obviously. Of course if you want it to be a fantasy, you want the person and the environment to fit the fantasy. In many cases you don't get that. You'd just as soon forget. It's kind of interesting because Elysia asked me, in an e-mail before I met her, what my favorite color was. I said, "Well, I like pink." She made it a point to have pink lingerie the first time. I thought it was pretty cool that she would take the time to ask and then actually do something with the information.

After about twenty minutes, Elysia went into the bedroom to change into the lingerie. She returned and took my hand and led me to the bed. She massaged my body, and she did a lot with her body in terms of moving it against me as she massaged me all over. Very sensual. To this day I remember how warm and comfortable her touch was as she moved her body against me. She's verbal during the massage, very encouraging, if you get my drift. I find that enjoyable. Again, that's probably part of her personality but that's something you don't typically get.

Sometimes the women can have a combination of attributes that a man is looking for but when you get into the sexual phase, they click off. They revert to somebody who's very cold, very distanced. In the case of Elysia, again that wasn't the case. Her personality and the things that I liked about her from the conversation continued through into that phase of the session.

E-mail:
From: Tom
To: Elysia
Subject: Thanks Elysia
Elysia, I just wanted to drop you a note. The session on Friday was outstanding, without question the best I have ever had. Your attention to detail (candles, music, food, drink, etc.) was unparalleled, even wearing the lingerie in the color I asked for! The introductory chat was a great ice-breaker. Following the wonderful body massage, I was ready for a disappointment for the next step, but it was so good, it was almost scary. And, as I am sure I mentioned several times while I was there, you are extremely attractive. Then, taking the time afterwards to allow me to unwind was greatly appreciated. And I did not feel rushed at any time. In fact, I seemed to watch the clock more than you. An overriding element was your great personality. After a few minutes I felt I had known you as a long time friend. I had many feelings during and after the session, but I want you to know I felt inspired, as I would be upon seeing a great athlete, a great musician, etc. Jeez, it looks like I have written a sappy fan letter, but what the hell. Anyway, if you do come here again, let me know. I would like to get a priority reservation. If you are considering a future trip and want to find out if there would be enough definite interest for future appointments, my answer would always be yes, but feel free to contact me.
Hey, stay out of trouble, keep healthy and safe, and do what makes you happy. Thanks, Tom

To the experienced, it may not seem enough to start a relationship. Meeting with her reawakened feelings I hadn't had about male-female relationships for some time. Actually, with her it was kind of like going back to high school. Not from an immaturity standpoint, but from the excitement and that youthfulness standpoint. That's what it triggered in me. It was kind of exhilarating.

The interesting part is from that first session, Elysia became my inspiration to lose weight. I have to laugh, could this be a new diet plan never heard of before! For years I had contemplated going on a

91

diet, but I never got the motivation to do it and I thought it would be too hard. But I felt awkward with Elysia because of my physical size and even though this was a professional relationship, I thought, 'Well, what can I do to make it easier for her and less offensive?' I thought I probably needed to get myself in shape. At the time, of course, I didn't know if it would be more than one session with her but I thought, even if it was just one more time, I would start down the diet road. I knew it wouldn't be immediate, but she just inspired me at that point. She made me feel that I wanted to improve myself. I'm sure it came out of the very first conversation I had with her. Eventually I ended up losing 120 pounds, with Elysia cheering me on. Almost every time I was with her she would comment on how much better I was looking. She was very sensitive to that all along. Once I started losing the weight, of course the same reasons that got me started made me want to continue. At some point my own feelings kept me going, knowing it was the right thing for me to do.

For the diet books, besides seeing a prostitute, what I found worked for me was essentially to eat the same thing that I had before, but smaller portions. Then I stepped up the exercise. It was kind of like becoming alive again, to be honest. I mean I had been plodding along for many years. I thought I was happy at the time, but I didn't realize the gap between where I was and where I came to be, until I met Elysia. It was like a key had been turned for me.

I could have just kept seeing her on a professional basis. Certainly, in many ways, it would have been easier to just pay the money and leave. But as I said, Elysia is amazing. I wanted more. Quite apart from the enjoyable sex, I guess it was her sense of energy that first hooked me, no pun intended. She seems to be an extrovert and I like that. She's very self-confident and there's playfulness there too. She has a slight sense of challenge about her. She'll say things like "Are you really up to being with me?" which is a very intriguing challenge. At the same time, she's not intimidating because she's so warm and friendly about it. One had better be on top of his game if he's going to be with her.

For instance, one session she was rubbing my feet and said, "Oh, I'm going to take you to get a pedicure." So I said, "Oh, I'm not sure I want to do that," thinking the 'man thing.' She said, "That's okay. I'll go with you so we'll do it together." She comes up with these things that are just, well, things I wouldn't think of. We eventually did go, well, almost. I paid for side-by-side massages with two masseuses so I could watch her being massaged. Then she had the pedicure, while

I slept.

I would say from my experience, not that I'm a hard-core veteran in this, but one of the things I've found is some prostitutes are physically very attractive but not very bright and some have pleasing personalities but are not so physically attractive. To find one with the perfect combination is rare. Most of the them put on a bit of a stage production just to make you happy while you're there, but Elysia didn't come across like that.

Another reason I kept seeing Elysia and took her on trips with me, was our friendship. She remembers our conversations and we can pick up a conversation we've had before. She listens to me. I feel close to her. We are able to communicate openly about things. I mean I actually, in some cases, felt more comfortable communicating with Elysia than with my own wife.

One of the things I like about Elysia in a sexual role is she can be a very assertive person. She kind of takes charge, which is fun at times, so I don't have the usual male thing where I have to be in charge and do this or that. In some cases, she leads the way with, "Let's try this or let's do that," though it's not always a verbal suggestion. She communicates in physical ways by moving her body or putting my hand where it will bring her pleasure and it's so enjoyable from that aspect. Not only is the pressure off me, but that difference in roles is fun too. I mean it's something different, and not all of the women in that profession do that. Many are docile. They just kind of let you do whatever you want and don't offer anything to the situation.

She's also kind. I mean, in the kind of relationship that Elysia and I have, there's a lot of things a person could do to take advantage of the man or to manipulate things. If she was a certain personality type, she could even cause him some discomfort. But Elysia's very sensitive and kind. That's a good way to describe her. Once I got to really know her, her kindness kept me at her feet.

Of course you don't get something for nothing. Sometimes, in human relationships, there's a higher price to pay than money.

Once my wife noticed I was losing weight, she jokingly suggested that I'd probably go off and find somebody else. I had been taking some medication and it had induced me to talk during my sleep. My wife told me I talked about this or that, just rambled on. I couldn't remember a thing. She is a smart and savvy lady and became aware of a younger, very attractive and worldly lady. She 'gathered' without my telling her explicitly. At that time my relationship with Elysia was more of a typical relationship with a prostitute. My wife was upset about 'my friend.' I told her it was a friendly colleague at work. I didn't articulate the physical part. We talked it through and I explained it well. She demanded, "Well, you've got to stop this!" and so forth. I tried to be very diplomatic but I told her that I really wasn't ready to give up the developing friendship. We had a lot of discussion about that, as you might imagine, and finally it evolved to the point where she would tolerate it, given she understood the relationship was a friendship at work. I did not feel good about being dishonest with my wife. I did not feel good about sneaking around. I'm not proud of that but I couldn't give up my sense of rejuvenation either. Later, my wife was to find out the truth.

In the meantime spending time with Elysia became my inspiration for a lot of things. I have, what I will characterize, a top-level job in a highly competitive business. It's not an easy job. It's very demanding and challenging so I tend to focus only on what I'm doing at work. It's interesting though, because sometimes, Elysia would pop into my mind. I would think of her vivaciousness and her energy, amongst other things. I began enjoying work even more, and I attributed a lot of that to just the change in me and of course I attributed that back to Elysia.

Our first trip occurred when Elysia told me she was planning to make a prolonged visit to New York City. I decided to visit her there. Frankly, I wasn't prepared not to see her for any length of time. I had some business I could do in New York but primarily I was thinking of having a mini vacation with Elysia. I also knew my wife never wanted to visit NYC. She had chosen not to go with me in the past. I decided it would be safer and more honest to be up-front with my wife and tell her that I would be visiting Elysia there. I discussed it with her. Surprisingly, it went well. She acknowledged she never wanted to visit New York and said fine, go and have fun. In fact, she told me not to do something stupid like just go for one or two days. Wow! So I approached Elysia with the idea. She also said it sounded like a good idea. There was no discussion of my hiring her for sex while there. It seemed like two friends planning a mini-vacation. It looked like a 'go.' Amazing.

Now the logistics had to be handled. I booked a flight and after searching the web, I decided to stay at a high-end hotel off Times

Square. Then I made choices for the restaurants and entertainment. I wanted everything to go smoothly. On the web I researched the plays on Broadway and it looked like *The Producers* and *The Lion King* were the top two shows. Naturally, *The Producers* was sold out through the entire year. The secondary market prices reflected the popularity. In other words, not exactly cheap but I bought them anyway. For another night I was also able to get tickets for the *The Lion King.*

The departure day arrived. The flight was good. NYC is always impressive from the air and impressive from every aspect. JFK is laid out surprisingly well and I soon found myself headed for my hotel in an infamous NY taxicab. I personally think the Boston taxi drivers are much scarier! The hotel proved to be an excellent luxury hotel.

After I checked in, I decided to pay a visit to Times Square. I wouldn't be meeting Elysia until the next morning and I needed something to do to take my mind off things. My brain was overloaded: thinking of business, about the visit with Elysia, the things we were planning to do or things that had yet to be planned. For being such a forceful, decisive person, Elysia always leaves the planning to me. I have never really figured that one out.

Times Square was colorful, as usual. The computerized lighted ad displays were something else. I've always found New Yorkers to be surprisingly friendly. Several times, when I must have appeared to be lost or looking for something, someone would ask if they could answer a question or provide directions. I walked and walked and looked at everything. I decided to take in a movie, so *Zoolander* it was. I always liked the lead, Ben Stiller. It was just what I needed and I left in a good mood. By now it was late at night, but I decided to walk. In the back of my mind, I thought of the NYC stories of muggings but there seemed to be a very visible police presence in the area.

When I returned to the hotel, I reviewed my notes for our itinerary, checked to make sure I had the Broadway tickets and then laid out my clothes. I tried to sleep and the next morning came way too early, from a sleep standpoint, since I got to sleep at 3:00 AM. Morning couldn't get there fast enough from a standpoint of wanting to see Elysia. I held myself back from calling her too early and later learned that she was disappointed I hadn't called earlier. I could have kicked myself. Minutes with her are precious, more valuable than gold, and I speak of value from an emotional satisfaction perspective, not financial. Sooner than I expected, there was a knock at the door. I approached with exhilaration and not a little apprehension. I opened the door, there she was. All my negative thoughts immediately vanished. I was with Elysia.

This wasn't about sex. I wasn't sure about that part yet. For the moment we were friends in NYC. We chatted about the trip, the weather and decided to catch some lunch. Around two, I put her into a taxi, gave her some money to pay for it and headed downtown to do some business. I also scoped out Fifth Avenue because I knew we would be shopping there the next day.

That first day we had tickets to see *The Producers* and had dinner reservations at a restaurant in the Trump Plaza. Elysia arrived around 5 and changed into an unbelievably sexy leather dress. I asked her about it. She said she had bought it for an event the year before, the Canadian equivalent of the MTV Music Awards. Apparently one of her conquests was a movie actor. She headed into the bathroom to put on makeup. The hotel had put fluorescent lighting around the bathroom mirror and fluorescent lights aren't flattering to anyone. Elysia yelled, "Tom, I'm getting old, I can see wrinkles." That caused a strange but pleasant reaction in me. First, it was a comment that a couple who was comfortable with each other might make, kind of like we had been 'going together' for quite awhile. That was very pleasant. The other was to actually imagine Elysia when she was older. It just didn't seem possible. Strange thought, that even she will get old someday. For tonight though, her long blond hair hung loosely over her back. I wanted to kiss the back of her neck under all that shimmering pale gold fragrant hair. I had to remind myself we were friends for the night, going to a play.

The bellman at the hotel flagged down a taxi and we headed to the restaurant. The meal lived up to expectations. For some reason I remember the dessert most. It was presented on two white plates, each of which was square and about fourteen inches wide. On each were four smaller plates, also white, which nearly covered the larger plate. Finally, on each of the smaller plates was a series of different desserts. At first I thought the items on each of our plates were the same. We discovered that they were different. Very cool! We shared each other's desserts to get a sampling of all of them and we kept washing it all down with champagne.

We decided to walk to the theatre. It was chilly. Elysia had on a coat over her dress, which was somewhat short to expose her

96

beautiful legs. She had on really high heels to make the outfit complete - or turn me on more, I'm not sure which. We had to walk fairly fast to get to the theatre on time, but Elysia walked in the heels as a hiker would in boots. No problem. It is fun driving or walking with Elysia. She likes to be in command. It was 'turn here, turn there, cross the street, wait,' always spoken in a most assertive and confident manner. Being in the position that I am at work, it is enjoyable to have someone else take charge once in a while. We got to our seats just in time, and it was good to see the show before the main leads (Nathan Land & Matthew Broderick) rotated out of the show. It was a quality show, very Broadway. Afterwards, I put Elysia in a cab and she left.

The next morning, we met at my room and decided to head over to Fifth Avenue, where we could do some serious damage to my credit cards. We stopped at a few stores such as Armani, DKNY, where she bought some sweaters. At times I felt like I was in some surreal movie. Elysia would try on the clothes and then parade them for me as I sat in a chair. She wanted my opinion. A couple of times she opened the curtain and flashed me with her body clad only in a g-string and bra. Of course I loved that. Still makes me smile.

We headed over to the Gucci store, which was what a NY store on Fifth Avenue should be like. It was very elegant, all the salespersons were dressed in black and there were plenty of them, and they were helpful but not intrusive. They seemed to know when to approach and when to leave us alone. We first stopped in the purse section. Elysia had a definite idea of what she wanted. She wanted a glossy leather purse with the right combination of color, leather finish and hardware color. She had the poor salesperson frantically searching the back room. I didn't give a damn what she bought. Finally after much discussion Elysia agreed that the leather finish, which the salesperson recommended, would actually be better because it would show less wear. We then walked by the shoe section. I noticed a section of boots. They were all black, very tall and had high, stiletto heels. I commented to Elysia that they looked very practical. Course, I meant it as a joke. She gasped and said she had always wanted a pair. Well, you know where this was going. She asked to try some on. She did. It was amazing how many heads turned in our direction as Elysia casually, yet confidently, strolled around to see how they felt and looked. Every single head, male or female, turned to peek at her long legs and beautifully appointed breasts, which seemed to be even more pert with those shoes hugging her legs. She said they felt good and, well, I don't know how they felt, but God, did they ever look

97

good. We weren't going to leave the store without them. And we didn't! Twelve hundred dollars was worth it for what happened later.

We headed back to my room, running late as usual. We started to relax for a few moments, looking at what she had bought, but we didn't have long before we had to start getting ready to head over to our next five-star restaurant dining experience. We were sitting there, somewhat tired, and dreading to start rushing out again. She looked at me. Then she said, "Tom, why don't we pass on the restaurant and stay in your room." What a great idea. I wish I could say I had been thinking the same thing. Silly me, I had honestly thought it was important to cram in as many 'events' as we could. We ordered up some cheese, fruit and champagne. Elysia pulled out a little recreational, agricultural goods that could be smoked and we did relax – really. We spent some time having a great conversation about life, philosophies for life and many, many other topics. I continually found things to be amazed about when it came to Elysia and I continued to underestimate her. Well, it was finally almost time to get ready to leave for the show. She looked at me in a sly way. "Tom, think we have time for a quickie?" I was just floored. What a marvelous, marvelous suggestion. I just couldn't believe it. It was HER idea and not mine! She headed into the bathroom as usual. I waited for her on the bed. She walked out of the bathroom nude, wearing nothing but the Gucci long black boots with the stiletto heels. There aren't words to describe the sight of her. It felt great to be a man. I don't think I could imagine, in my wildest dreams, a sexier image. Blonde hair, thin, long smooth body, creamy white skin and boots to her thighs. Can you imagine? I was glad I didn't have heart problems. I could just see the headlines. Tourist found dead in hotel with strange smile on his face and the largest dick ever seen. Unfortunately, it truly had to be a "quickie" but felt so enjoyable. A fantasy come true.

Tonight we would see *Lion King*. We didn't walk to the theatre this time. I was too mellow to walk fast. I wasn't sure about this play. It claimed to have a wide age-demographic appeal. In other words, suitable for kids as well as seniors. I thought it might be too juvenile for Elysia. You know, her 'woman of the world' image and everything. It started and I was really enjoying it. I liked it more than *The Producers*. It had dramatic sets, lighting, music, and wasn't just a few people on stage reciting lines. I became engrossed in the show. At some point I glanced at Elysia. She was gently rocking to the music with a slight smile on her face. It was a smile of joyful innocence. She was engrossed in the show. I had never seen Elysia like that. It was an image I will enjoy to my dying day.

After the trip to NYC, Elysia and I continued to see each other. In my mind, she and I had moved beyond the original provider-client relationship. To what, I guess I didn't really know, but we had gotten to know each other well. I started flying her to visit me, sometimes just for dinner, then popped her back on the plane the same night. When she visited for work, we spent the entire first night together. I'd give her a couple of thousand dollars, or basically whatever she asked. I started buying her presents: a snowboard, ski outfits, a fully decorated Christmas tree delivered from a florist in her city, a stereo, a guitar, a car, a full-length fur coat, whatever she wanted. I even sent flowers to her grandmother's funeral in Elysia's name.

Then one night I mistakenly took a double dose of my medication. The next morning my wife acted kind of funny. She told me that I had spent the night talking about a woman named Elysia. I had no recollection at all but I recognized she was describing exact conversations. She asked me if Elysia was a prostitute. I said,"Yup." She asked for more information and I told her just about everything. I guess the thing I had talked most about in my sleep was how much I liked Elysia, the friends we had become, and strangely enough, that was what my wife reacted to. In fact, this whole situation's been kind of strange because she was upset by it, but wasn't as upset as I would be if I were finding out something about her. I think I would have gone ballistic. I was surprised by her tolerance. It seemed like one of those things that goes against the laws of nature, kind of like having the laws of gravity suspended. I expected to come crashing back to earth at any time. In the end, there were no secrets between us on this situation, really, so it was not based on lies.

Amazingly, my wife gave me free rein on my nights with Elysia. She didn't ask when I would be home from my 'meetings' with her, she just requested that I not wake her up when I got in. She now seemed to be looking out for Elysia. At one point I hadn't heard a specific time confirmation back from Elysia and I told my wife that maybe I should just be quiet and see how long it took for Elysia to realize it hadn't been firmed up. My wife said, "Now, Elysia is your friend, don't do that to her. Go ahead and confirm a meeting time." Elysia also knew that my wife knew and found this situation "unusual." During this time my wife and I remodeled our downstairs and Elysia suggested hardwood floors, which we went with. She said to thank Elysia, "It really was a nice touch with the floors!" All of this was beginning to appear like some comedy routine!

My birthday arrived and Elysia sent a handmade invitation to my office inviting me to a surprise birthday celebration she was preparing just for me. The invitation was incredibly thoughtful. She had painted it and there was her personal hand lettering on it. She had pasted on some attachments, I recall a little metal heart. I assumed we'd probably go out to dinner and to a play. My wife had given me a small birthday party with friends the weekend before, so it turned out I was free to be with Elysia on my actual birthday which was kind of cool.

This time I flew to her and checked into a hotel. Waiting in my room was a small vase with a single yellow rose with a card that was yet another invitation for the evening. There was also a voice message from her saying to be at her home by six. I dutifully showed up and was expecting to pick her up and leave for another venue. When she opened the door she invited me in. We hugged and greeted. Then I noticed there was a gentleman standing there. She introduced him, "This is 'Mr. Chef' (I'll use that name for a well-known chef in her city) and he will be cooking for us this evening."

Luckily, my birthday is in a month when the weather is nice. Warm but not too hot. Elysia led me through her house to her backyard. It was decorated magnificently. She had moved her dining room table outdoors to her patio by a little fishpond. The table had a formal bluish velour tablecloth, formal silver cutlery, flowers, formal china dishes and lots of candles. Elysia has a candle fetish. There were candles floating on the pond and hanging candle decorations in the trees and candles tucked in the moss. She had a little love-seat rocker under a tree where we sat. Beside it she had placed a huge basket full of unwrapped gifts. There was a toaster because she knew I was about to move out of my home into a bachelor apartment. There were lots of homemade things such as strawberry jam, which she said she made herself. There was a jar of honey, muffins, real Canadian maple syrup and a whole variety of Canadian food items.

Once I had looked at everything, she led me back into the living room where we sat down on her couch. She proceeded to bring out more gifts that were wrapped up in fancy paper with all sorts of exotic ribbons. The one I treasure the most was a framed photo of her in a blue swimsuit. That was a very special gift. Tame for public viewing, but probably a little much to put on my desk at work. She had made Asian-styled plaques with symbols for power, patience and justice, which were framed. She knew I like Chinese food so she had some chopstick holders and some chopsticks that apparently she had bought years ago on a trip to Japan. There were other presents related to Chinese food too.

It was really special, that present part. I mean it was different. It took me off guard totally. I had assumed we would go out and I would buy the dinner and that would be my birthday celebration. There was more. After I opened all the presents, we returned to the patio and 'Mr. Chef' commenced serving appetizers and handed me a printed menu card.

Appetizers: Shrimp.
Tuna tartare in cucumber cups & peanut oil, lemon, & celery.
Duck fois gras warmed on croutons with honey thyme
cream cheese with herbs & purple radish garnish.
Salad: Arugula, goat cheese, thyme, pear, & raspberry vinaigrette
& almond oil.
Entrée: Halibut with lemon/orange, basil Nugget potatoes
Asparagus
Dessert: Homemade brownies

As well, fruit sorbets were served between courses.

'Mr. Chef' was apparently very knowledgeable because he explained the region of France where the two bottles of champagne came from and other pertinent details. He was cultured and gracious. His dinner was fantastic, which he served over several hours. There was no reason to rush it. I remember a slight breeze came up which caused melted wax to flow over the tablecloth. Some candles would blow out occasionally and we'd re-light them. Sometimes, 'Mr. Chef' did. We had such a relaxed fun time, just talking out on the patio in her twinkling fantasy-land.

Unfortunately, my present didn't include sex that night. I'm not sure why not. I was content to not push it and happy for her thoughtfulness in doing what she had. A taxi took me back to my hotel at eleven.

E-mail:
From: Tom
To: Elysia
Subject: My birthday dinner last night….
My Dear Elysia,
For me last night was a night I will remember forever. It was just something that was unbelievable. I mean, it was a fantastic, fantastic experience in itself. The topper was that you were so thoughtful and willing to take your time to plan it and bring it off. And the details! The invitation, the flower sent to the room, the romantic and peaceful

setting, the candles, the decorations, the .... it just goes on and on! The chef is a treasure, the meal was superb. And it continued with the gifts. The thought that went into them was incredible. They are so special to me. They do have that Elysia-touch. You seem to know exactly the things to pick out. The heart is fantastic – thank you! And thanks for sharing the photo of you as well. I can never get enough of those! I still can't believe it today. You are outrageous.

We didn't finish our discussion about how to program your MP3 player. If you can tell me the make and model, I can probably download the manual from the Web. I can then figure out the quick way to get it done. As I said on my phone message, I know we had talked about possibly getting together for breakfast today – nothing firm, I assumed. I just thought you were probably tired/busy so I'm heading out. It was great to get your message. It perked me right up for the flight home.
I remain extremely satisfied and happy, Tom

In this world of coincidences, I had to open a branch office in Elysia's city of all places. My wife knew what city Elysia lived in. I told my wife that I needed to make a quick business trip there for one day. My wife suggested I don't push it so hard and spend the night there instead of flying back the same day. I decided not to, but wow! Another time my wife and I were going to travel together to the city where Elysia lives. Something came up at work at the last minute that required me to cancel. We had tickets to a play that I thought would be non-refundable and my wife asked me if Elysia might be interested and, if so, we could give them to her. Then, around the first of December, my wife reminded me that I needed to be thinking about a Christmas present for Elysia. Sometimes I felt I was in a Twilight Zone episode.

I've thought a lot about it. I think that my wife felt she couldn't compete. She was trying to diet too, but wasn't having much success. She wanted us to stay together, so she was willing to or would tolerate the ongoing situation with Elysia. I know it just seems so strange. I actually saw a therapist about it because I wanted to talk to somebody who had an objective viewpoint about my marriage. He said, "Well, almost anything's acceptable these days, so if you two are happy with it, more power to you."

Eventually I rented my own apartment though I still spent many nights at home with my wife. I began dating as well. I truly don't think my seeing Elysia was a major factor in the demise of my marriage. The marriage had really been over for several years. We both needed to move on.

I debated whether to tell Elysia about my divorce. I probably could have kept it from her. However, I did feel we had a relationship that would stand this type of news. She often referred to me as her rock, a calm voice in the storm. I hoped I might be able to derive a little of the same benefit from her. I think somewhere in the back of my head I wanted to marry Elysia, if she would ever have indicated such a mutual desire. I knew for certain I wanted to be involved with her for a long time. I knew it wasn't practical, but that's how I felt.

E-mail:
From: Tom
To: Elysia
Subject: loss
Hi Elysia,
There has been stuff going in my life that may have made me seem a little strange recently. You may not want to know all this but it helps to "talk" about it to someone I feel very comfortable talking to. And, I have come to realize, you are someone that probably knows just about the most on some of my thoughts about life, problems, joys and other personal things.
Well, my wife and I are getting a divorce. First off, it is not as upsetting as one might imagine. The marriage has really been over for some time. Several years in reality. So to give up something that didn't really exist any longer maybe made it easier when the decision was finally reached. She is a good person, I have a strong sense of commitment, both of which probably contributed to a willingness on both our parts to have it last as long as it has. It is a most amicable split and was a mutual decision. Yes, I know this seems kind of crazy but we both seem to have the right attitude about it for now. We both feel a heavy weight has now been lifted from us.
I imagine you have some questions about whether my relationship with you was the cause, or a major part of it. No, it really wasn't. I am truthful here, Elysia, I don't think I would have a reason to lie to you about this. I have always tried to be straight with you and I don't plan to change. We have always shared our good news and bad news. You have told me I am your rock, the calm in the eye of the storm. I have also realized that, believe it or not, you have often acted as that for me. I really need a little of that from you right now. Don't worry, I am not going to be moping around feeling all sorry for myself when we get together. See you soon.
From one "rock" to another, Tom

Eventually my wife lost sixty pounds but there was no turning back. Our relationship was in trouble before I met Elysia. My marriage broke up for reasons other than my visiting a prostitute or any weight problem. But I still feel guilty about it, though I believe our marriage should have ended. Our divorce wasn't acrimonious, just kind of sad.

When I was interviewed for Elysia's story, I was asked what I would tell women to do to make themselves more appealing to men. I don't claim to have 'THE ANSWER' as there isn't one. But I will say 'to not take your partner for granted.' Naturally, that works both ways. One develops a certain level of comfort with your partner, such as not being afraid they will run for the hills if you come home in a cranky mood. One should always think they really need to work to keep the interest in a relationship. Don't settle for the least common denominator or the least work in a relationship. Always consider yourself at least in a pretend mode to be competing for your partner's interest with another. I don't mean living in a jealous sense of insecurity all the time. While not the same as a 'regular' relationship, I mentioned how the sexual aspect of the situation with Elysia had settled down to a predictable routine. This is an example of taking someone for granted. You do not always have to try to maintain interest, but you should.

Ten

TOM - Part 2

Obviously, our relationship started because of the sex. Elysia was very professional about being an escort, but she was also very good about trying to respect me in our personal relationship. It transcended the 'john' relationship and was fun. I really thought she was a great person, but sometimes I was a little sceptical about her. I think she was a good manipulator. I can laugh about it but there were times when I wondered if I stopped spending money on her like I did, if she would still see me. If the money is what it was all about, I think if she really had wanted to, she could have played me for a lot more but she took it easy on me.

Due to the unique relationship between Elysia and me, I realize I have only myself to blame. Yet I have no regrets, not even in the fact that I eventually experienced a few different takes on the old "Not tonight, honey, I have a headache!" With time her sexual details toned down considerably, and our relationship became much more mundane.

Sometimes I felt stupid about the amount of money I spent on Elysia. For example, if I gave her a thousand dollars for the evening, and we had dinner together, and then we decided to go buy her a new outfit, I would think to myself, 'Well, I didn't really need to do that. I have already paid her a thousand dollars to spend time with me, so what did I do that for?' I knew I was living a fantasy life when I was with her, and buying her expensive things was a part of it. I realized it was about my wanting to contribute to the fantasy, which was a different, more opulent type of lifestyle than what most men experience. Taking her to NYC, to the plays, to dinner, and buying her expensive presents was certainly not something I felt was required in order to have sex with her. It had everything to do with having a gorgeous blonde with an astounding figure on my arm to show off, and my enjoyment in spending time with such an exquisitely sophisticated sexual female. Honestly, I also enjoyed pleasing her with things she wanted. It all made me feel good, and obviously I felt it was rewarding enough to keep up the spending.

A few times I was struck by the fact that Elysia didn't forget about the money I paid her to be with me. We mostly tended to dance around discussing it. She never once said, "Well, Tom, I've been with you 'X' number of hours so I expect 'X' hundreds of dollars for that." When I was seeing her in a traditional escort relationship, we worked out a price of $1,000 US per evening, with dinner and a sexual act included. I always tipped her another hundred. We'd spend about three hours together. After we became more personal, I continued to give her that, despite all the gifts and money I tipped her. Yet we did have definite times where no money was exchanged. One example is the birthday dinner for me in her home, and we spent time together on shopping sprees without my paying her for her time. But some-where in between paying for sex and spending time with her were gray areas for payment. At least I thought so. I lost sight of when money was necessary because I certainly was thinking of her as a friend at that point. So there were several awkward occasions where I forgot to give her the money, and she used a tactful reminder that I owed her. I wasn't surprised, but it did cause me some degree of hurt because I realized I personalized our relationship more than she did.

I suppose a part of me hoped the extras would help make her really care for me. The downside is, of course, that I will never know if she really enjoyed my company, or just liked the fact that I was willing to spend lots of money on her.

Sometimes it bothered me. I have wondered what would have happened if I had said, "Well, gee, Elysia, I need to pay my rent this month. Maybe if we don't go out and shop for the clothes, or stereos and other gifts, would that affect our relationship?" I didn't know if the relationship would change. To be honest, I was sure it probably would. That was something I was concerned about. I knew I had passed the point where I could say, "Let's just stick to the usual fee and leave it at that." I had only myself to blame. I really didn't have any illusions about that.

Unfortunately, as in a stale marriage, the sex became like that too.

From a fantasy sexual standpoint, if Elysia hadn't been so beautiful, it would have become just plain boring. When I was 'the client,' she put on a show because she felt she had to do her job to get paid. I no longer wanted to be thought of as a 'john' even though I was, but on the other hand, I wasn't sexually getting much out of it. In the beginning there were special appetizers, long conversations on the couch, and sexy lingerie. She often did an erotic strip dance around the bed to show off her body. She would loosen me up massaging my back with body oil, and the oral aspect was a work of art. After a year it had become more mechanical. She would change out of her street clothes in the bathroom, come out naked and basically just do a bit of oral sex before intercourse. That was it. Even the typical rubbing of her body against my body didn't happen any more.

Whatever I lost in the sexual aspect, Elysia was still a lot of fun. Spending time with her in NYC and on other vacations was certainly satisfying. I knew she was also working, but it didn't matter. I remember a shopping spree, which may not sound dazzling but was a new and enjoyable experience for me. We were at Zaks, and Elysia was looking at a pink jogging suit and size two jeans that she wanted to try on. The salesman directed her to a dressing room, and as she was walking to it, he said, "And, sir, if you'd like to go back there, you certainly can." I was a bit surprised but followed Elysia in. There was a chair inside and I sat there while she tried on all kinds of clothes the salesman picked out and brought her. It was almost like we were a couple. Elysia said things like, "What do think about this? How does it look on my butt?" She liked her jeans tight and she was having trouble finding ones that fit tight enough. I enjoyed watching her struggle into them; pulling them up over her legs and g-stringed bum. Of course, from time to time, she was nude. She flashed her breasts, and I wanted to have sex with her right there on the floor. Unfortunately, it was impractical because the salesman kept returning and knocking on the door with new clothes. I know I ended up spending over $2,000 on her that day.

I also remember shopping in Toronto the day after my surprise birthday dinner in her garden. It was a beautiful day so we slowly walked along the street in a downtown area with expensive stores. Of course, she did attract attention and, of course, I loved walking with a beautiful woman. We had an hour-long lunch with lots of champagne and eventually I said, "Well, okay, we had my birthday yesterday. Let's go get you something now." She said, "Oh yes, sounds good to me." Ever practical I said, "What do you need?" She laughed, "Well, I don't know. I could use some sunglasses. We can go look." We ended up buying her a nice fashionable pair of designer sunglasses for $270. Elysia was never cheap with herself, though I laugh because she would often say something like, "If I was paying for this myself, I wouldn't be paying this much." I'd lapse back into my fantasy and remember her nude.

We continued our walk and eventually ended up in a small haute couture boutique. I said, "Why don't you get a couple of dresses or pants." It was slow in the store that day and I sat down on the only chair while Elysia went into the dressing room. I was surprised when she pulled back the curtain and stood there with nothing on but a mischievous smile. I wasn't expecting that. I laughed and said, "Yeah, I'll take two of those, Elysia." She kept flashing me, and every time I laughed. I spent about $1500 on clothes for her that day. Absolutely worth it too. I have no idea if the saleslady saw, or the other customers, and I didn't care.

Elysia may have been a good manipulator, but I suppose everybody is to some degree. I laugh about that because I'm sure she probably was. It would bother me if that were all it was about but, if it was, she was very good at it because I didn't get the sense that I was only a 'wallet' to her. The experience of buying her a car is a good example. I originally planned to have her come visit me to go looking for a car, buy the car, and then I'd give it to her to take back to Canada. Well, I researched it with US and Canada Customs, spent money on tax attorneys, and learned it was complicated, almost impossible, and not worth the effort. She ended up buying a car in Canada and spent far less than I had offered her. I wanted to buy her a newer car because I didn't want her in some piece of junk, but she said the amount I offered was too much. I legally transferred the amount she requested and she bought the car.

So, you ask, is it worth having a personal relationship with an escort? Would I tell the men of the world to stick to the price and keep it to an hour? I would say, "Don't do what I did." Yeah, I would say, "Keep it a business relationship." I mean, that's easy for me to say. I didn't do that and, of course, now that I've come to know Elysia more as a person, I'm glad I didn't. However, if you're looking at it from the sexual fantasy/excitement angle? For me, making the relationship personal produced an inverse return. I gave her lots of money, trips, gifts, and my return became wham, bang, we're done. The sex was not enhanced by any means. In fact, it regressed.

I guess I fell in love with her. Given I'm over fifty years old, I'm not sure what love means. When I think of stereotypical love, Elysia met all the performance specifications, and that's probably what clouded my judgement, but it wasn't real love. She obviously saw many, many men, and not all of them fell in love with her, so I accept there was probably something in my makeup, something that I wanted in her which was more than sexual. It's something deep inside my character, I suspect, that needed the 'gorgeous' dream a little more than the next man. I enjoyed the fact there was this beautiful younger woman who, even if it wasn't true, seemed to feel an attraction for me, and I could call her up, ask her out, and have her spend time with me. If I felt a need to analyze if it was healthy or not, I suppose it's not, but that was what I got out of it. And it was fun because she was fun, creative, daring, and upbeat. Obviously, I'm not speaking just strictly about the sexual aspect.

I guess it's kind of ironic that after my divorce I gave Elysia my wedding ring and high school graduation ring. I no longer wore them, and because they amounted to a chunk of gold, I offered them to her to recycle into a new ring. Elysia wearing a form of my old wedding ring has some kind of quiet justice!

No matter what happens, I'd like to keep in touch with Elysia. It would be sad if we didn't e-mail each other every once in a while as friends, especially if we threw away the money aspect. If it was about her wanting more money, I'd have to question that, at least giving to the degree I was doing.

You get what you pay for. Elysia gave me my fantasy and I have no regrets.

Eleven

ELYSIA'S THOUGHTS ON TOM

We met, wherever. He met me standing by his little shiny expensive, very expensive, convertible car which he had washed that day because he was going to see me. He opened the door for me and I sat down on the soft leather seats. I was wearing the fur coat he bought me and little else. He walked around to his side. He had chosen a restaurant and it was always five star. We sat at the best table. He ordered an expensive bottle of champagne and we ordered the most exquisite dinners. We sat there and talked for three or four hours. I talked about whatever I could possibly think of to talk about. He never suggested it was time to go to the hotel. We had dessert and then we left to go. It was like any other couple. He had an obsession with a fantasy. He had an obsession for me. But I'm not that person he took for dinner. I'm not that person he had sex with. Sometimes he forgot that. Occasionally I forget too.

Tom is such a good man. There's no question about that. He treated me fabulously and, right from the start, indicated he wanted more of a relationship than the usual client-provider relationship.

E-mail:
From: Tom
To: Elysia
Subject: February visit & scheduling
Elysia, Whew! I've been catching up on my work e-mail, decide to take a break and what do I find? A most special Valentine note causing great anticipation for an appointment with you! Now, as to a good day and time, last time we talked about maybe going for a little extra time (2 hr. session?),

and maybe out for a few drinks first. If I stick to my usual day but moved it to 5:00 PM start, would that work for you? Sticking with the usual time (4:00 PM) would work for me also, I just don't know if that restricts our choice of establishments that would serve our favorite "adult beverages." Would another day be easier for you with this arrangement? Just for grins, would you be open for going out to dinner sometime? That may be a little tight for a two-hour slot though, and I don't know how much flexibility you have in scheduling. Could you handle a three-hour slot, or at least 2+? You know me, I wouldn't stay around for the full time just for the sake of it. Same question as above, if this were feasible, which day is preferable for you?

You mentioned no transportation yet. I can certainly understand what a pain that would be! If you end up deciding to fly here, I happen to have an old sports car, in excellent condition, which you can use. I would be more than happy to leave it at the airport for you to pick up and use while you are down here and then leave at the airport when you return. It's insured, licensed and gassed to go! Or is a car rental your preferred option? I would be willing to pick up the tab for that too.

Well, I lucked out and had a meeting cancellation, but it is almost time for my next one. So, I await your reply. Then I can impatiently wait for the time to pass until your visit. Love, Big Bear Tom

From: Elysia
To: Big Bear Tom
Subject: My Big Valentine's Bear!
Hi honey! I would love to go for dinner with you! Thursday night would be great with me. We could meet at 7 and we can celebrate our Valentine's together then. I am sure it will be no problem to keep me past my curfew for as long as you like. :o)
Looking forward to seeing you, I miss u. Love, Elysia xoxo

From: Tom
To: Elysia
Subject: Thursday arrangements
Elysia, I can't wait. Just a couple of quick logistical questions: Assume we head out to eat first, say 7:30 appointment? Any type of restaurant you like (e.g. steak, seafood, Pan-Asian, etc.) or don't like (etc.) or want to be surprised? I know most of the top-end restaurants here and many get booked pretty quick. Let me know, Love, Tom

From: Elysia
To: Tom
Subject: Champagne arrangements!
Hello my darling, Sorry to take so long to get back to you. I am in the middle of moving! I am really looking forward to our evening together tomorrow!

111

7:30 sounds great. As far as the place to eat .... hmmmm ..... My friend Sapphire recommends a place called 'Champagnes' (I think?) but I am open to anything. Seafood is always great! Please, you choose. Can't wait!! Love, Elysia

From: Elysia
To: Tom
Subject: sweet kisses.....
Hello there Big Bear xoxo
Thank you so much for such a wonderful night! I really enjoyed myself and time just flew by. I had no idea how late it had gotten! You were more than generous as well. You are so good to me and I thank you.

Well, I spent this wonderful sunny Saturday playing in my new garden. It was loads of fun. Sapphire came over to harass me too!! I am sure you can imagine us two nuts out back digging around and planting bulbs. I treated myself to a few new flowers and such for the spring and summer. I can look forward to lots of pretty flowers now. Anyway, I hope to hear back from you soon. Let me know how things are going with you. Lots of love, Elysia

From: Tom
To: Elysia
Subject: Fun in the sun, thinking of you!
Elysia, I'm very glad to hear you enjoyed the night. I certainly did! It was fun being with you in a great restaurant with a nice environment. I did make it home safe, sound and with no "curfew" violation. I didn't realize the time situation either. In retrospect I almost chuckle. Here we are first having a nice, leisurely dinner and then it is time to hustle. Although a little more balance would be desired, it was wonderful and definitely a memorable night for me. I just hate to 'rush' anything when I am with you.

Glad to hear you were already able to start with the new garden. The new place sounds like it has a lot of possibilities. Although I have not yet met Sapphire, from how you describe her and knowing you, I bet it was something to see you both in gardening mode.

I'll write again soon. And getting a note from you just lifts me up, so drop me one sometime to let me know how you are doing – I do care.
Love as always,
Tom

From: Tom
To: Elysia
Subject: dinner?
Elysia, If you are up for it, I would like to do dinner again. I don't know if things have changed with your availability since your last note, but how about we meet at 5:30 with a 6:00 PM dinner reservation? While last time

was definitely memorable in a slightly humorous way, I would like to not have to rush the other again. I know this was my problem, not yours! If you can support the earlier start, this might help some. Let me know if the time or plan doesn't work for you.
Tom

Eventually, having dinner became the norm. We dined at all the best restaurants in Toronto. What started out as a three-hour date turned into five hours or more over time with no extra payment for those extra hours. I never asked for more money. Any presents he gave me were supposed to be extra, not a part of my hourly fee. We had lots of conversations about anything and everything. I was spending so much time with him, I showed more of the real me than I did with other clients. It wasn't completely the same acting, plaything, because it's difficult for me to keep it up for five hours. I felt somewhat close to him but I never crossed the border into wanting more. I never crossed that line. For me, the money kept it a professional relationship, although on one level it became deeply personal. Afterwards, when we went to the hotel, that was when the 'escort chick' thing starts and I had to have sex with him. It's part of the deal. He was always generous with money. There were always fresh, brand new one hundred dollar bills. Usually he gave more. He never gave less. He paid for dinner and it was always at least $200+. We ordered an $82 bottle of champagne every time and every time he wanted me to order the $200 bottle. I would say, "No, no, no. This one's fine" because I was thinking *I want that $200. Give me the $200 and I'll drink the water!* Having said that, I did enjoy sampling the different kinds of champagne.

Right from the start of our professional relationship, Tom brought me presents. One of the first ones was an expensive, limited edition pen in honor of Frederick Schyler, supposedly a great German playwright and gifted poet. I had never heard of him before. The pen came in a separate leather case, which must have cost a lot too. I was surprised and thought it was something more than a guy would normally pick. It was beautiful and so nice of him. Well, I lost it on a flight back from San Francisco. I must have left it in the plane when I filled out my customs form. I had no idea what it was worth, but I knew it must be worth a lot and I didn't want to lose it. I was just sick about it. I phoned Alaskan Airlines and said to the girl, "I know I'm wasting my time, but I've got to ask, did anybody turn in a fancy pen?" Amazingly, somebody had. The next week, when I returned to California, I walked up to the counter and it was there! I was so happy someone was honest.

He also bought me nice lingerie. I liked that. I remember the first one he gave me was a set with a lacy pink bra, a matching g-string and a little cami-princess top with a drawstring under the bust and spaghetti straps. Of course later I put it on for him. It pleased me he had gone to the effort of picking it out and buying it for me. Did he get extra service for the effort? Well, of course gifts do add a certain additional enthusiasm and I always rewarded good behavior. Tips of money are appreciated more.

E-mail:
From: Tom
To: Elysia
Subject: Friday confirmation
Hi Elysia, Just wanted to touch base to make sure we are on again for this Friday at 3:00 PM. I really do enjoy myself on the evenings out with you and appreciate them sooo much. While we are certainly different people from different backgrounds, we do share some common things, little things like observing that Victoria's Secret seems to be conservative (don't think Joe Suburban and Suzy Homemaker would typically think that) to some of the bigger things like some shared philosophies towards life. We also do some different things like popping down or up from another country, having a five-star dinner and drinks and flying back the same day. Anyway, throw that in with some other things like your energized personality and it makes for a fun, interesting, enriching, learning time.

Remember I am only a phone call or e-mail away if you need something. Like if you get in the mood again to toss all your CDs or lingerie (Heaven forbid!) I will talk you down off the ledge!
See you soon!
Tom

From Elysia xoxox
To: Tom
Subject: Friday confirmation
Date: Wednesday morning
Hi Tom honey! :) Yes! We are on for 3:00. We could be sitting at McDonalds and I would still have a great time entertaining you with my stories! :o) Can't wait to see you. 555-4321 - right?
Love,
Elysia

From: Tom
To: Elysia
Date: Wednesday afternoon
Subject: Re: Friday confirmation
Yes, 555-4321. If I'm not there to answer, go ahead and leave a message.

Friday can't get here fast enough.
Tom

From: Elysia
To: Tom
Date: Sunday morning
Subject: Thanks
Dear Tom, You sure looked great! I am so happy to see you getting healthier by losing the pounds and taking care of yourself. The twinkle in your eye is fantastic! Thank you so much for the extra, sweetie! Wow. I didn't realize until after you had left, thanks! I am your lucky charm tucked into your pocket close to your heart! I hope to be back soon. Until then stay warm!
Love,
Elysia xoxoxo

From: Tom
To: Elysia
Subject: Re: thanks
Elysia- Thanks so much for the note. I really appreciate your thoughts on my lifestyle change, it's added encouragement for me. Although I think the twinkle in my eye had a little to do with your proximity! The "thanks for the extra" is really something I say to you. It just kind of hit me Friday as I was driving into downtown after I left you. The "it" was how you always seem to make me feel special, and bring such enthusiasm and vitality to our meetings, even though you have to keep things organized, balanced and moving forward while here. Elysia, you continue to astound and amaze me! Now I certainly understand your scheduling for visits doesn't revolve around me.... but if for some reason you are only able to make one more visit this year, please (oh please, oh please, oh please!) don't make it during Nov. 15 – Nov.26. I will be in Atlanta losing money (probably) but having fun.

Now remember, unless you want a fruitcake for Christmas, drop me a couple of suggestions. Well, you actually gave me good suggestions on Friday, but if something else strikes your fancy as a possibility let me know.
Love, :o) hey, I get to use this too! "A friend" sounds too formal.
Tom

He told me that because of me he felt more like a young man again. He said he had a different kind of energy now and a more positive image of himself. What I noticed was the weight he was losing. The weight loss was an amazing transformation for him. He really cared about looking great. And he did. I remember one time when he arrived, I noticed he'd been using bottled self-tanner. It never looks natural and I didn't like it on him but appreciated the fact he was trying to look great. Really, gentlemen! Don't use the self-tanner lotion. It looks too fake.

E-mail:
From: Tom
To: Elysia
Subject: Monday
Elysia, I was a little concerned that I hadn't heard back from you since my note to you at the beginning of the week. I was just sitting down to send you a note to make sure you were okay and that we were indeed on for a visit. I was just sitting here thinking of your wonderful personality and how joyous, spirited, energetic, - sometimes wistful, sometime sad, yet always interesting and entertaining you can be. Unless you tell me otherwise, I will meet you at 5:30. Somewhere, maybe the usual place? I have a new place for us to try for dinner that sounds interesting. Let's both relax, enjoy and forget all our daily troubles and woes! I suppose you are on the usual arrival schedule so there will be no time to squeeze in a little mini shopping expedition? Need any clothes, stereo equipment, body jewelry :), etc.? Oh well, maybe next time.

Oh, I really want to thank YOU. For so, so much .... on this crazy journey we call life, you have caused a major course correction in mine (yes, a good course correction!). And I am indeed always here for you – do remember that. With much love and anticipation,   Tom

During one of our evenings where dinner and dancing was in order, Tom told me that his wife knew about me. I already knew something was up because during our past four appointments, he mentioned he no longer had a curfew and that it was no big deal to stay out late. He was obviously pleased he no longer had to sneak around. I didn't ask why, I didn't want to know, but that night he told me he had mentioned to his wife he had met a woman through work (me) and we had lots in common. He'd painted it as a platonic friendship. I said, "WAIT A MINUTE, she's probably not stupid. She must suspect." And he said, "Yeah, I'm sure she does." It was so creepy. I really didn't want to hear that. I didn't ask why she would put up with it. I didn't want to know. I like being in a bubble of pretending. I thought we had a good thing going and I didn't want the boat to rock. He did too and that's why he wanted more. I assumed it was because she wasn't having sex with him so she accepted that someone else was. Maybe that made it easier for her. Since he told her he had met me through work, and she didn't know what I looked like, perhaps she pictured me as some old ugly hag. In the meantime, it seemed he was falling in love with me. I was worried that he thought something might ever come of it. I was confident he wouldn't leave his wife for me. Well, mostly confident, right up until he sent the following e-mail to my friend Sapphire. Tom knew Sapphire because the three of us had dinner together several times.

E-mail:
From: Tom
To: Sapphire
Subject: Enjoyed last night, and ..... I am glad you were able to make it last night. I appreciated your company and it is always nice to be able to share a great dining experience with friends! I certainly know Elysia did as well.

Last night seemed to drive me towards a decision I have been considering for a few weeks. People, with what I suspect is far greater wisdom than I, have said that it is an inviolate law of nature that Person A, who seems to have ESCORT stamped on their forehead (apparently permanently and indelibly), cannot have a relationship with Person B, who seems to have CURRENTLY MARRIED on their forehead (apparently permanently and indelibly), beyond a certain nature and limitation. I tried to make that last sentence even longer and more convoluted but I couldn't! Maybe part of the "far greater wisdom" is a desire to protect the feelings of other individuals – who knows?

Anyway, decision? I think I need to test that assertion this year. I hate to give up the ball game without really ever getting into it. I feel it truly is possible to change one or more of the variables ("stampings") in the equation. I am not a masochist so I would like to minimize the pain I may have to endure as part of this experiment. So, I am always welcome to comments, suggestions, or a good old 2 x 4 swung against the head or other parts of the body! I have found that head wounds of this nature are actually preferable to wounds of the heart in the long run. So, if you desire, you have my permission to inflict any of the above to me. Again, thanks for last night and for being a friend to Elysia and maybe to me in some small manner. Tom

I found it bizarre. You must understand that we were coming from totally different places. I cared about Tom as a person and I'd never intentionally hurt him but I realized he saw me as a girlfriend. He had called me his girlfriend. Things like, "Here I am going to dinner with my girlfriend," or as I got out of the car to leave, "Love you Elysia, take care." He'd lost sight of reality. It was the money that kept it from crossing the line and he'd forgotten that this was my job.

* * *

E-mail:
From: Elysia
To: Sapphire
Subject: What is Tom thinking?
Hey there, I think he is highly intelligent but he is naive as so many of them are. If he thinks that our relationship is going somewhere and that we have a 'future' together, then he is dreaming and wishful thinking. If he thinks

that he is 'in love' with me, well, come on, he doesn't even know me! I pray that he has the sense to keep things in check. Poor guy. He has no clue. Yes, we certainly have moved from provider/client to something else. He has forgotten, or chooses not to recognize, the fact that he pays me!! How can these boys, and we know there are others that are like him, believe that we working girls actually like and or want to be with them. They forget that it is all about the cash!

If he is looking for more, then he is only setting himself up. I have not, at least sincerely tried not to lead him in that direction. I sure hope that I have been honest enough with him that I can remain guilt-free, well okay, somewhat guilt-free. I am worried about the future in regard to having to one day burst his bubble. It will hurt him and I would be sorry about that, but come on, he is married, not to mention he lives in another country! As if we, even if I were interested, would have a future. What relationship would last if he had to hurt and dump his wife to be with me. No thanks.

Just another weird factor. He doesn't know about me or my life. It's not like I am about to talk to him about my personal life: ie. dating, my relationships. That is just taboo and would destroy the ILLUSION that I am there only for them. How can they not realize this? You see how fucked up it is! Does he actually believe that I am alone all the time or what? I wonder. Could he actually accept or discuss something like that? I know that he is married and I accept that and we acknowledge that, but is it a two-way street? I think not! Yet he claims to care about the 'real me' and not Elysia, and yet Elysia is only part of the story he knows.

I am not sure how to proceed. I will just carry on as I have. He wants to 'help me' buy an apartment. Does this mean that he will forever be a part of my life and feel because he has helped me buy one that it is OUR love shack and that he has a claim to it? Does he not think that I will have a boyfriend, lover, and husband in the future and that it is not going to be him? Does he think that I will forever be his what? Mistress? I guess that is the term for it. If he is not 'paying me' to be with him but 'helping' me does he think of me as his girlfriend. You cannot have a girlfriend and a wife. Isn't it amazing how men don't get it!
Elysia

Sometimes men think of paying an escort as a 'helping-her-out' thing. I don't mind that but that's usually how they gloss over the fact that they've hired an escort and helping her implies a kind of extended friendship. Tom would pay me $1300+ Canadian dollars to spend five hours with him and go for dinner. He must have thought of it as helping me. That's how I came to see it. Maybe he wasn't forgetting he had hired me, I couldn't be sure. Maybe he was just playing the fantasy game. Men of the world, it's wonderful when you help a service provider

118

out by tipping her generously for the fantasy you enjoy, but it's probably not a good idea to fall in love.

The surprise was that Tom decided to get a divorce. I was almost positive that he had no delusions that he would leave his wife and we would get together and live happily ever after. I convinced myself it was not about spending time only with me. The week before his divorce announcement, he had e-mailed me that he was going to Cleveland to see a new friend for a date. Whatever he was thinking, he still kept making appointments with me professionally.

I didn't want to discuss Tom's divorce with him because it could potentially ruin our relationship and I didn't want it to change into something else. I was happy the way it was. Becoming better 'friends' would have made it more difficult for me to treat it as my work. I had treated him better than any other client, and I was concerned he had more emotional feelings for me than I did for him. He was generous with me and I didn't want that to stop.

E-mail:
From: Tom
To: Elysia
Subject: Gold anyone?
Dear Elysia,
Whew! Just got in from what I believe is my last birthday party for the year. Needless to say, none have even come close to the current record holder for the most outrageous birthday party I have ever had.
Okay, it's late, but before I crash just a reminder that I have two big old men's gold rings that could be recycled if needed. If not, I guess I could use them for fish lures or something? Good night!
Tom

From: Elysia
To: Tom
Subject: YES! Gold anyone?
Hey Darlin' Just a short note as I am running out the door! I am glad to hear you enjoyed your birthday celebration (s)!! You deserve all the love and attention you received!
Yes!! I am definitely interested in your rings. If you are willing to give them up send them along. I will put them to excellent use and you can take comfort in knowing that they are loved and appreciated and worn daily instead of sitting in a box somewhere in the dark. Ok my beautiful bear! I am off to do a million things before work tonight!
Thinking of you as always with lots of hugs and kisses, Elysia xoxo

Around this time I was leasing a car. I didn't want to invest in a new car so I told a friend, who knows about cars, to keep an eye out for a sharp used one. At this time, I was working for World Trading Finance and they had run out of money and owed me numerous paychecks. I still had to pay the rent, buy groceries and pay bills. I decided to arrange some escort work again.

E-mail:
From: Elysia
To: Tom
Subject: ANOTHER VISIT!
Hi there Big Bear, It's your Miss Elysia here. My job at World Trading has been put on hold until they get their big financing. Until that comes they can't really afford to pay me so I have had to tell them to call me when their situation changes. Shit :(I thought this job was going to work out better than it has. But …. Things should pick up some time in the near future. Until then I seem to be on hold again and stuck in career limbo.

My plans for the immediate future are to come to Ferndale in Feb. I still have no transportation, which is REALLY a problem. I feel trapped all the time and I am not sure how I will get there but I will cross that bridge later, I guess.

Let me know what day and time is best for you and I will patiently wait for time to pass so we can spend some time together again.
Chat with you soon, Elysia xoxo

From: Tom
To: Elysia:
Subject: January visit:
Elysia, Fantastic to hear you are planning a visit! I, of course, can't wait to see you again. I get a great energy and psychological boost when I know you are coming. I need to figure out a way to bottle that or something! I don't know if you are ready to work logistics, but if so I would like to go for 4:00 PM on the 26th. If that doesn't work for you, let me know.

Yes, I remember you said you would have to give up your leased vehicle unless the lease could be extended, which probably wouldn't happen. Now having Elysia without wheels is not good! Like you didn't know this already! While I know you aren't destitute and living in the streets!!!, you mentioned you had taken a hit in the old income stream due to your trip and now World Trading is letting you down. I will be willing to kick in some money for a car rental or something if need be. Elysia – understand I don't think you included the info about your car as a plea to elicit an offer like this, so please don't be offended. I also know you are fiercely independent. Just tell me to keep my ideas on this to myself or something ;). I wouldn't want you to start censoring things you might tell me so I don't make something out of *them that wasn't intended. However, if you would appreciate help sorting out a longer-term solution, let me know.*

Well, I'd better go. Drop me an e-mail anytime you want. Let me know if the 4:00 PM time works on the 26ᵗʰ or if your plans change.
Love, Tom

From: Elysia
To: Tom
Subject: Hi honey,
I was just thinking about you today with the sunshine here and all!! Hello there my big bear :o) I am glad to know that I am still in your thoughts. I still have more things to do around my new apartment but it is coming along. I could use a few new things .... always a girl!

You definitely have my attention with your transportation idea.... hmmmm .... what could it be :o) Things are tight around here right now. I had really expected to be paid by World Trading by now and as you know it really stresses me out. Grrr .... so let me know what you had in mind, I would love the help.
Thanks,
Love, Elysia

From: Tom
To: Elysia
Subject: read now please...car
Elysia, Jeeezzz.... I have really been busy this week. Have some interesting things to tell you the next time we meet. Work is hectic now, but fun as hell. I love stress and challenges. I had hoped to have time to draft this and get a chance to carefully edit it, but won't have the time. So, if it comes out sounding too formal, legalistic, just plain "cold," or other negative aspects, I didn't intend it to be! I just want to get everything on the table so there is less chance of misunderstanding. I think I am a pretty good judge of character, and you definitely have it! So, some of the details cover things that I don't think you would even consider, but I wanted to get the "worst case" situations on the table. I may have forgotten something. If so, I will blast you an e-mail ASAP. If anything is unclear let me know, I will clarify it. And, please offer any suggestions. I am not trying to dictate, but had to start somewhere. Or, if it isn't something you want to pursue, I understand.
Proposal:
Bottom line, it would amount to something like a two-year free vehicle lease.
Gory details and fine print:
How? I would buy a late model used car within certain price parameters and provide it to you to use for a two-year period. To minimize my cash flow impact, I would finance the car. The financing period would extend beyond two years. My bank is providing great terms at present and I have completed

the pre-arrangement. I arbitrarily chose the two-year period. At the end of that period we would re-evaluate the situation and make a decision at that time as to what happens next. Options would be I take the car back, I extend the period, you get the car or something else.

Why don't I just give you the cash and you handle the rest? Well, as stated, I don't want to impact cash flow that much and the financing does require association with a specific car. You can, of course, return the car anytime you wish before the two-year period. You would be responsible for maintaining adequate insurance on the car, licensing, maintenance and repairs. The insurance is required to maintain the financing. I intend to honor the two-year period (at a minimum as described above). If something comes up that requires me to shed payments and debt, I may ask for the car back. I don't know what that would be and don't foresee that happening!! If any of these situations should happen, I would give you as much advance notice as possible and be as reasonable as I can. If I should lose contact with you and am unable to ascertain your whereabouts, I would need to take action to recover the car (e.g. issue stolen auto report, etc.). I would also like to know on a regular basis that you still have the car in your possession. I haven't thought of what time period would constitute "loss of contact," two months??? Also, out of respect for any future direction you may feel compelled to take, our meetings do have to be of exactly the same nature as in our past. Don't get me wrong, I am not suggesting a change! They would however have to be face-to-face.

There are some constraints and limits on how much I am able to juggle finances unilaterally in my personal situation. Hope this isn't too vague. In any future financial situations you and I arrange, could we take this (the vehicle arrangement) into account in some manner? Not necessarily a dollar for dollar match, but some consideration, at least for meetings like we had last time. Again, with the exception of some timing changes or overall longer sessions, I really enjoyed last time. They have all been great though.

Okay, just what kind of vehicle are we talking about? This is something for which I do need quick feedback from you. As part of the feasibility analysis, I looked at a wide variety of vehicles that would fit the financial scenario I set up. Obviously, supply and demand apply, so with more exotic vehicles you get less for your money. So, for example, I picked one that would be safe, not an econo-box, reliable, reasonably stylish and economical. Part of the measure is whether I would enjoy driving and being seen in it myself. I did find a very low mileage (13K miles) Ford Taurus in what appears to be great shape and has the remainder of the factory warranty. It is dark red metallic, camel interior, is automatic, has air conditioning, power windows, etc. It is being sold by a very reputable local new car dealer. I did check it out in person. If you do want to go with the overall proposal and are willing to drive this car, I will go ahead and lock it in and hold it. I can e-mail a photo. Otherwise, more looking and talking is required which is not a problem.

As you might imagine, I have never actually done this specific type of arrangement so I don't know if there is something I haven't yet considered that would make this impractical or impossible. As an example, I don't want to know any more personal details about yourself than you are comfortable providing to me. I don't think this would cause it, but there is also the Canada/U.S. angle to consider. I am thinking back to your border crossing car escapade.

Whew! I think this outlines it. Let me know where we go from here, if anywhere.
Love ya, Tom
PS. We had the discussion about which name I could use with you. You said the non-Elysia name was okay and was what I preferred. I notice you nearly always use Elysia in your e-mails with me. Still okay with my other choice? I do understand if you want to continue to use it with me in e-mails for probably several reasons hopefully not directly related to me. Oh, I don't feel this way, but I don't want to be thought of as primarily a walking wallet by anyone. You have never caused me to do so (feel like a WW), but I do like to think we are friends as well. You didn't ask for this (vehicle) so don't think this is causing me to start feeling like this. Just a place I don't want to get into.

From: Tom
To: Elysia
Subject: Don't know what to say
Well ....since I haven't heard back from you yet, I assume I have inadvertently managed to make you angry, disappointed, concerned, hurt, or all of these and even more. Maybe you are still just thinking about it, or are out of touch enjoying the sunshine, but I suspect not. If my assumption is unfortunately somewhere in the ballpark, is there anything I can do at this point to undo this? My intentions truly were to help. If you could either confirm I have now read the situation correctly or not, I would really appreciate it. Tom

From: Elysia
To: Tom
Subject: We are okay Bear!
Hi Hon, I am so sorry to take so long to get back to you. Because of my recent move I have not had access to my computer until today. I am sorry I have left

you hanging.

First I want to send you my most sincere thank you! This offer you have made is far beyond my imagination and I did not expect such thoughtfulness! I have not really had a chance to process your offer and I know you are looking for some immediate feedback. My first thoughts are WOW! And my second thoughts are concerns for our friendship. I do not want to do anything to jeopardize us. I am glad to hear that I have not made you feel like a walking wallet. I have tried to always be real and sincere with you and although you have helped me get by financially, I do not think of you in terms of that.

Now as far as this wonderful, thoughtful idea you have had ... my initial thoughts are this, I will be unable to cross the border with a car that is from the US that is registered in your name. That was the problem with my friend's car that time. I am not legally able to cross the border with a car with US plates and not be the registered owner in the vehicle. So you would have to bring it up here and I would then not be able to come down and see you with it :(. I would be more than happy to take care of the maintenance and insurance (etc.) but I can not insure a car that is not in my name and then there is the US car Canadian insurance thing. I don't think I can insure a US car in Canada .... I don't know.

I think that we should talk about this more. I know you want to move quickly, but I do not want to rush us and screw things up later. I really appreciate your kindness and thoughtfulness. I have not had anyone think of me or try to help me out like you have. Honestly, that is really more than I would hope for. As you know, it has always been just me taking care of me. It is nice to know that you are there to talk to.
Thank you, hon.
Love, Elysia xoxo

From Tom
To: Elysia
Subject: Yes!!!
Yea!!! It was sooo good to hear from you. I mistakenly thought things were back to normal for your e-mail since you had recently sent me a note. This was one time I actually was extremely happy to be wrong.

Now for my apology. Yes, it appeared that I was moving too fast. I felt and still feel confident that the details can be worked out. Don't worry, I am not stressing about this. I was worried I had possibly ticked you off. But it has turned out to be a challenge. So, I have been researching options. I have had a series of interesting phone calls this afternoon. Including calls to the government of your province, to the Superintendent of motor vehicles, Canadian Customs office, US Customs office, an attorney in international law who's a personal friend, etc. Didn't take too long, but came back with inconsistent answers from two Canadian offices. As in; one says yes, it is possible, one says no. I am always amazed at some of the arcane rules and regulations that bureaucracies have come up with. Oh, rest assured only general, innocuous, hypothetical scenarios were used!

Yes, we should talk about this more. I do understand you still haven't reflected on the offer and had a chance to come back with other feedback. I am not in an unnecessary rush and appreciate your patience and understanding in however this might conclude. I definitely do not want to do something to screw us up. And I don't want to be in a position to have this jeopardize my ability to provide for you on your visits like I have in the past.

Okay, switching gears (no pun intended). Well, since you don't want me to introduce my new car to the great Canadian north to visit you for a couple of hours some day, I am left with no choice but to await your next visit. No, you didn't really tell me not to. Of course I wouldn't think of coming until you get the cozy hot tub you described last time. I am going to a great restaurant this weekend and going to do some other things to unwind. I should be able to hit it again next week with some recharged batteries. I'll write soon when I get more info. Remember, you and I have a lot of fantastic restaurants to experience so get down here! I am still going great on the diet so I can afford some haute cuisine now and then. Love, Tom

From: Tom
To: Elysia
Hi, I haven't had a chance to check personal e-mail since Friday. What a great surprise to get your note about coming! Thursday sounds fantastic, same place, same time. I really need the dazzle of your smile and energy of your personality to help recharge my batteries. Also, as a friend, it sounds like you have been busy; don't get stressed out trying to get down here too fast. I would willingly wait longer if it helps you in your planning. Understand I don't want to wait longer, "immediately" is not fast enough!

I had lunch with my legal friend and we discussed the car situation. Actually his friend, who is the head of a State Bar Association, is checking something out for me too. Things appear to be working as I had hoped. He said he would be able to get back to me on Monday at the latest. Then we can talk more about it either before or wait until Thursday. See you soon! Love, Tom

From: Tom
To: Elysia
Subject Follow-up

Hey Elysia, I have included the attorney stuff below. Any questions or suggestions, let me know. I love talking to you, anyway, but like I said this was somewhat uncomfortable. It is new to me as well and a little scary, but we can both work through it. I know I am probably being redundant, but this act is only intended as something to help a friend, no obligations, no strings beyond what is on the table.

My fortune cookie says, "Elysia's life is now entering an upswing cycle." Well, I'm not sure that sounds Chinese, but what the hey!

Keep in mind my offer for you to be an international jetsetter swinging in, to dine out at a great restaurant and jet back out, along with a little spending money. Hey, you have offered in the past to show me around your city sometime. You know I could do the same, except in reverse. I blip to you, we go out to lunch/dinner or event of our choice and I make tracks back to the U.S. Unless there is something I don't know, it shouldn't matter if someone you know sees us. All we will and would be doing is having dinner as friends – literally.

Here are the recommendations from the attorneys:
Proposal: Bottom line, it would amount to something like a free vehicle lease for an agreed-upon time period.
How would it work? I would provide you with an amount of money to purchase a car.
-Locate and purchase car in your name
-The vehicle information is provided to attorney
-A one page promissory note is prepared, we sign
-This establishes a security agreement on vehicle
-It is filed with provincial personal property registry
-Anyone that does a search on vehicle serial # will learn that there is a promissory note.
-Promissory note would state: At the end of a period (TBD) the vehicle would be provided to me, or an agreed-upon amount of money
-At the end of that period we would re-evaluate the situation and make a decision at that time as to what happens next.
-Options could be I take the car back, we extend the period, you get the car, or something else.

You can, of course, return the car anytime you wish before the period, no "return penalty."

They suggest some wording about returning the car in a reasonable condition. I think this is probably overkill – remember I trust you!
-Or it could end up that you keep the car in some manner anyway.

Dollar Amount:
Currency conversion results:
-Using cash exchange rate —
$10,000 US dollars equals approx. $15,670.00 Canadian
-After vehicle tax, effective amount for base purchase is approximately $13,500.00 Canadian.
-Federal and provincial taxes in participating province must be considered.
-My bank would perform a wire transfer.
-No dollar restriction on transaction (unlike some Web services)
-Money will be transferred in U.S. dollars (only way they can do it)
-Some Canadian banks can receive direct transfer, some will have it transferred through an intermediary bank in U.S.
-I will need to provide wire transfer instructions from Canadian bank to my bank.
-If request received before noon is done the same day. After noon is performed next business day.

From: Tom
To: Elysia
Subject: Crap! Missed call
Hi, I just pulled my cell out of the charger and saw I had a missed call. I checked and found the message from you. Darn. I would have liked to talk. Anyway, thank you so much for calling and letting me know your flight made it home okay and for the thanks. I don't do it for you to thank me (I enjoy it more than anyone), but the acknowledgement is much appreciated. I know flying back to your city isn't like making a world trip (safety-wise), but I wanted to know if you made it okay. I was going to send you a note about last night later today. I tell you Elysia, I just really enjoyed it. The last time at the waterfront and last night at the restaurant were just magical (ouch, clichéd term, but true!) for me. I was still running around today on my high from last night and felt so good I thought I would send you some flowers, but realized asking them to be sent to 'Elysia' in 'Toronto' probably wouldn't be real effective. Well, we'll get that little detail worked out if and when you are ready.

Once again, thank you so much for being willing to fly down and spend some time with me. Let me know about the car when you have had a chance to talk to "your" people. Love, Tom
p.s. I really can count normally, but hope you ended up with the 11, not 10 bills like I told you — if not then I misplaced one!! If you ended up with it, great — use it for partial payment on one of those classes you wanted to take. But then I do expect a flamenco/guitar/ballet/painting performance next time.

From: Elysia
To: Tom
Subject: OK, listen
Hey babe, today the sun is shining and life is a lot better. I feel spoiled and relaxed. The pressure is off for the minute.

As far as the car thingy goes, I will go to the car lot this week and speak to my friend and see what he has available and for what cost. I will update you with my progress. I am hoping that something fun, safe and fabulous will pop up for your favorite gurl! :) I have just no idea about cost, only looks ....what colour does it come in and does it match my nail polish? LOL
Have a great weekend Bear! Lots of love, Elysia

I tried to cut all the strings attached to the car offer and he agreed on the surface. However, I kept remembering he wrote "Don't let me down," and that was a string. And that I "must stay in touch." Another string. I wondered, if after he bought me the car, I could expect less of a tip if he was going to spend that kind of money on a car for me. I decided I would risk losing it all by subtly telling him I would only accept money and no other (legal) strings attached.

E-mail:
From:Elysia
To: Tom,
Subject: No strings attached.
What else .... The car stuff. I have had a tiny look on the trader site. I looked at Cabriolets and for fun Mercedesezz. You know, this whole car thing is a little weird for me. Why are we so uncomfortable when we talk about the money? I don't want to hurt you and say the 'wrong' thing and sometimes I am an elephant in a daisy patch. You have said more than once that you are doing this as a favour to me and that there are no strings attached. I am grateful and thankful for your kindness! :) You have so generously offered to buy your princess a new carriage and I accept! What you must do, ma-lord, is give your lady a budget that you are really comfortable with and she will shop accordingly. I thought perhaps since you said that I could keep my carriage, paint it pink and have the name "My Princess" airbrushed across it, that you might reconsider your original idea. Please feel free to give me a Canadian dollar amount and I will find us a couple of choices.

We have a hot date next week! Yum! I will be getting into town on Wed. I will rent a car and get a room somewhere. Sometimes I leave things to the last minute ... so silly. But it's just you and me on Wed. So, same time?! Anyway, I'm a sleepy girl.
Talk to you later, Love, Elysia

From: Tom
To: Elysia
Subject: Just the facts and only the facts – right
I am considering two dining choices for dinner that are fairly different from each other. If you wish, let me know if you lean one way or the other for these two mystery choices – "hip without pretension, contemporary but not intimidating" or "elegant restaurant providing a grand setting for important dinners. It's unique, harking back to a more regal era." If you don't let me know or don't care, I will choose all by myself.

Okay, on to the car. Yes, it is weird for me too. But I don't want you or I to be too uncomfortable about talking about the money. I appreciate your thoughts about not wanting to hurt me. But hey, unless you make it "personal" it shouldn't (hurt that is). If we are "only" talking money, I should feel free to tell you "no" and the same for you. I also don't want to hurt you either by having this seem more business related. It isn't at all. If it was, I probably would have "abandoned the feasibility options analysis" long ago! The only real "string" I want is just a desire to keep in touch. But since you said yourself last time that would happen anyway, I guess even that isn't a "string," is it?

Okay, let's try up to $12,000 Canadian total. This assumes the exchange rates don't make huge changes in the next few days! Understand, I don't throw this amount around lightly. I realize I may be naïve, crazy, hopelessly hopeless, misled, or all of the aforementioned. Just don't let me down, Elysia. I also realize this won't buy a new Cabro or something. Of course I do want to see the pink paint job with "My Princess" across it. That was a contractual commitment, wasn't it! We'll need to decide how to best make the transfer. How about a really big pile of quarters? You could tell Customs you won big in an Indian casino or something (oh ya!). I'm open to suggestions. Otherwise we can do it as I described before. Now let's have some fun with this.

Travel safe, don't be late though! Yup, same time could work for me, though if dinner gets really slow, we'll have to take the Foie Gras and entrée out in a doggie bag so I don't have to rush back home after we get back to the room (Oh no!). Oh, remember the two choices I was considering? They are Wendy's and Burger King. They do serve Foie Gras don't they?
See ya soon!
Tom

So he had offered $12,000 Canadian and no legal agreement! He did say the car was a favor to me and in no way, shape or form was it an exchange for sex or time with me. It was a gift, no strings attached. He said so.

E-mail:
From: Elysia
To: Tom
Subject: Update
Hi there Tom, I just want to drop you another note regarding the car. In your last e-mail you said, "Just don't let me down, Elysia." This seems like something I feel I must ask you about. I would like to know what your hopes and expectations are so that I don't let you down. My ESP is not what it used to be and I think that it is important for us to talk about. Sounds so serious but it's not really. The written word is open to so many interpretations and I want to be clear.

Now as far as all this converting and stuff you are up to .... just so you know, I am not looking at anything remotely close to $12,000! That is just way too generous for me to accept considering you said I could keep it. I am going to see a car tomorrow though! I think he wants $6,000 Cdn. I am hoping I can do a little lash batting and get it down a little/a lot more because I will still have to insure it. Well, my love, I will leave all of the details for dinner up to you. Let's hope for some nice weather.
See you soon, Elysia xoxo

About a week later, my friend called to say he had found me a car in a private sale. Believe it or not, he saw it in someone's driveway with a 'for sale' sign in the window. He checked it out and thought it was a bargain. I bought it. I called Tom and told him I had found a car. I told him that the car was $3,000 and that the insurance was $1,500 and I had to get some repairs done. He ended up sending me around $6,000 Canadian! You know, I could have taken him for the whole $12,000. Later, a part of me wished I had. But, really, he was very good to me.

* * *

As life is apt to turn, just when you think you're on top of things, I was really shocked to learn Tom was seeing other escorts professionally for sex. I found out from a close friend, Tracy, who worked in the massage parlor. She had said to me, "I'm seeing Tom." I said, "Oh, okay, sure." I automatically assumed it was a casual friend thing. Sometimes, for safety, Tracy and I would travel together to work in other cities so occasionally we ended up having dinner together with each other's clients. I would never turn one of her special clients without her permission. It doesn't seem right. Yet I had unwittingly given her my permission. To this day, I don't blame her. Later, when I told her I thought she was seeing him just for dinner, she said, "Oh, Elysia, you know me better than that. It's always business with me. I'm not just going to go for dinner with Tom."

Tracy said Tom had said to her, "Well, I think we should probably keep this from Elysia." I had no idea. I was pissed off. I thought all that time that I was the only one he saw but he was paying other girls while telling me he loved me. The other ones he just fucked and paid? Or maybe he had six of me around that he wined and dined and told them all he that loved them. Who knew? All that bullshit just meant I was still a prostitute, that he gave gifts to me so I'd entertain him for more than just sex. I didn't ask for the gifts, the flowers, the car, the clothes, or any of it. I felt he was something different than any other client. I was so angry but he was cheating on his wife with me, what made me think I would be the only girl he was seeing! This was a pivotal moment in our relationship for me when things began to change. I now harbored resentment and no longer felt special and it reflected in our sex.

Maybe he did love me in his own way. Who knows? Whatever. When I thought it was just me, it was a different kind of relationship. It was kind of like a girlfriend thing and he gave me money and it wasn't just a pay thing. He should have never let me find out that he was seeing other girls. What an asshole! He made me feel cheap. He made me feel like a prostitute, and I hadn't felt like that before.

If he was paying me as an escort, he needed to pay me more money! I charge by the hour. He gave me only around $1500 and I would spend at least 5 hours with him, over dinner and back at the hotel. I spent nights with him where I never charged him by the hour. He made a mistake. He fucked up and I was furious. You don't mess with a high class escort. He had crossed the line.

So I switched to the other Elysia. How was I going to do that? Easy. Business. Well, a thoroughbred never gives up on the home stretch. He referred to himself as my boyfriend. What happens when a boyfriend cheats? Well, the games begin.

E-mail:
From: Elysia
To: Tom
Subject: You bought a new car!!!
Oh my! Once again I am totally impressed. A JAG! Well, my dear, I am sure you have worked very hard all of your life and you deserve all of the treats you have. Good for you! An Elysia and a Jag ....oo la la! What are the neighbors going to think? I am trying to not appear so green and at least I get to go for rides. I can see it now, there we will be, me in my fur (subliminal

message) with my hair and scarf blowing in the wind and you with your driver's cap and a big "Who's bigger than me" grin going through the McDonald's drive-through on our way to the Theeeahtur! :0) Oh, my birthday is coming up. You'd really be mad at me if I didn't remind you. I really just wanted to help you out and do you this favor by giving you a few helpful hints. Remember, there are 87 shopping days until my birthday."

It sure will be nice to be in your strong arms again.
Your Elysia xoxo

And I sent him the internet link to the most expensive fur store in my city.

I was feeling in my 'Ice Princess' mood. He said he was going to come to town on the 14th. He said he would be staying at the Four Seasons Hotel and "I sure would like to see you for an hour or two, maybe go sightseeing." I told him I'd meet him for lunch. He said, "Make sure you order up some sunshine." You know what I said, "I'll try but, oh, we'll find something to do. I know the inside of every mall in the downtown." He remarked, "I better bring my big fat expense account card then." I said, "Yeah, let's rub the numbers off it."

E-mail:
From: Elysia
To: Tom
Subject: Fur shopping :o)
Dear Tom, Well, I made it to Regal Furs today and had a great time. You are so thoughtful with such an outrageously wonderful birthday present. I missed you and was sending you my vibes. I was greeted by Lisa and she helped me try on probably 15–20 coats! I was able to finally narrow it down to several choices. I really liked the Silver Fox coat. It is big and fluffy and really posh! They only had a medium and it was too big. It was difficult to imagine what it would be like smaller but they said that they would alter it. Seems like a lot of coat to alter instead of starting with a small to begin with. But the princess in me really likes this one although it is big and a cumbersome coat. Still ....

Sapphire and Tracy were there with me too! I tried on a beautiful mink coat! There is something very elegant and regal about the feel and weight of mink! I really liked this one too but found it to be too conservative for me. I tried on an awesome mink jacket with black fox collars and wow!! I love this one, but the style ... it was a bit too restricted as to what I thought I could use it for. As I was trying on the plain mink again, Jon the alteration guy walked in with a selection of fox pelts! And he began to drape them over my shoulders and WOW!! That was it!! What a difference it made. The plain coat my mother would wear was suddenly cozy, cuddly and way more my style. He said he would make me a big collar and cuffs like the jacket for the mink coat.

It was a tough choice my darling!!!! And honestly there were only a handful or so to choose from without going custom. I did take a peek at the price tags as I was going along and the coats I chose were all within our price point except for the collar and cuffs, this I knew would be extra .... So Mr. Acropolus got out his handy little calculator and tapped away. Jon had priced the collar and cuffs at another $600 and change and the coat was $5985 U.S.

I hope you like what I have chosen! I am still waffling a little but I am happy with my choice. It was not easy! I took a picture with a full length Canadian lynx just for fun!

Wow Tom!! Thank you sooooo much!! I can hardly wait to show you!!! I will be talking to you again soon.

Your Elysia xoxo

From: Tom
To: Elysia
Subject: From across the country

My dear Elysia, Wow, I hope you ended up with a fur coat you really liked. I was a little concerned in that it sounded like you liked the Silver Fox "really liked this one although it is big and cumbersome. Still ... " and "I am still waffling a little but I am happy with my choice." Girlfriend, I hope you didn't feel rushed to make a decision. I realize your imminent departure kind of drove it but to me (but what do I know about fur!) your design with the custom touches and additions sounded cool. Thanks for the great pictures. I almost felt like I was there. You looked outrageous in all of them. However, I don't think I will ever have the same feeling when you joke about being a princess. After seeing that picture of you in the full-length fur, when I think of nobility, being regal, etc., that photo pops into my mind!

I did call Acropolus and he said you sounded happy when you left. I liked your tactic of getting the coat chosen and then saying it just needed a few "changes." Good going Elysia! Acropolus said it was important for him to honor his commitment to stay within the price point we had discussed, so he just accepted a little less profit on the sale. He also said the coat would be very attractive. Somehow I think he will still be able to pay the rent! I had only intended that as a guideline. I mean when I went car shopping I knew the base price, but just couldn't resist the options! He said you were all very nice people by the way. He said he would have it ready by Saturday. I just can't wait for the time I can see the coat worn by my most favorite model, live and in person!

Okay, time to sign off for now. I miss ya! Hope to hear from you soon.
Love, Tom

* * *

Up until now, I had always rented an apartment. I knew it was time to buy my own. If I owned my own home, my car, had a steady job, then I could quit escorting for good. I decided to see if Tom would help me out with a down payment. I also started looking for a nursing job. I knew I needed a straight job to get a mortgage. This time, a job I liked came through. I was ecstatic and wrote to Tom with the good news.

E-mail:
From: Tom
To: Elysia
Subject: YOUR NURSING JOB!
This is truly fantastic news! I am so happy for you and so happy to hear this. I knew (no b.s.) that you could ace the interview. You have all the right qualities to be very effective in an interview situation and it sounds like that person was perceptive enough to realize this. Enjoy it, but it is only the start of many good things (I can feel it!) I want to hear all about it. Now I am assuming you don't start TOMORROW so we are still on. But, now it is a multi-purpose trip! We can celebrate your success! So, I do want to go somewhere special. If you have somewhere you might want to go, let me know. Otherwise I will confer with the concierge at the Four Seasons and pick somewhere. Also, I think we talked about a shopping excursion, who knows, maybe a little celebratory gift (practical or impractical may be in order :).
CONGRATULATIONS!!!
Love, Tom

* * *

I never did ask him for help with the down payment and I never received a gift of money for my apartment from him either. I earned every dime to pay for it myself. Our relationship began to drift from here on.

Twelve

POLYAMORY

"You know we really love you and we never expected anything like this to happen to us. We want to share our lives with you. We want you to be part of our family. When you come to Boston we would like to go to the jeweler who made our rings and have one made for you as well." She took her ring off and put it on my finger. And it fit perfectly. I didn't expect it at all. From the very beginning I had been bothered by their rings. They were their wedding rings. They reminded me of 'what the hell am I doing?'

I can't even explain the relationship to myself. It's not traditional. But we were so happy. Laughter flowed easily. How do I explain it? How do I explain it to the real world, or my family, or anybody outside of us who hasn't seen it? Let me start at the beginning.

* * *

We met at, let's call it, Club Erotica. The first night I arrived, Cecilia and I were in the bar where a band was playing fantastic acoustic guitar music. The band members were cute. It was hot and the sunset cast a warm glow into the cabana beachside bar. Jake's band, based in Boston, had been hired to play there for two weeks. Joelle came along for a vacation. Weeks before this, they had come to the conclusion that they were content and happy with just the two of them and that they no longer wanted anyone else in their relationship. They hadn't been monogamous. They enjoyed sexual relationships with other women, but that's all it had been, sexual. No joining of the hearts before me. She had gone off birth control and while they weren't trying to get pregnant, they weren't avoiding it anymore. Evidently, they had decided to stick with just the two of them in their relationship, right up until Jake saw me sitting on a barstool listening to his music.

My best friend, Cecilia, and I were drinking Coronas from bottles with limes. Cold bottles of beer. If the bottles became warm before we finished, we'd laughingly clap our hands for buckets of ice. It was hot. I like my drinks cold. We were on that kind of vacation high where you are half excited, half-exhausted, and full of expectations for some fun. Fun finding men. Fun seducing men. Fun manipulating men. Whatever. The lead singer stopped to dedicate a song for his 'beautiful wife in the blue dress over there.' I was so attracted to him. I turned around and there was his wife, Joelle, sitting next to me. And she was beautiful. I thought, 'Okay, too bad, they're married' and I just wrote him off. I started looking at the other band members, hoping they were single.

When I first saw Joelle, I thought she was beautiful. Not lovely in the tall thin model sense, but in a lean strong muscular dancer sort of way, with all the curves a female should possess. She wasn't tall, only 5 feet 6 inches, but she was strong in both body and spirit. Her smile was wide, with enviable paper white teeth, which are made all the whiter by the contrast of her long black hair. She was graceful, gentle and confident, which is a definite attraction. Everyone feels comfortable around her. I swear if anyone could walk on water, it would be her. I fell in love with Jake first, and because he had this wife, who I knew he loved deeply, I hoped that we would all get along. The fact that she would allow her husband the opportunity to be loved by another woman amazed me. She was a phenomenal woman.

The second night we were well into our party phase and by now Cecilia was already hooked up with 'Woosh Boosh,' or so we called him, which is 'head chef' in French. Well, maybe not, but then who really cared? He was the head chef for Club Erotica. Wooshy didn't speak English but his infectious smile and discernable high levels of testosterone made up for any lack of communication. He was twenty-nine. Cecilia was forty and gets this 'perfect abs' chef and they don't even speak the same language. He spoke a little English and she spoke a little French and they both spoke a lot of hand-touchy language.

We felt like dynamite. We were it. We were the party. It was low season and there were only about 300 people there. Lots of them were fuddy-duddies and there we were running around with no tops on most of the time. We would go down to the beach, lie in the sun for a while and eventually untie our bikini tops and slide them slowly to one side. It's all in the presentation. Sometimes we'd just tear our gear off in the water. People would watch us, both men and woman. Some would be quite standoffish, but they were watching all the same. Eventually we were voted best boobs on the beach. No kidding. It was entertaining, totally. Cecilia's smaller than me, but she didn't care. Her thoughts on that were, 'These are my boobs and I just turned forty and I'm screwing a twenty-nine year old and happy birthday to me.'

So the second night was even hotter and the band guys took their shirts off. It was totally cool to watch those guys sing. Jake, Joelle's husband, had both his nipples pierced, which to me is a turn on. The band sang and the atmosphere was romantic. After they finished playing, Jake came up to me and started chatting. I was completely attracted to him. He had that kind of animal magnetism which makes otherwise normal men into Adonises. He was flirting with me and I was kind of going along with it but didn't think anything of it because he was married. I didn't even consider him at first. I don't do husbands. In my personal life, never. I am not interested in having an affair with a married man. It is not my gig at all.

My relationship with Jake was different from my relationship with Joelle and it was different when all three of us were together. There was a connection with Jake that went deeper than the bonding we started in Club Erotica. It was as if I had loved him in a different lifetime. I don't really buy into reincarnation, I mean who really knows, but our relationship made me think it was possible. It felt like I'd loved him deeply before, but I couldn't be with him then for some unknown reason. My love for him was not just about who he was: handsome and sexy, a musician who wrote music, or his aura of protective strength. I can't help but feel it had something to do with an unknown connection. He had that Sicilian look, that 'don't-mess-with-me-cause-I-don't-take-no-shit' kind of roughness. Raw at the edges and lots of testosterone. He was 5' 11" and there isn't a part of his body that wasn't solid muscle. He had the look of a boxer, not a musician. His skin always had a tanned glow, with mountains of surprising blonde thick curls that frame a cheeky, 'I'm-up-to-trouble' smile. A blonde Sicilian? Well, believe what you want but picture him sexy. I adore him.

Eventually, he invited me to his room to smoke a bowl. He gave me his elbow, like a gentleman, and I put my arm through his as he called out to his wife, "Hey, Joelle, I'm taking Elysia and we're going to smoke a bowl." She smiled and said, "Okay, see you later."

I walked with him to his room. I knew I shouldn't be going there. I knew what I was walking into and I didn't care. Whatever was going to happen between us was going to be worth being with him. How I felt at the end of it didn't matter. We started smoking pot and talking. All of a sudden he began his little seduction, I guess that's what you'd call it. Things like, 'You're the most beautiful girl.' Well, I really can't remember what he said, it's a blur, but I remember his lines were good. He was totally coming on to me. I told him, "I can't do this, man. You're married. You have a wife and I'm just not into it. I can't go there." I kept saying no, no, no. I was saying the words, but the next thing I knew I let him pull me beside him and we were kissing and I was into it.

I still recall the moment where I thought, 'This is not what I want in my life.' I remember that moment where I had a choice. I chose. I thought, 'Stay here.' Part of it was because he kept saying it was okay because his wife knew. He tempted me with, "She told me to go and talk to you. She knows what we're doing. She thinks it's okay." I tried to remind myself the importance of making the right choices and sticking to them. But I couldn't do it. I couldn't walk away. I knew that I should walk away. His strong stocky muscular body flowed into me and we were having sex. And then there was a knock on the door.

I panicked. I pulled the sheet over my head. Jake said, "It's okay, it's just Joelle." He got up with a hard-on, opened the door and came back to bed. Joelle came in. She said, "It's okay, it's okay. I'm just going to shower." She stepped in the shower and her eyes moved to focus in a mirror that slanted so she could see the bed. She showered, slowly lathering her body, while watching us. He was on top of me, fucking me, and I was watching her watching us.

I suppose I'd like to justify it by thinking that the universe ordained it and said, 'Here you go, enjoy.' Did I want this in my life? I didn't go looking for it. It just happened. Either I accept it or I don't. I chose to accept it. I came to a fork in the road and I said okay. I knew exactly what I was doing. I knew that somewhere down the line it was going to be me who was going to get hurt. I knew it and it just didn't matter. It was all worth being with him.

The rest is a bit of a blur, but I think I called to her to come. Perhaps he said it. I remember her coming to bed, her lean lanky athletic body molding into ours, her long black hair showering us with a tickling sensation. There was just enough warm water left on her body to allow her to slip easily between us. She didn't hit on me right away. We moved slowly with lots of touching, kissing, flowing exploration, engorging with need. I was in that twilight land of hot intensive animal desire. Things started happening between Joelle, Jake and me. It was better than it had ever been.

She couldn't have known how I would respond to her sexually. Maybe she was hoping. I didn't tell her I'd had sexual experiences with women over the years. Funny thing is, I've never considered myself gay. I've never even really considered myself bisexual. I've never considered myself straight either. I've just considered myself, me. If somebody comes along in my life that I choose to love, okay. If not, okay. It had probably been ten years since I had had a relationship with a girlfriend and in all those years I had never gone searching for a female lover. And I certainly wasn't looking for this to happen.

It was this first night that I fell in love, the first time we made love together.

* * *

It was almost premeditated. I was to later learn that first night they saw me in the bar, Jake told Joelle that he was attracted to me. He told her, "I have to get to know this girl." His need had blown her away. She saw how important it was to him. She couldn't say no. She said, "Go for it." She always let him go and do and be and explore whatever he wanted, just as he had allowed her. She was attracted to me as well, but I think it was more that *he* wanted me, whereas before she was always the one who brought the girls into the relationship.

All week we made love together, all three of us. It's just the same as two people making love. It's just an extra person. If it was my turn, they were both doing me and vise versa. It was very sensual. It was very erotic; a lot of kissing and hands touching everyone's parts and taking turns. It was an equal participation thing. You don't sit off to the side and watch. We stimulated each other all at the same time, in some way or another. We used lots of lubrication to keep things slippery soft. That's kind of how it works, generally. I guess I could say we turned into a 'glob.' Three equal bodies, though most of the time it was 'someone in the middle' kind of thing. When we were in bed together, I made sure I had both of them with me, on me, under me, in my brain and in my heart. Whatever was going on, I stayed involved. When I was with the three of them, I was equally into both of them, always. All three of us were very good at it.

During the day, while Jake and Joelle were learning to scuba dive, I spent time on the beach with Cecilia. We suntanned or swam in the pool or the ocean and then we all met later. Jake left around 4 to get ready to play with the band between 5 and 7. Afterwards we had dinner together. I was usually still in my bathing suit because we stayed on the beach to the catch the last rays. Cecilia and I would show up at the bar in our sarongs and bathing suits to watch the band play. At night after dinner, the hotel always had some kind of entertainment but none of us ever saw it. Cecilia left with her chef, and Jake, Joelle, and I were off having fun swimming in the pool or the warm ocean waves, stargazing, or in their room smoking pot and having sex.

I abandoned myself to hedonistic pleasures. One night the three of us went skinny-dipping in the hotel pool and had sex as we floated around. Another night we drank too much and we started dancing. Raunchy dancing. We received a huge applause. Huge. Everything was all lovey dovey as we danced in each other's arms. Joelle and I kissed in the corner sometimes while Jake watched. Or he and I would be in the pool playing with each other while Joelle watched. It was no secret that the three of us were together. We talked endlessly, Jake told me about his life as a song writer/musician. Joelle talked about being a school teacher. I told them I was a nurse. I didn't tell them I was an escort.

Jake and Joelle met me and fell in love with me without knowing anything about my life or me. I fell in love with them without knowing them either. We accepted each other for whoever we were at the time. It was just supposed to be a week-long booty call. Who could guess then that it would turn into more?

One day Cecilia and I sailed on a boat to another part of the beach. We drank sangria on the way and were feeling no pain. There was a sandcastle contest and since there were about fifty people, they asked us to form groups. Cecilia and I teamed up with another girl. One group started building a sexual position, a big cock between tits, which of course inspired us. I suggested we have a girl going down on another girl. This guy, who happened to be standing near us, said, "I'm in on this. I'm joining you girls." He eagerly followed us to our spot on the beach. I drew the outline of a girl lying on her back with arms, boobs and her legs spread wide and then another head, bum and legs formed between the legs of the first girl. We only had so much time. On the second head we made long hair flowing down her back because her face was going to be down, and then we built her a really nice ass. Anyway, we won. It was very funny, and we were the talk of the beach. Then someone took group pictures and of course Cecilia and I were bare tits up. There was no titty action anywhere until we took off our tops. Well,

I went to have a swim in the ocean and a guy got my top. This big huge hairy guy was wearing my teeny tiny little flame bathing suit around his chest. Well, the top part anyway. It was very funny.

Towards the end of the week I decided to try scuba diving. Jake told me to go with Dale because he was a professional diver and would help me. They were friends. Jake was the reason Dale had come to Club Erotica, to hang out with him and the band. Dale seemed quite willing to take me diving and, after we dove, the next thing I knew he was hitting on me. He said, "Well, between you and me, what's going on with you and Jake?" I said, "Oh, you know, we're just having some fun. Nothing serious. He's married." He said, "I want to know if you want to stay next week. Just forget about him. Stay with me. I'd make you way happier than he ever could." I didn't expect it from him. I thought to myself, 'What am I? The blow-up doll that gets passed around Club Erotica? I knew his attitude was 'Oh, she'll sleep with them so she'll sleep with me.' Well, hello, NO. There was no way. I was really shocked. I said something like, "Why don't you leave it with me. I don't know if I'm staying." It was my polite way of telling him to fuck off. Later he came up to me again and asked if I'd thought about things. Well, hello, NO. Meanwhile I told Jake about it. Turned out they had words about it after I left. Jake had told him, "Don't fuck with my girl."

One of the first things I remember about Joelle was when she said, "I want Jake to know what it's like to be loved by another woman." To me, that was profound. Why would you encourage your husband, the man you love, honor, and cherish, to go and be loved by another woman? That astounds me. I'm completely opposite. I am possessive and think, 'He's mine and you ain't going to be allowed to get near him.' I can be a ghetto girl sometimes. Ghetto girl is being a hooker and protecting her man. It's possessive street talk I picked up from being around, because escorts are very possessive of their men. The last thing they do is share him. So that's a real part of my thinking, and when I heard this from her, I was amazed and astounded that somebody would think that way. I didn't understand it. How can someone be so secure that they can set free the very person they love believing that it will be all right? As in 'I trust you enough.' She trusted Jake. She trusted me. She trusted herself.

At the end of the week, Joelle had to go back to work in Boston, while Jake stayed on for another week. The night before she left, I was in their room and all of a sudden I felt really uncomfortable because I remembered this was their last night together at the club. I thought they should spend it together. I left. I felt awful.

The day she left, Jake asked me to stay the rest of the week. I was supposed to leave the next night. When Joelle got on the bus to go to the airport and said good-bye, I thought, 'Oh fuck. I can't leave tomorrow. I can't do what she just did.' The saying good-bye part hurt. I didn't want it to end. I arranged to stay the extra week, but didn't tell anyone right away, not even Jake. When we were in the pool that evening, I told him and he became a bit weird. He seemed to have a problem with it. Finally, he said, "Okay fine. Let's go back to my room." I could sense something, but I didn't know what it was.

We started to make love and then he stopped. He looked into my eyes and held my face in his hands and said, "Don't fall in love with me. You can't fall in love with me. I'm married. I can't be with you." He held up his left hand and showed me his ring and said, "We can't have a relationship." The part of me that wants to make things right said, "No, this is just a booty call. It's just Club Erotica. It's no big deal." I didn't mean it. My eyes gave me away as I said it. He said, "I plan to write some music and spend time with my band members this week." I said, " What? You know what? Don't even fucking worry about it. I'll just cancel it and let's forget it." I was peeved and angrily retreated to my own room.

The next day I made sure I didn't see him. I drank a lot of beer and smoked a lot of pot on the beach with Cecilia and her chef. I agonized. I felt so hurt I cried. Eventually we decided to swim in the pool to cool off. Jake was there hanging out with his buddies. I just ignored him. I was thinking, 'You want space? Have some fuckin' space.' I dove into the pool. Jake swam over to me from the other end and said he felt badly that he had blown me off and that he was just as unhappy as I was. I wanted to kick him in the balls, right there in the pool. He hadn't changed his mind though. We talked and basically said our goodbyes. Funny how fate can decide otherwise.

Cecilia and Woosh Boosh came over and told me Boosh had arranged a discount on the room we were renting so she could stay another week. I considered the dramatic impact of leaving Jake in a huff of indifference, in fact, right in front of him I told Cecilia I wouldn't be staying. The next day, I decided for certain to stay the extra time.

So surprise, surprise. Jake and I spent the rest of the week together. It was 'life as a roller coaster ride.' The first couple of days were uncomfortable because we struggled with how we felt. I said to him, "You know, it's too late. I already love you." I told him it was not about my love having expectations of living with him or getting married. I told him I loved him as Jake, as Joelle's husband, as a person. It took him a few days to let go and acknowledge what he was feeling because he said, "It's not you. It's me. I'm afraid of how I feel for you and of being unfaithful to Joelle. I never thought I'd love anybody but her and now I have you." Over the course of that week, he repeatedly told me he loved me.

Jake once told me that before they were married, Joelle would periodically leave him because she needed to be connected to a woman. She found some kind of connection with women that she didn't get from him. She left him to fill that part of her. He knew that if he wanted to be with her, that was something he had to accept. He loved her so much, wanted her that much, that he was willing to live with her having other women. He knew she would never have an affair with other men. He knew he was the only man that she wanted. Before they married, they talked about what kind of openness they needed. They realized and agreed that she needed other women and therefore he should have the same freedom too.

We talked about everything. I told him about my child and he had a real understanding because he became a fathered as a teenager and was unable to raise his child too. He told me about his shadowed past as a drug dealer, as well as other crazy things he had done and what he had gone through to change. Somewhere in that conversation I slipped in that I had charged $500 an hour. I tried to make it as casual as possible. He acknowledged it with, "Well, you got paid more than most." That was the end of that conversation. He was streetwise. He 'got' what I had told him. Another day, when Cecilia told him straight out that she was an escort, he asked if I was one too. She said, "Elysia's not working right now." He was totally accepting of it. I was later to learn that Joelle had been an exotic dancer who danced around a pole at men's bars.

All good things come to an end, but after that week, only Club Erotica ended. I invited Jake and Joelle to come to Canada and visit me. They accepted.

E-mail:
From: Jake
To: Elysia
Subject: loving you from Boston
Hey Baby, I've always been the luckiest person I know ... because I know the face of love. I've held its hand many times – stared longingly into its eyes, felt pain for its lack and amazing bliss at its return.

I've been thinking about you in the last few days as I've been walking around like a grump (at least according to Joelle). The thought of you has made me smile more times than I can count.

No, I do not regret taking you back to my room that first day. No, I do not regret one second of our relationship. I love you and I hope you know that. I know it's hard for you being alone there, so far away from us but be strong darling, we'll be together again soon. I know you get depressed, but we'll be seeing you soon in Canada. The only thing I regret is that I can't take you in my arms and love you the way I want to. I wish that my life kept us out on the road so you and Joelle could come with me and our life would be a rolling summer camp.
I love you and I miss you,
Jake

From: Elysia
To: Jake
Subject: Thinking about you …
Hello there Jake,
I am sitting here thinking about you, of course. You are always on my mind and in my heart. I love you so much and wish I could make this easy for us all. We are all struggling with our feelings, reality and the distance between us. We cannot undo what is already done, only try to find peace with where we are now. Whatever happens between 'we three kings' will happen with love, truth, and the best intentions. Even the most dark and difficult times are protected by the love we have for each other. At least that is what I am telling myself these days. I miss you so much Jake. All this love inside of me for you is overwhelming. It's intense and must freak you out! How about one of my poems:

A circle
Hand in hand in hand.
Linked together
Life, heart, soul
By love
Carried away by thoughts
Of completeness
And peace
And grace.

Take care of each other, Love Elysia xoxo

* * *

Something really nice happened when they came to stay with me in Toronto. Maybe it was the best of our times together. It was probably the happiest we were to be. Every night was romantic. We had wonderful dinners. Every candle in my apartment was lit and we drank bottles of champagne and listened to music. We gently kissed, touched and caressed each other with an emotional and sensual affection that made anything possible. Jake played his guitar and we talked. Don't think for a minute it was just about sex. We began talking about them moving to Toronto. I want to remember that week, forever. I wish life could always be like that.

I organized a scavenger hunt for them as a fun way for them to get to know the city. They had to find clues, which led them to places for lunch, or to see a particular view, or to shop down funky little streets.

More than ever I was amazed by the strength of their relationship to handle a third person in such a loving bond as theirs. I believed they had been together for such a long time, since age thirteen, and therefore had such trust in their commitment to each other that they could both sit back, without jealousy, and watch each other make love to me. They were so sure of their love that they were able to let go. They had been friends and lovers who had come and gone from each other's lives and now knew, no matter what, there would always be 'Jake & Joelle.' I remember them telling me, when we first met in Club Erotica, that they would always be 'Jake & Joelle,' as in 'bacon & eggs.' I never doubted that for a moment. They are the center for each other.

I certainly don't think their kind of trust is the 'norm' in relationships. It's hard for me to admit that I am a jealous person but our relationship forced a spotlight on it. I had to deal with it and think about it. For instance, when Jake would say to Joelle and me something like, "Oh, you remember when I went to that show and that really cute sexy girl was there and I was flirting with her all night ...." My reaction would be; "Fuck this! How dare you!" Joelle's reaction would be, "Oh yeah, I remember you telling me about her." I don't know for sure where Joelle's security came from, but one day while sitting on a park bench in the sun we discussed it in an intimate safe conversation as women can do with each other. My relationship with Joelle was different than mine with Jake because I easily related to her on a female level. When we spent time together alone, we talked and touched and looked into each other's eyes. We conversed about things that were important in our hearts, our feelings, and we connected on a girl-talk level which is different than with men. I remember her telling me that day, "You know, I'm only human and of course I do get jealous sometimes, but I don't let it rule my life." She was a saint.

I love the way she looked. I love the way she loved us. I love how smart she was. She was very strong and completely in touch with her male side. She and Jake had switched roles in a certain way. She was the main breadwinner. Those were all things that attracted me to her but that was not why I loved her. It was her profound gift of being okay with letting someone else be themselves and do what they needed to do. It amazed me how open, loving, understanding and giving she was. Her ability to share me with Jake blew me away. I don't know why she feels the way she does but it's essentially her kindness and her non-judgmental way of accepting people that attracted me to her. I've always wanted those kinds of characteristics in myself.

One night, towards the end of the week, something really nice happened. I didn't expect it at all. The three of us had enjoyed a romantic dinner, which we made together. We smoked some pot and slowly drank a couple of bottles of champagne while listening to music and talking in the living room. Jake played his guitar often and we were really relaxed. Surprisingly, at one point, Joelle asked Jake to join her in my bedroom. My first reaction was 'uh-oh, that's kind of weird.' I tried not to give it too much thought. I reminded myself, 'Oh, okay, whatever. Whatever's between them, fine.' After a few minutes, they came back in. They sat down next to me on the couch, one on each side of me, and they seemed serious. Very serious. Each one took one of my hands and Joelle gently said, "We really love you and we never expected anything like this to happen to us. We want to share our lives with you. We want you to be part of our family, and when you come to Boston, we would like to go to our jeweler's to have a ring made for you like our wedding rings." It totally blew me away. I realized she had summoned Jake into the bedroom to ask him if it was a good idea or if he minded. Then she took her ring off and put it on my finger. And it fit. It was so amazing. She said, "Just wear it until I leave. We'll get you one of your own as soon as we can." Jake took it further than just giving me a ring. He suggested that we have some kind of a ceremony when we got it, where we exchanged some kind of vows. I think I said "Wow" for about a half an hour.

Somewhere in the back of my mind a light flashed 'What am I doing?' as I absorbed the symbolism of a ring and marriage and all that stuff. My overall reaction was that I was overwhelmed and totally blown away. I didn't see it coming. Now instead of thinking of them as a couple and me as some sort of a friend, I felt like we were a circle. They expressed that. Now it was the three of us. It was no longer them and me. It was 'us,' belonging together. It was that feeling we all live for.

146

I loved their wedding rings. I guess you would call it some kind of nugget jewelry. They were designed by the same designer, but were not identical because of the way they were made. When one looked closely, two figures were kissing surrounded by textured gold. We talked about having three figures somehow connected on my ring.

After ten days they flew home to Boston. At first, I couldn't bring myself to tell anyone we were engaged. Not even my closest friend, Cecilia. Honestly, a part of me worried what people would think. It was not 'traditional.' I mean, how do you explain it? We knew we were happy and that there was a 'fit,' but try and explain that to the real world, or my family, or anybody outside of us! Even I was struggling with my role in our relationship and couldn't define it clearly to even myself. There was no rulebook to consult and no guidelines. Our relationship just was! I wanted to fit into society and not be judged as a freak. I knew it couldn't be out in the open, except with good friends who were non-judgmental. Everyone was going to think we were weird to a certain degree, and yet who's to say what's weird and what isn't? I mean, lots of heterosexual relationships are brutally weird, so who's to judge?

E-mail:
From: Elysia
To: Jake
Subject: Missing you
Hello My Love,
I am sitting here at work watching the sky change and the planes that pass by and imagining you leaving. I am filled and full and content and still very, very happy. I know that when I get home my sanctuary will never be the same. Just as my life hasn't been the same since we first met. I left you at the airport quickly, because I know that you do not like to see my tears and sadness and I could not hold my happy smiling face for you any longer. But I wanted to fall into your arms and stay there forever! To feel your kisses and to hear you tell me everything is going to be ok. But, alas ... I ran instead.
What an incredible ten days we had! So much was said and felt! The more time we spend together, the more a part of me you become. And the connection with Joelle is now more than I had even hoped for. I love her. I am not looking forward to the next weeks without you both. I'm so happy we will be spending Xmas together. I know the wait will not be easy for you either, even with Joelle beside you. I love you so much Jake, and thank you for making me feel so happy.
Loving you always and forever,
Elysia xoxo

From: Joelle
To: Elysia
My darling,
I am glad that I can say we got to spend time together and get to know each other. You are truly beautiful and a wonderful woman. Leaving you in Toronto was harder than either of us expected. We spent some of the hours on the way home designing your ring. How do I describe who you are to everyone? I haven't tackled that yet. I better get to thinking about it, although personally I just think of you as "our Elysia." It seems to describe you and us. Let other people decide how to label you/us. Sweetheart, when you miss us, don't go to the dark side. Just close your eyes and hold us in your heart. Remember you are part of the circle and the circle stretches many miles – but never breaks.
Love, and goodnight for now.
Joelle

With them gone, I quickly realized the toughest part of our relationship was not the fact I was involved in a ménage-à-trois and not the fact they were married. The tough part was that we were not living in the same city or country! Nothing else was difficult compared to that. I desperately missed them. We were not sharing our lives. Our togetherness was limited to the telephone and e-mails. We began exploring the idea of living together in New York City, L. A., or Canada.

Before they left, we briefly talked about my being an escort and about HIV/AIDS and assorted ailments.

E-mail:
From: Joelle
To: Elysia
Subject: Thoughts from last night!
Did you get all your Christmas shopping done? If you did ... Congratulations 'cause I haven't at all ....
I'm glad you told your friend about us – she's one heck of a lady! Engagement is as good a word as any - since none fit just right! Jasmine, the jeweler, is having a show/party during the time you will be here for Xmas. I thought you might enjoy meeting her. Anyway, what more appropriate way of celebrating Christmas, then going for a ring fitting/design meeting?
OK, to tackle the larger subjects at hand. HIV/AIDS and assorted ailments... Both Jake and I have had AIDS tests, but not terribly recently. In terms of anything else we're clean. We both know the people we've been with (over the summer), are still in contact with them and are confident that they've been "straight" with us. But another test couldn't hurt, especially if

it makes you feel more confident. In terms of your health, I assume you would have said something as our relationship deepened (I know that's not very proactive of me). You mentioned getting your AIDS test and I guess I just assumed that you probably got one regularly ever since you started 'working.' Considering Herpes is easier to get than AIDS, I'm not too worried about any of us, but you're right, we should all of us decide on guidelines/protocols.

Next, you 'working.' I can't speak 100% for Jake, but he did mention it briefly so I can say that it doesn't thrill us that you would share your body with someone else. BUT (big but) it is your body and we won't judge you for your decisions. And I know how hard it is to get out of a cash for play business. I can only imagine that its 10xs harder for you than it was for me to stop dancing. So, if you decide that it's something you want to do then do it (even if this means that you will be visiting someone while in Boston). That's my side. I won't speak for Jake.

I know that neither Jake nor I thought that you had "officially" stopped as recently as you had. Cecilia had intimated that it was a longer period of time, so if you need time to transition out then take it. You know we love you for you and that work and love are two completely different things. So the reverse is true, you should feel okay about talking about it with us too.

I wish we were together also. I hate talking this way.
Love, Joelle.

Suddenly, my life became a reality check. I carried a secret, which now haunted me. Their relationship with me was honest. I needed to return that trust.

E-mail:
From: Elysia
To: Joelle.
Subject: HIV and tests
Hi Hon,
I am not really sure what to say at this point. There is so much to the topic of my being a working girl and I don't really know where to start. Part of me wants to say nothing about it at all. The fact that I have worked in the past has always been a huge secret, as you can imagine. Me, in the straight world, trying to live with part of my life hidden. Anyway, it is not something I have shared with most people.

I do not want to have any secrets from you. That means I have some things I need to tell you and probably some things we should talk about, so that there are no creepers or surprises later. This is not a comfortable topic for me, just so you know. While we are on the topic of HIV – yes, I went and got my results and they were negative. I know that I am negative. What I did not tell you was I went also for a liver enzyme test. Last year I found out

149

that I have Hepatitis C. I had no idea. I don't really know where, when I got it. As I am writing this I wish I didn't have to tell you, I wish I had told you sooner and I wish it wasn't so.

I am sorry I am telling you in an e-mail. I am not there but the time seems appropriate. I feel left out of the loop. I don't get to see your reaction, how you feel, the conversations you and Jake will have about it and I will imagine the worst! I am not sure how you will react or what you will think or if this changes things for you. I am sure you will let me know soon enough.

What I have done in the past and what I have gone through has made me who I am today. I can't take any of it back or undo any of it. All I do now is try to move forward, try to be aware and not to make the same mistake a million times and be good to people.

I miss you terribly tonight. I wish I could be with you.
Love, Elysia

I confessed and they freaked out, of course. Deservedly so. At first we had used protection during sex, but it was such a free form of love that we started cheating, though he didn't come inside of me. At Club Erotica we had unprotected sex all that time. I know now they have a 'thing' about it. They do not have sex with other people without using a condom. The first time we were in the pool at the Club and he looked up at Joelle for permission to have sex with me, he asked me if I was safe. I said yes.

I had my own reasons for not telling them, which was basically I was in complete denial about my having Hep C. I hadn't processed it or accepted it properly. When I was diagnosed, my brain said, 'No, I'm not accepting this information.' I put it in Pandora's box and locked it away. I was not ready to deal with it. It wasn't until later when I met Jake and Joelle, even when they flat out asked me, "Are you safe?" and I said, "Yes, absolutely," that I realized my boldfaced lie to them and to myself. I had to look at myself and say, "What's going on here?" That's the psychological reaction, well, I don't know what to call it, but I think ones' brain can protect itself from what it can't deal with. I had done this to them because of my own denial. After this happened, I went through a grieving process about it. Yes, I screwed up and I take responsibility. I didn't keep them safe. And Jake had asked me. I guess my lesson in the whole thing was if I chose not to tell it's up to me to keep the other person safe, meaning practice safe sex until they chose not to. As a working girl, I practiced safe sex. As their lover I am ashamed to say I did not.

At first they were devastated. Then they did their own research and started reading and learning about it. Hep C. is not highly contagious sexually, except during menstruation. It's about the transfer of blood. At first they weren't sure about our relationship. Jake, especially was concerned.

E-mail:
From: Joelle
To: Elysia
Subject: Fucked up and everything else.
Morning Sweetie!
I am going to address the condom issue. As you mentioned last night, Jake and I have to get used to this also and we are working on it. (Think we're doing pretty good too!) The questions that keep coming up to us are – wouldn't you feel worse if by some freak chance he (or I) did contract it? Isn't it better to be safe than sorry? And how can we (the three of us) work together to make everyone feel comfortable? For us, the answers to the questions are: yes, yes and when we are all together then the three of us can use condoms. Is that a fair compromise? I don't know. From what I understand, so long as you aren't bleeding and either of us has an open cut in our mouth or on our hands, then oral sex and finger play is cool. So we really aren't worried about that (so no we don't think you should be hermetically sealed!) I don't know, I'm just throwing this out there. We welcome your input since you've lived with this longer then we have. And just in case you still have thoughts about not coming to Boston: GET THEM OUT OF YOUR HEAD!
Love ya muchly, Joelle

Eventually they accepted me again and we decided to use condoms. I was going there for Xmas expecting that I was never going to be able to see his dick again unless it was covered. That's what I thought. The extreme. I felt humbled and guilty.

* * *

Christmas Time

I hired a cab to take me from the airport to their apartment. The doorman, Beerbelly, let me in. I could see why he was nicknamed Beerbelly. He brought my bags into the apartment. A bottle of champagne and three glasses were sitting on an old oak round table with four oak chairs. Two chairs were pulled back, away from the table. An old couch, covered in plaid material from another age, sat beside the table, and in front of it was a coffee table with two coffee mugs, one half-full of coffee. It wasn't a large apartment. It was long and narrow with burgundy walls and cream-colored curtains for doors on the closets. It was nice, but humble. 'Stuff' was pretty much scattered everywhere. I didn't care what it was like.

Their little dog yapped at me. I'm not an animal person. I don't much care for cats or dogs. I'm really not into caging animals for my own personal benefit. Besides, dogs and cats carry worms that can infect humans. I petted her. She didn't slobber much so I didn't mind her. She seemed to welcome me and we agreed to get along.

A window looked out on a huge tree behind which began the building blocks of apartment buildings. I walked down the hall to the bathroom. Two towels, two washcloths, two glasses, two toothbrushes, soon to be three. The toilet seat was in the bathtub and upon closer inspection I could see the hinges were broken. I walked into the kitchen. It was messy, looked like a rushed morning. Breakfast crumbs, scattered coffee filters, a lidless jar of orange marmalade, and dishes with leftover food all needed attention. The garbage can was overflowing. Pretty cobalt blue dishes lined the cupboards. I felt slightly uneasy, as if I was snooping and intruding in other people's stuff. I mean this was not my turf. I reminded myself this was Jake and Joelle's home. It was my first realization that wherever they were, either in their apartment or mine, or sitting in a restaurant with them, I would feel at home. Wherever we were together, that was home. I went to the table and opened the champagne. I poured myself a glass and sat down on the couch to relax and suck in their space, savoring the excitement I was feeling. There is nothing like the sweet anticipation of developing love. I was eager for the reality of us.

To cut to the chase, of course that first evening in their apartment was full of celestial spaces of cosmic heavenly feelings. I'm laughing. Well, isn't that the way budding love is supposed to be described? To be honest, it was all of that, but slightly awkward too. At times we were unsure and insecure. This wasn't the vacation 'mindset' of Club Erotica. This was their turf. Normally the habitat of two. We spent time developing our lovemaking at the same time we were developing our relationships.

In fact, for all my worrying about how they would handle my Hep C., we went back to the way that we were doing things originally, which was not using condoms except during my period. That happened. I was just at the end of it. There was a point where he put one on and I knew it was happening because I knew where they were kept. He reached over top of me and behind Joelle. She tried to distract me by saying, "It's okay. Don't worry. It's no big deal," because we all knew what he was doing. Really at the time, it didn't hurt me at all. I thought it was going to really bother me and make me feel dirty, nasty and awful, and it didn't. I was prepared to accept those feelings for their benefit. I was fully prepared to do whatever it would take so that they would feel better about me, no matter what. Because I had done this. I had put us in this place. I'm the one. I'm the reason that they're feeling that need to protect themselves, so I had to live with my feelings until they were comfortable. I thought they had forgiven me, and, you know, they really had. They let it go.

I think the universe presents people to you. They come into your life for a reason. I believe Jake and Joelle have come into my life to teach me things so that I will be a better person. I figured I'd learn something that's not for everybody to learn because what we were doing was so different. We were experiencing a new order. We were pioneers in a way. About the only thing we did know was that when the three of us were together, we were at peace.

In the three weeks spread over Christmas, we lived as close to normal as anyone. We enjoyed all the things a couple would do. Interaction times three. I wish I could paint some kind of exciting co-existence that would leave you, the reader, eagerly relishing the next paragraph, but life just wasn't extreme. About the only thing unusual was that none of us got around to fixing the toilet seat. It remained non-attached to the toilet; a free spirited joke, often sliding off onto the floor, sometimes while I was sitting on it. Jake kept putting it into the bathtub. Joelle and I kept putting it back.

Mornings we struggled out of bed into the cold kitchen to make coffee and toast with cinnamon sugar. Sometimes we returned to bed to eat it. We shopped at delicatessens for treats, and enjoyed long walks followed by a late dinner. We rented movies and talked into the night. Jake played the guitar for hours on end and Joelle went to work. I read a book. In fact I remember reading *Memoirs of a Geisha* and enjoying it. We had individual time together and I was as comfortable with all of us in the room as when I was with just one of them. Our relationship became so much more than sexual, though the sharing of sex between us was fantastic. We fell in love all over again. It just happened and we were open to it. All three of us. At least that was my impression.

The whole time I was there I dreamed about renovating their apartment, but that's me. I wanted to move the wall unit, paint the cupboards, and pile all the clutter. The 'neat freak' in me became a bit of a joke, whenever they couldn't find anything they'd ask me where I had put it. They felt the place needed so much renovating that they kind of gave up on it. Some people are just like that. But not me. My bathrooms are always immaculate and there is no sign hanging outside my door claiming 'Martha Stewart doesn't live here.' I like to decorate. I like organization. So I cleaned and piled all the clutter.

They hadn't put up any Christmas decorations so I made them haul them out and took control of creating some Christmas spirit. I insisted we get a tree. We took a drive to a tree farm somewhere north of the city, as in a Bing-Crosby-Xmas-Hollywood-experience-kind-of-thing. It was snowing and we wore gloves, knitted hats, pink noses, rosy cheeks and cheery attitudes. The owner of the farm had jacked up an old car, a DeSoto, covered it in lights and put a Santa in the front seat. Large plastic reindeer were pulling the old junker car. We could barely see the colors of the figures because they were lightly blanketed in snow. It was such an American decoration. It was cool. We mucked around amongst the trees and picked a big fat seven-foot tree and chopped it down. Jake tied it on top of the roof and we were quite the cheery little trio driving home. There's something about a Christmas tree that does that.

While our lives were fairly normal, I can't say our Xmas gifts were. I brought gifts from home with the intention of spoiling them. I had shopped for days. When Jake saw me place my presents under our tree he literally drooped. I knew he hadn't been doing many gigs, so cash was a problem. I told him to get creative. Then I gave him a hundred bucks. I could see his mind working.

I met many of their friends and a lot of their family. After all, it was the holidays with lots of celebrating and Christmassy spirited parties where we always dressed up. Everyone I met was warm and welcoming. Even Jake's mother. It was fun and we participated like anyone would during the holidays. We went Christmas shopping together. It was snowing, which made it very festive, and we made a point of looking at all the special Christmas window displays and the decorations ornamenting the town.

Christmas morning I opened Jake's present. It was a homemade coupon book for full, unlimited access to Jake's cock for a lifetime. I remembered telling him to get creative. It also included ten body massages, either therapeutic or erotic as my choice, several pedicures, a coupon for an evening of submission, another for a fantasy night and finally there was a picture of his penis in full salute. In fine print, he wrote on the back of each coupon, "This coupon is non-transferable." He bought Joelle a year's pass to yoga classes. Legally, she already had unlimited access to his cock.

By comparison I suppose mine were normal, except for the gift of

1500 seed stock shares in an offshore start-up mining company. The company I worked for was promoting this investment. With any luck, I hoped they would eventually earn enough to get them out of debt. To me it was a paper dream. If it all came in, I would make lots too. I also gave them sweaters, martini glasses, a bottle of Canadian Merlot Ice Wine, and other little items. We spent the rest of the day cooking a turkey with all the trimmings. The best gift of all was my feeling of belonging.

You know, it was as natural for them as it was for me. It was not this inconceivable thing. I know people think of a threesome as a wildly bold, sexually crazy situation, like it's fantasy material. To us it was perfectly natural, normal, and do-able because it wasn't about the sex, because we'd all had lots of sex before. It's nice to be loved by two people. We saw all of the good things in our relationship; the love, the togetherness, and support for each other. It was all about how good it felt when the three of us were together. I believed our natural high would overcome anything that might happen.

We decided it was time to get my ring. There was an open house wine and cheese party at the studio, which happened to be on the very day of my birthday. Joelle and I got up early to catch the train for a little town somewhere outside Boston. It was pissing cold rain, trying to snow. A miserable day. Jake decided not to come; the bed was warm from our three bodies. "Too good to abandon," or so he said, the bastard. It was my BIRTHDAY and I wanted the fucker to get out of bed. The ring should have been enough reason, but my birthday should have made it all the more reason for him to come. Joelle and I decided to go anyway. We watched the rain-flooded fields zip past from the sweaty windows of the train. Joelle's aunt met us at the station and took us to Jasmine's, the jewelry store where Jake and Joelle's wedding rings were made. Her aunt didn't know what was going on between us.

Jasmine looked like a sixties hippie displaced from California, complete with the over-exposed suntanned leather skin and flowing flower print skirt. She knew Joelle, of course, because she had made their wedding rings. Joelle already had explained to her she would be bringing someone who wanted to have a ring made. I'm not sure Jasmine understood that I was a part of their relationship but she knew I wanted a ring in the same style. She showed me lots of unusual pieces to get an idea of what I wanted. She served us wine and we took our time drooling over all the jewelry. Finally we had started talking about the ring, when Joelle's aunt moved within earshot. I tried to get my point across to Jasmine with the least number of words as possible so that she would understand without the aunt finding out. She showed me a ring with three figures cast in gold, similar to what she thought I wanted. It was of a mother, father and their child. Jasmine finally said, "You need to talk to me about this ring and what it means to you and give me a feel for what you're looking for." You know, just what an artist would say, 'Describe your feelings.' At the best of times I have trouble describing my feelings about our threesome. So I said simply, "Well, it's a love relationship. I want three figures with three hearts." Descriptive, no? I could see her mind slowly going 'ding dong' and she commented slowly, "Ooookkaay." I knew she understood. She suggested kissing figures with one head here and one head there and one head under, and bodies around the ring. "Or how about hugging?" she asked. The aunt by now was busy refilling her glass of wine over in the corner. Finally Jasmine came up with, "How about if I try something with the two smaller figures being two females and a bigger one hugging them both?" I said, "I don't really know. You're going to have to figure out a way to put the three together and it's important to me to have hearts in it. Hearts are my favorite shape and I want hearts in the ring." I gave her $200 US, half the final cost. The aunt drove us back to the train. If she suspected anything, she must not have cared, because we all chatted in a most normal manner.

New Years

New Year's Eve arrived and Jake had a gig in a club, along with several other bands. His band was one of the first to perform on stage. Afterwards he joined us. Joelle and I were dressed up as space girls in skimpy costumes of shiny metallic silver cloth with low-cut tight tops, which left little to the imagination. We felt like the belles of the ball. People watched us, obviously noticing the three of us were together. At times it was bizarre how much people stared. That said, when we were together we were not particularly aware of other people around us. I mean we were respectful of everyone else but mostly we were just us.

Joelle and I were having a drink while Jake circulated with his music friends. He kept coming back to be with us and he'd kiss and hug us both. We were physically affectionate with each other in public but not in a pornographic kind of way. We displayed a normal affection, common to couples at a club. A girl came up to us and said something like, "Wow, you guys. People are watching. You guys put on a great show." She ranted on about us doing 'it' for the effect; that draw of one guy with two girls. She then asked, "You know what, why don't you guys come up on stage when I'm performing?" I snapped back, "Get the fuck away, man." I couldn't believe it. To me it was insulting. I felt intruded upon. She wouldn't have noticed had we been a twosome.

It was not about being scandalous to draw attention. While we didn't feel a need to keep it secret, we didn't want to advertise it either. I was aware of other people's reactions. Well, I suppose it was fascinating to see the obvious affection in a ménage à trois. But lots of men accommodate two women: a wife and a lover. They just don't usually know each other. We happened to know each other very well.

Another time we had some friends over to party and the three of us were in the kitchen hugging and kissing. A guy came in and muttered something like, "Wow, Jake, I had better leave you alone with your women." Jake looked at me and I knew exactly what his thoughts were. He was thinking the same thing I thought on New Year's Eve: 'This is our family and it's not some big macho bullshit thing. It's not a show. There's no 'look at me, I've got two girls.'

It bothers me the way the world's going to look at our ménage à trois. I'm insulted that they'll put a pornographic slant on it, that it's all about two girls and a guy. It's a big deal to people, especially men. The guys will think the man's a king because he's got two girls, two beautiful smart girls, to play with at once. I can hear the envious laughs from some men reading this. Obviously sex is important in any relationship, but the sex is the easiest part. Anybody can crawl into the bed and have sex. Our relationship was much more than great sex.

The New Year's Eve party was an eye-opener in another way. All three of us were downstairs in the bowels of the club. We were partying, doing drugs, and drinking. I don't mean doing a lot of drugs, mainly smoking pot. I think I did a couple lines of coke but nothing major. We were standing there and I was talking to somebody. Jake was standing beside me when this girl, this groupie, got up off the couch and came over to talk to him. The next thing I knew, they were necking. They were kissing each other, and I was a foot away. I immediately felt repulsed and mentally freaked out. It was like, 'Oh my God, I can't believe he just kissed her in front of me.' I was disgusted. It just grossed me out, especially the working girl me, who never kisses except in my personal life. I was furious. If I had been at home, I would have left. Definitely. I found Joelle and said, "He was just necking with a chick." And to her, it was no big deal. She kind of blew it off and she casually said, "Really?" I freaked out more. To him it was no big deal, obviously, and to her it was no big deal and it was a really big deal to me. We were in a room with fifty people and a band. I couldn't say anything more even though I was boiling inside.

We took a cab back to the apartment. I still didn't say anything because I knew it had to do with their relationship and their rules of playing with other people. I realized my limits on personal relationships were different from theirs and I was creating my own pain. I was the new guy. I didn't know their boundaries. But I couldn't help being angry. Part of me wanted to scream, 'How fucking dare you do that in front of me, in front of my face?' I thought it was so disrespectful. 'Here I am, your new girlfriend/wife in front of your band, God and everybody, and you're sucking face with some other bitch. You don't even know her name.' I was thinking, 'Screw you. You don't think you're going to come and kiss me now, do you?' I wanted to get away, 'cause if he was going to neck with her, he was going to do it with a hundred other girls.

For me, it's the one thing I don't do. To them it was the one thing they could do without each other's permission. For anything past kissing, they had to get specific permission from each other. They had worked out a code where they could say no if either one of them felt uncomfortable. That was their understanding. To them, kissing anyone was just no big deal.

We arrived back at the apartment and I looked at him and said something to the effect, "So, I guess I'm going to have to get used to you kissing other girls." I suppose it was oozing with sarcasm. He didn't get it. He said, "Oh gees, don't you know, it's no big deal. You're the one I love. You're the one I'm sharing my life with. I was tripping on E and was just necking with her." To him it was perfectly rational, acceptable behavior because I was the one that he was in love with. In his mind, that proved the necessary devotion, making it okay to kiss other girls. I didn't say anything else. What could I say?

The next day when Jake was gone, I talked to Joelle about it again. Well, it turned out the girl was Silva, The-Slave-Chick. Turned out she knew Jake on another level. I remembered one time when Joelle and I came home from one of her overnight business trips. The place was a mess. The kitchen looked like a party had rolled through, with dirty dishes in the sink from when we left. Joelle was furious Jake had left the place in such a mess. I noticed different things were out of place in the apartment, especially the bedroom. My suitcase was moved from the corner. A blanket, pillow and the laundry basket were on the floor and under the bed. Things on the table by the bed were gone. A light was missing and the bed was slightly moved. At first, I didn't think anything. I rationalized maybe Jake was working out and needed more space. When I noticed torn wrapping paper and unwrapped gifts on top of the dresser, I asked Joelle what was going on. She looked at the gifts and said, "Oh, Silva must have been here." I said, "What? We were away overnight and he had some girl over here?" Part of me hissed, 'What the fuck? He's got a wife, he's got a girlfriend, and now he's got to go and get somebody else?'

We sat down and Joelle explained how it's not sexual. Jake had her over for an S & M thing, the whole slave-submissive dominating thing. It was strictly for pleasure. It was Silva-The-Slave's idea. He would tie her up and do a power, aggression trip on her and deny her whatever it is she wanted. Well, I don't really know what they did. Everyone's different. Joelle assured me he never actually screwed her. I'm thinking, okay, this is Jake. Everything is sexual to him. A bar of soap is sexual to him. I said, "You can't sit here and tell me this doesn't turn him on, being with another girl in this way. Doesn't it bother you?" Apparently not. Joelle was pissed off because the apartment was a mess, and he had obviously not picked up anything all weekend and he hadn't even done the dishes. I was pissed he had this chick over to string up from the ceiling, or whatever they did.

That's when we talked about kissing other partners. I said, "This is more than I can handle. You know, the kiss on New Year's Eve? It really bothers me." We talked about fidelity and she reminded me that they have never been monogamous with each other. She said to me, "If this bothers you, then the answer is very simple. It doesn't happen. If that's how you feel, then it doesn't happen." I answered, "I don't want to be lied to about this. I don't want you to just go behind my back and do this and then just not tell me. I don't want you to think, 'Well, she's not here.' How's she ever going to know?" I said, "That's critical to me and I'm telling you that right now because I'll find out. It doesn't matter how hard you try to bury a secret, I will know. How can you make those promises to me?" She said, "If Jake and I disapproved of your being an escort, what would you do?" And I said, "Well, I'd quit. Simple." She replied, "It's the exactly same thing." And that's all she said to me. It was all about her desire to do something for the other person if something bothered them. Out of respect for that person, or the relationship, she would stop it.

To Jake, it was no big deal. But monogamy, fidelity and kissing is important to me and I really needed to say that. I asked him if he planned on continuing these activities, whether it was kissing while being with other girls or Silva-the-Slave or whoever. I tried not to say, 'Okay, if you do this, this is what I'm going to do, or whatever.' Basically he said that it was fine. He implied it wasn't going to be an issue and the New Year's Eve thing was just a kiss and nothing to worry

159

about. He assured me the slave thing with Silva didn't work out and not to worry about it either.

When it was time for me to leave from our Christmas together, I didn't want to leave but I had to return to work. It was during this time that the company I worked for was discussing sending me to Costa Rica to manage their office there. A couple of days after New Year's, I flew home to Canada.

E-mail;
From: Jake
To: Elysia,
Hey Babe,
I understand how you feel and I'm sorry that I "blew you off" but New Year's Eve was just a kiss and that's it. It was mostly because I was tripping. To Joelle and me, kissing/making out isn't a big deal and I didn't realize it would bother you so much. As far as Silva goes, I'm not seeing her. I played with her and there was no sex at all involved. It was a Master/Slave thing and it didn't work and won't be happening again. I think that for right now it would be best if we just kept things between the three of us, a kind of extended monogamy. Joelle and I both feel that things are really great the way they are and we don't want to screw anything up between the three of us. Joelle mentioned you were considering going to Florida to go working (hooking.) If you feel you need to, then I think that you should go ahead. I love you and I hope this answers some of your questions, I'll speak to you soon. Jake.

Jake's a guy. Isn't that how we women blanket a man's insensitivity because we believe men don't approach things the way we do? That a certain amount of insensitivity is normal? Isn't that how we justify mistreatment of our sensitive female emotions? I reminded myself Jake was a base knuckle-bashing straightforward guy. I justified his behavior by believing that to him, as most guys, his apparent slack approach to emotional exclusivity did not affect him the same way it affected me. At least he had given me his word not to kiss other women so I could move on.

About a week after returning home, I wrote a long e-mail to Jake, expressing my concern for his kissing other women. After I sent it, I decided it wasn't appropriate. Actually it was my second e-mail to him on the subject. Since I knew Jake's password, which he had given me at Xmas, I went into his Hotmail e-mail site to delete it. While I was in there, I saw a "Need to know" subject line, which I thought was my original e-mail asking him whether or not he was going to be with other

160

girls. I hadn't saved it and I wanted to refresh my memory. I clicked on "Need to know" and it wasn't my e-mail. It was private from Jake to Joelle. I read it anyway.

E-mail
From: Jake
To: Joelle
Subject: Need to Know ...
I remember our deal and definition of monogamy as being – we would still play with others together and no more "solo adventures" which is fine with me. I haven't gotten much out of my solo adventures except for a second wife that I'm not really sure I want. I've always wanted a second girl, you know that, and you have always agreed with me. I really want to just cut and run for awhile, fuck the consequences. But here is the honest to God truth about our monogamy; I don't want to lie to you. I've NEVER been able to keep it in my pants.... NEVER!!!! And I don't want to tell you that I'll be faithful and then lie to you if I fuck up. I love you more than anybody – you know that, and our marriage has always kind of been based on this idea that we had an "open marriage." I hate that term though. As far as Elysia goes and the idea of living with her for a while, it'll only really work for me if she's in Costa Rica or if we're all on the road a lot. Having her around for almost a month, without the chance to be alone with you, almost drove me fucking nuts. Yes, I've always wanted a second woman in our lives and if it's Elysia then that's fine. I have to admit that if we have to leave her at some point, at least I won't get my heart broken by her. That's it for right now.
I love you always, Jake

I was devastated. My heart was pounding and a rush of anxiety almost dropped me to the floor. I was completely shattered. I thought, 'Wait a minute. First of all, I didn't ask for the fucking ring and I didn't ask to be called your wife and now all of a sudden, it's a fucking problem.' I then read Joelle's answer.

E-mail:
From: Joelle
To: Jake
Subject: Re: Need to Know ...
Ok, so our definitions are different. I thought we went to Club Erotica saying "traditional" monogamy. But that's neither here nor there. The bottom line reason I want to be monogamous (with you & Elysia) is that we have had enough "scares" this year. Elysia and Hep C is all I want to deal with. I don't want to worry whether one or the other of us is going to contract something accidentally. In terms of the second wife thing, I don't think Elysia even knows how long this is going to last. She said in one of her

161

last e-mails to me that she hasn't decided whether she can give up the "dream" of a husband and "normal" family, especially since we (you and I) are going to have one regardless of whether she is in the pic or not.

Can you keep it in your pants? I don't know either. Heck, I don't know if I can – you know my history on that! But I would like to try. Obviously with the understanding that a "slip" requires full confession – we can't lie to each other or Elysia about it.

Another reason for "monogamy" is that I'm tired of the games people play and I don't want to be a "middle-aged swinger" or a "player." It takes too much emotional energy to chase tail and frankly I don't think it's usually worth it.

Elysia is going to Costa Rica – she confirmed that the other day. Whether we stay in Toronto while she's there is up to many factors – obviously your music is the main one. And I think if we need to spend time together alone, then we just need to be honest with her. Not try and "sneak" around, but to just tell her. This way she has the same freedom with us and no one feels shut out or hurt. She and I have talked about this a little bit. There are lots of things to work out. This is a huge move for us and a major adjustment to how you and I run our lives, but I do think that in the long run it will make our relationship better.

I love you too. You are my soul mate and my lover and my partner and my friend. Neither of us are good at change and we are both scared of making life changes, but here we are facing our fears and while it's really strange right now I think it will be great in the end.
Kisses and hugs,   Joelle

I freaked out. I lost it. I was so angry I spontaneously e-mailed them to end our relationship.

E-mail:
From: Elysia
To: Joelle & Jake
Subject: GOOD-BYE
Well, it took me a little snooping but at least I know that truth about how Jake feels. I have known it all along and you actually had me convinced otherwise. I didn't realize my being in Boston was so difficult for you and Jake. So sorry!! It's nice to know you feel the only way this was going to work is if I am not around! Warms my fucking heart! Well, you do not have to worry anymore because I AM DONE. Thank you so much Jake for coming into my life and wreaking havoc. You did this and I hope you have enjoyed yourself. Anyway, you are definitely not the one with the broken heart. I hope that makes you feel better!
Don't bother calling. E.

Then I left for the day. I was basically hysterical, crying, bawling and messed up all day. I visited Cecilia and cried my heart out to her.

E-mail:
From: Jake
To: Elysia
Subject: Good-bye
So you went behind our backs and read an e-mail that wasn't meant for you to see and now you claim to be brokenhearted. Well, boo-fucking-hoo for you. I don't know what made you feel it was necessary to check up on us and honestly I really don't fucking care. I hope you're happy you found something that proves all your little abandonment fears reality, because that is what you must have wanted or you wouldn't have gone looking. How many times have you checked my e-mail? I left the password because I TRUSTED YOU!!!! Apparently I shouldn't have. Joelle was thinking of making you her business partner, we introduced you to our families and did everything we knew how to make you feel welcome and loved in our home and that wasn't enough. All this after you fucking lied to me abut the Hep C., put us both at risk, let me pull my dick out of you and stick it into her and we FUCKING FORGAVE YOU FOR IT. But honestly, none of that shit matters to me right now because you're alone and you'll be alone because even though you felt like we were the ones who couldn't be trusted, obviously you were the sneaky one. I'm just glad we found this out before we moved together. You know I could always tell there was this insane jealousy thing inside of you. I think that is what always reminded me of my ex-girlfriend. The fact is I don't know what made you do it. I am truly sorry that you did because whatever you may have read, the fact is Joelle and I both love you a lot. We will miss you but I'm also very relieved simply because I'm now spared any ridiculous emotional bullshit that might have happened in the future. The truth is the only person in this whole thing that I feel bad for right now is Joelle. Whatever shit I wrote was just whatever was on my mind at that moment. It wasn't meant for you to see. It was only meant for her to read and you snuck behind our backs and broke your own heart (Curiosity killed the cat). But now Joelle is also sitting here heartbroken because of your stupidity. I hope you don't expect me to try to justify or explain what you read (I'm not really sure what you read) because it's your fault you saw it. I really hope that you find happiness in the future. You'll make someone a great wife someday. You just need to learn to trust the people who love you (not everyone is your dad).
Goodbye forever,
Jake

From: Joelle
To: Elysia

Subject: don't delete this out of hate
Elysia,

Black and white once again fails to deliver the emotions I'm feeling... What the hell are you talking about?!! What snooping? What did you do? Jake and I know how we feel, at least up and until tonight. Some of your language sounds familiar as if you read an e-mail that was a part of a much larger discussion. Why did you do this? I don't even know how to react ... when you were here I told you my fear about this relationship that you would pull the plug and here you are doing it. Convince you of what, Elysia? I haven't convinced you of anything. I have always told you what Jake has said to me to be the truth --- yes there are versions before the final one and some not so nice --- did you want to hear them all? I don't think so. Maybe I was wrong. Did you want to hear that when you told us you have Hep C that we both said, "Fuck this!" No, the real answer is that we thought about it and did research and talked to our doctor and came to the conclusion that we could live with it and that you were worth the risk. Now you read something out of context and don't even say ---- hey, fuck you both but ...That's not love. We have been willing to try and adapt and overcome and open up our life to you and to find ways to make you feel welcomed, loved and wanted, and you throw it away just like this? What happened to the unconditional? What happened to talking? Learning to communicate? Maybe the Ice Princess finally won --- welcome home Elysia!

I can't believe you gave up just like that! Maybe you have meant to all along. Maybe you really have been in this waiting for me to divorce Jake. I don't know. I wish I did and I wish you had the courtesy to tell me. I know Jake's mind, I thought I was getting to understand yours. So, you want to talk about wreaking havoc in a life? Take a step into my shoes babe. I'm the one who left my husband with you during the day for three weeks over Xmas. I'm the one who left for work every day knowing you were fucking him. And not caring! Believing that you truly loved us for us. Hoping beyond hope that my marriage wouldn't be blown apart because of Jake's feelings for you --- yes, Elysia. Believe it or not, he does care for you. Same goes for me.

This is not all about what Elysia perceives. Or what Joelle says in a rambling rant. Or what Jake says in an e-mail. This is what the three of us agree to, eyeball to eyeball. And when you were here, we agreed that we loved each other. To the two of us that means through everything. What does it mean to you? Don't end it this way.
Joelle

I came home late and there were two messages on my answering machine from Joelle. "Phone us." "We need to talk." So I did. Jake answered and said something to the effect, "I thought you didn't want to talk to us or have anything to do with us." He was seething. I didn't want to deal with his anger so I asked to speak to Joelle. She was crying as much as I was crying. They thought I was snooping and spying on them. She kept asking, "Explain to me what happened." I told them about wanting to delete the second e-mail, and reading their private e-mails was initially accidental and with no devious or sneaky intent. To me, it was so innocent that I didn't even see it as an invasion of privacy. Joelle and I talked for two hours on the phone. We were extremely hurt and devastated. Jake briefly said, "Look, we still love you. But we are really hurt and we'll just have to see what happens." I got the impression I had crossed his line.

The next couple of days were difficult. We e-mailed each other and things began to settle down. We basically agreed everything had been moving too fast. Decisions were being made too quickly and the 'zit' popped. I always call it the 'zit theory.' You know, things will build and build until finally they pop and then the healing can happen. This was one of those situations. In four months we had decided to give up our lives, as we had known them, to be together in a threesome.

Jake never explained or defended the things he said in that e-mail. The only thing he admitted was that I was insanely jealous like his ex-girlfriend. He said, "Yeah, truthfully, that is how I see you sometimes."

So I thought about that. I probably was jealous of their relationship and it did create a lot of insecurity in me. I guess that was there, but I don't think I'm like that all the time. To me, being jealous and insecure implies a really negative image and I was not prepared to take that on. I think my feelings were justified. His e-mail said I didn't 'belong.' It was not my reaction that was necessarily wrong; it was reading someone else's personal e-mail, not sent to me, that was wrong. Obviously, I fucked up. There was a lot of other ways I could have handled it. Spontaneous raging never works. I accepted responsibility for that.

Well, what goes around, comes around – as the saying goes. When I was with them over Xmas, I checked my e-mails through their service provider and on their computer. In Hotmail, which I was using at the time, there was a little button on the front page you could click which said something like: 'Keep my Hotmail open all the time to network neighborhood.' I had clicked "Keep open until I turn it off," or whatever it said. I didn't deactivate it before I left which meant unopened e-mails to me would pop up on their computer screen to indicate their existence.

Joelle apparently opened her computer one day and up popped my e-mails. She claimed she just read the subject line, that she didn't open my letters to read. I had recently e-mailed some of my tricks to make appointments, trying to come up with some money. My "subject" headings were suggestive for sure. The problem was I had been telling Jake and Joelle, until I was blue in the face, that I hadn't been working since I had met them. I actually had been working for World Trading Finance so the e-mails she saw were contradictory. In fact, I was trying to come up with some money for our planned trip to California and I hadn't received a paycheck from World Trading for several months.

E-mail:
From: Joelle
To: Elysia
Subject: ok, so I guess we're even.
Elysia,
I'm not sharing this with Jake. I went into the Internet via your way – going into Network Neighborhood and what popped up automatically was your Hotmail inbox. So I peeked. Should we talk about this? It looked like you are hooking still ....but I trust what you've told us – that you're not. I don't know. I feel bad about peeking and I'm going to try and figure out how to get rid of the automatic entry. Let's talk about this.
I love you, Joelle

From: Elysia
To: Joelle
Subject: Re: ok, so I guess we're even.
Hi Hon,
Yes, well … what goes around comes around and I suppose we are even. I had it coming. Once again, things are not what they appear to be. I don't know if I can really explain this but I will try. Working was a game of cat and mouse. With quite a few of my clients I did not have sex. Believe it or not. A lot of them were friends who have been there for me in many different ways. I quit working before you and Jake came along and I have not worked since we met. I have not been with anyone else but you. I have no intention of going back to it for my own reasons regardless of what happens between us. This is the truth and I would not lie to you about it. Why would I? You have always said that whatever I decided would be ok. I would not jeopardize us for that! Or tricks or money! Having said this, it is obvious from my e-mails that I have been in contact with some of my old clients. It is/was part of the 'game.' Mostly I was feeling them out to see where I stood with them. I was leading them on and if I lead them on in a certain way … like I "need" them or "miss" them, they can be generous without me actually having to do anything or go anywhere. Basically, I was trying to trick them into coughing up some cash. (Now you know why tricks are called tricks) Sometimes just an email will 'stimulate' them into taking care of me for their own fucked up ego reasons. Is that working to you? It isn't to me, but

166

if you feel differently then please let me know. Believe me, I have plenty of opportunities to work. It has been hard to say no to the cash but I know that I will never have sex for money ever again! Even saying that to you is difficult for me. Admitting out loud, and in black and white that that is what I used to do gives me feelings of great SHAME and makes me feel really, really shitty about myself.

Nevertheless, I hope that you believe and understand what I have told you. Considering what we have been going thru lately I am sure that this has been difficult for you. I know that trust is a big issue right now for us all and this probably didn't help. As you know, it is hard to give each other the WHOLE picture.
I love you, from one peeker to another. Elysia

Of course she was concerned that I was lying to her about going back to escorting. Meanwhile, I was feeling; what the fuck is this all about? We went through all that 'trusting turmoil' because of what I did with Jake's e-mails and she did the same thing to me, only I'm supposed to pretend it's no big deal? They gave me hell and now a week later she was reading my e-mails? I asked her if she had told Jake. She hadn't. I demanded, "You better tell him what you did. I want to know what his fucking reaction's going to be." Apparently she didn't. I waited and there was nothing.

Two days passed. I went into my Internet chat line. Jake was online and we started chatting. I asked him what he thought of Joelle's snooping. He said, "I don't know what you're talking about." I told him what had happened. He indicated it was not her fault the e-mails popped up, that she couldn't help but read what the subject line was. My take was: "She got off on a technicality and I got the electric chair for basically the same crime." Jake's comment was, "Oh, I'm not real happy about it." I said, "What do you mean 'not real happy' about what she did? You fucking roasted me. And your wife goes and does a similar thing and it's not a big fucking deal?" Hello!

Whether she opened the actual e-mails or not is a technicality. She had opened up the network neighborhood and read what was there, rather than just closing it. And I know the temptation to peek and to look. Well, I was lambasted by Jake and told I was the fucking lying sneaking bitch and she got a slap on the wrist. As for hooking, I had nothing to hide from them. I didn't care about that. They knew all of my secrets. They knew the skeletons in my closet. Before this happened, we were planning a trip to California and I needed money to go. Joelle's mother was paying for their trip. I didn't have anybody to pay for mine. It was just me taking care of me. It's always about the money.

E-mail:
From: Elysia
To: Jake
Subject: STILL DEAD
Dear Jake,
So much has happened and been said and I guess it all just smarts still ...
ouch :(It seems when I bring things up with you, you've already had a chat
with Joelle about it. Having said that, I know I fucked up and I am
responsible for us being here but there are some things I am having a hard
time letting go. I take what you and Joelle say personally and to heart. (over-
emotional? Overly sensitive? Opposite of Ice Princess). There are no
conversations here, the sorting out, the healing/loving or any of the things
that we do for each other for comfort that would make this easier. (boo
fucking hoo as you put it.) I cannot help but wonder if the things you said
are really how you feel. Like having a second wife that you are not really sure
you want, and that the only way you're moving to Toronto would work for
you is if I was in Costa Rica. The most difficult thing was my thinking all
along that we had all wanted the same thing and reading that you didn't.
That you wanted me gone. That having me around for almost a month was
so difficult. That you wanted another girl around and if it was me, then that
was fine. (consolation prize) That at least if you had to leave me at some
point you wouldn't get a broken heart. There is usually a grain of truth to
things that are said out of anger and so far nothing has been taken back.
There has been no 'I'm sorry, I didn't mean that' so I have been left to
assume that you really do think that I have abandonment fears and that
there is an insane jealousy thing about me. You have referred to our future
in terms of "ridiculous emotional bullshit" and yet mostly it was your apathy
that really got me. How little you cared.

So now it turns out our Miss Joelle falls prey to the temptation to 'peek'
as she called it, and it is hardly even mentioned. In fact, not at all from you.
For someone who had such strong convictions and harsh words for me
regarding this issue, to not even hear a word about it from you I find
poignant.

You told me you have been thinking about me a lot. Honestly, I have no
idea what you are thinking or feeling or what I can/am prepared to believe.
With great love comes great heartache and last weekend was more than
enough. Joelle said you shoot to kill, I am out shopping for a coffin.
Love, Elysia

From: Joelle
To: Elysia
Subject: More thoughts.
Good morning,
I didn't sleep last night. I hope you're not pissed, it really was an accident,

which I did take care of (this computer will not get into inbox again). And frankly I don't want you to answer the questions I asked. They aren't my business since I shouldn't have seen anything AND I do trust you.

As weird as things are right now, Jake and I have been talking about what happened and our reactions to it. We are still excited about seeing you and being with you. In some ways, I think this was important to go through because it forced Jake and me to realize that if you are going to be included fully then we have to be aware of when we aren't being open. It occurred to me that you have been really open about when you haven't felt included and therefore we should be more open about when we do need time alone. Whether it's me and Jake or me and you or you and Jake. There is no reason why we shouldn't feel comfortable asking for that time. Being a duo instead of a trio doesn't diminish the quality of our relationship, but in fact might strengthen it. Does any of this make sense or am I just rambling?
Have a good day sweetheart!!!!
Love you, Joelle

In the broader picture, it had all started because they needed time alone. I finally understood that. I only saw within my point of view. I figured I was only with them for such a short period of time that I wanted us to be together all the time. I never realized otherwise. Joelle had a job to go to, Jake had his gigs and music business, and I had nowhere to go to prevent me from being in their face all the time. Certainly never occurred to me they didn't want me there.

After all this happened, Jake and I were chatting on an e-mail chat line when we decided to talk by phone. We planned our conversation for the next night because Joelle was going to be out. Jake told Joelle about our plan. It was time. The anger had melted away enough that we could actually speak to each other and say "I still love you and we need to clear things and make it okay." He called me and we had started talking when I heard Joelle's voice in the background. Jake said "Fuck, she's here. I really wish she wasn't because I really wanted to talk to you." He felt he couldn't with her there. We needed privacy too.

E-mail:
From: Jake
To: Elysia
Subject: Hey
Look, right now I'm really not sure what to say. I love you a lot, I really do, but we've gone really far, really fast. And as far as I'm concerned things just spun out of control. I hope we can work things out in the future if we give it some time. We both agree that we want you in our lives, but I'm not sure if living together is going to happen. I think we're going to have to wait until

after our trip to L.A. to figure things out. Joelle told me she invited you again to come and if you want to come then I think you probably should.

We should see each other to try and work things out. I just don't know how. I do think that all of this could be worth it. I don't know if we'll ever be able to get back to where we were. My mom always says that there are things that you say about people you love that they never need to hear, usually before she would say to me, "Jake, you stupid son of a bastard. You don't think I don't know?"

Anyway, try to keep a smile on your face.
Jake

From: Elysia
To: Jake
Subject: You must think I am nuts…
I dreamt about you all night last night and it was soooo real! It really fucked me up today. I don't know if I am supposed to turn to you or from you. I know that it's not your job to comfort me anymore but I am stuck between all this pain in my heart and wanting to have you in my life … knowing I should let go and not knowing how. So I am going on with my life and pretending that everything is fine, hoping that it will be one day. You know, I had a really good week. I am not completely devastated but today was a no-good-very-bad-day. I don't even know if I should e-mail you or tell you these things. I don't know what I am supposed to do or how to feel.
Love, Elysia

Things slowed down between us. There was no more talk about moving in together. There was no light at the end of my lonely tunnel where we were going to be one big happy family living together, sharing our lives. We again decided to meet in Los Angeles in a few weeks, since Jake had to attend a music conference there. I put a Band-Aid on temporarily, still hoping for the dream that, no matter what happened, we would find a way to be together. In truth, the milk had gone sour but we didn't have the heart to throw away the carton.

Thirteen

POLYAMORY - PART 2

Of course as it turned out, we kept trying. Jake's business trip to Los Angeles seemed like an excuse for us to get together and possibly do some healing. I flew in first and rented a sporty convertible. I checked into a suite at the Westin, had room service deliver some champagne on ice, and then went back to the airport to pick up Jake and Joelle. It was sunny and warm and it was really good to see them. Jake was Mr. Sherpa carrying his guitar and all the luggage. He greeted me right away with a big smile but he was loaded down, so he threw everything into the car and then came over to give me a big hug and kiss. He was very affectionate, extremely touchy-feely. In the car he put his hand on my leg while reaching over the seat to touch Joelle. We went back to the hotel. Though our issues were uncomfortably masked, our lust for each other remained strong and we enjoyed sex together. Afterwards, the munchies set in so while Joelle had a nap, Jake and I went for food. We drove around for about two hours talking. We drove through Hollywood and Beverley Hills in the warm sunshine with the top down.

He was the first one to say, "So you must be thinking about the e-mails." In fact, at the time I wasn't. I told him so. And then he said, "Well, maybe it's me then. It's on my mind and I really need to talk to you about it." He began to tell me what had gone on between Joelle and him after I left at Christmas.

He explained they had been having a rocky relationship before I came along, and problems had been building over the years. When I became involved, I made things better, but there was still an undercurrent of stuff between them. He told me when I was there for the three weeks, there were times when I would leave the room and he and Joelle would fight with each other. He said they would have a tense conversation and then when I came back into the room, they'd stop. I had no clue. None. They were really good at hiding it. The fact that they acted one way in front of me, and another way when I was out of the room, made me feel excluded. I began feeling like a fifth wheel. In fact, it pissed me off. I thought we were sharing a relationship. I was struggling to be a part of them. This was not having a relationship. This was not sharing. This was not their being honest with me. I said to Jake, "You should have told me you were fighting. I could have gone away for a while so you could have had a discussion to work it out." They never asked for time alone. They never asked me to go to the mall for a few hours. I felt like they were bullshitting me the whole time.

I was aware of trouble between them before I entered the picture. Joelle had once said, "You showed me again the good qualities in Jake. You made me value our relationship again." So now I was thinking that the only reason they kept me around was because I made their relationship sunshiny and nice again. When I was not around, apparently they were fighting.

He continued to unmask his feelings as we aimlessly drove around. He said the serious problems between them basically came to a head when I left after Christmas. He unburdened his thoughts. Joelle had liked me so much right away that it had made him suspicious. She had seen how attracted he was to me and when she, all of a sudden, had come onboard so quickly he thought it was all too easy, that maybe she was somehow faking it. Basically he felt that she was trying to buy him off by giving him 'me,' in exchange for him giving her a baby. That was his suspicion and that's why they were fighting so much.

Joelle never said as much to me. I don't know it to be true. But I did know she wanted a baby and that it was her idea and not his. I got the impression her biological clock was ticking and she was ready for a baby even though he wasn't.

What I did know was that they were not using protection. Jake would come inside of her, but not inside of me. They knew I was not on the pill. We had never discussed my having a baby and I realized I probably didn't have the option. It would be Joelle that would bring the children into this relationship because that was how Jake wanted it. I knew I probably didn't want a child, but I silently questioned whether I wanted the option taken away. I felt like the toast on the side plate that doesn't get the butter.

As we continued our aimless driving, Jake tried to explain further. I remember he was telling me the e-mail wasn't true, that it was said out of anger towards Joelle to basically hurt her in their fighting. He said I read the e-mail on the eve of them making up. That day they had sat down and both expressed their desire for me in their relationship, equally. They had just worked it all out that very day. They had come to believe each other's words of love for each other and for me and had renewed their desire for our threesome. There seemed to be no foundation for suspicion.

I knew there would be a price for reaching out. I still felt there was foundation in what was said in the e-mail. I remembered his words to her, "Here you're doing this and I don't even know if I want it." I felt disillusioned. I could barely breathe.

He said he was sorry I'd read all that stuff. He said he really did love me and was willing to do whatever it took to prove it to me. I apologized to him for invading his privacy by going into his e-mail and compromising the trust between us. I think for him, it really became water under the bridge. I'm the type who keeps dealing with problems, re-evaluating, re-living them longer than I should. To him, our conversation was closure. I was left 'guarding' myself. For me, it reopened a whole lot of other issues, which I never got to talk to him about.

We returned to the hotel and our room. Joelle asked us what had taken so long, since we were initially going for burgers and coming right back. When we explained we had talked about the e-mails she said, "Oh, that's good. I'm glad you guys talked. You needed to." Joelle and I discussed it later. She understood how difficult it had been for me. She was full of forgiveness. But now I was starting to get suspicious. Was Jake right? Was she forgiving me because she needed to know all the facts so she could control me and Jake and our lives so she can get what she wanted? I did apologize to her for hurting her. I needed to do that because I knew she was really hurt too and it was important to apologize for the sake of my own conscience.

When I think back, I can't remember any fun moments or even the things we did, except I did love driving around in a convertible with the top down. But I do remember conversations and feeling a need to protect myself from any more disappointment.

Jake planned to stay longer in LA than Joelle and me. I purposely booked my flight home two days before Joelle was to fly back to Boston.

I did that because of the e-mail where he expressed not having time alone with her. I made sure it was clear to them that I would be leaving early so they could have time alone. They had the opportunity to say, "No, we want you to stay until the end." It didn't happen. And neither one of them expressed a need to leave early so I could be alone with one of them. What did happen was that Jake agreed he would fly to see me in Toronto for a week before heading home to Boston and Joelle. We thought this was a good time for Jake and me to spend some time alone.

E-mail:
From Elysia
To: Jake
Subject: You're home? What?
Hi There, I hope you are home safe and sound.
Take care, Elysia

From: Jake
To: Elysia
Subject: Re: You're home? What?
Hey Elysia,
Yes, I'm home. Sorry I haven't called. I wasn't sure if you wanted to speak to me right now. I know how upset you must be about my coming straight home. Life has really been fucking strange the last few months. I just really regret that I couldn't come to see you. And that my needing to come home hurt you. I do love you Elysia, I really do. I'd love to come and visit you sometime soon if the offer is still open. I still think we need some time to talk through all this stuff together. Jake.

From: Elysia
To: Jake
Subject: Re: You're home? What?
Dear Jake,
I am glad you are home safe and sound. I didn't realize that you 'needed to go home,' you never told me that. Why did you need to go home? That is different than feeling the ticket price wasn't worth paying, which is why I thought you aren't here. I am so afraid to talk to you … to say anything at all … it just seems to cause problems.
Elysia

From: Jake
To: Elysia
Subject: Our relationship
Look, I have to say something once and for all here. I don't think the words, "I want you to come home," ever escaped Joelle's mouth. But truthfully, I

don't think it matters what she said - but it went something more like, "I need you, go to Elysia's but come straight home." Whatever it was, it was my decision not to come to you. Whatever else she may or may not have said is meaningless for one reason. She is my wife and that means (I'm sorry to have to put it like this) that my first loyalty is to her and it always will be, no matter what. I told you that at Club Erotica. That's the way it's always been and that's the way it will always be. I'm sorry if you didn't know that, but I know I said it to you. Yes, I really wanted to come to see you. Yes, I really wanted to spend time with you. Yes, the idea of you spending all that money on a ticket for me to come there seemed a little excessive. But the truth of it, when you get down to it, was that she told me she needed me and I knew that the only place I belonged at that moment was with her. I'm sorry that I didn't tell you at that time but I knew how you'd take it. And besides that, the money was a factor. I do care about you. I do love you but Joelle is and always has been the love of my life. I told you at the Club that it shouldn't go any further than what it was. And I never should have let it go this far. I really wanted to have all the things that we talked about — the three of us being together — and I let myself get caught up in those dreams even though part of me always suspected that they were just that. I know that we both love you and that we both want you in our lives. But it's up to you to decide now if that's what you want anymore and, if so, how. I'm sorry that it has to be like this. I wanted our lives to be like they were when we visited you in Toronto and at Christmas, but now I don't know if that's possible. I love you and I wish I could be there to say this in person so I could hold you and comfort you in some way. Please don't be angry at Joelle. It isn't her fault. I take all the blame for this. Joelle is too naive and honestly thought that our long distance thing would be easy.
Jake

From: Elysia
To: Joelle
Subject: Fw: Our relationship.
Dear Joelle,
There I was in the middle of booking a ticket to Boston thinking "Fuck it, if Jake couldn't come here, I'll go to you. I was thinking nothing else matters when I received this e-mail from Jake. There is nothing left that needs to be said. I truly love you more than you will ever know.
Be well, be happy,
Elysia

* * *

It was then, they found out they were pregnant. We all thought it was really good news.

E-mail:
From: Elysia xoxo
To: Jake
Subject: Now you really will be 'Daddy'
Dear Jake,
Congratulations!! Wow. Right now I am thinking WOW! YEA!! A BABY!
.... Immediately followed by feeling incredibly far away and not at all a part
of all the happiness and love you must be experiencing. I just sit here missing
everything! It's really hard. I am sorry! I know you don't want to hear this
stuff. I am very happy and very excited and a lot of other stuff too, just
climbing the walls a little. Missing you terribly! Just missing out. I am really
happy for you and Joelle and your new baby! You will be an incredible
family and YOU will be an awesome dad!
I don't know what else to say right now, the future seems so uncertain for
us.
I love you, Elysia

From: Jake
To: Elysia
Subject: Now you really will be 'Daddy'
Thank You Darlin'
I am really happy, more than I thought I would be. The sky is a little bluer,
the clouds puffier, etc...... Listen, as far as feeling uncertain about us, the
only thing I ask is that you try to take things one day at a time right now.
Let's get together and when we're face to face with each other in the same
room we can go from there.
Like I said before Elysia, I don't want you out of my life. I want to have
a romantic and sexual relationship with you. If YOU can handle it. I do not
want to put you back into the position where you feel alienated and lonely
and depressed because we live so far away from each other. If you want and
can handle a long distance relationship with me/us, then I think we should
continue. But that's the question that I have to pose to you. Can you handle
it? And is it something that you'd even want to try? Because I know how
hard it's been on you all this time. I love you too much and at this point I'd
rather endure the pain of losing you before taking the chance of ever hurting
you again (maybe because I feel like I deserve it).
I love you and miss you,
Jake

From: Elysia
To: Jake
Subject: BRAIN EXPLODED ....
Hey, hon,
Wow, talk about blowing me out of the water. I thought you did not want

to continue our relationship. I thought that is why I/we are going through all this heartache. I thought you felt you could not give me what I wanted and that you just could not be there for me as my lover/boyfriend (whatever). That I was not the one for you or you for me because Joelle is the love of your life. I am truly confused! I do not know what to think or feel. Have I missed something along the way? It seems you have changed your mind. Maybe not … if Joelle is and always will be the love of your life, then where does that leave me/us? You thought I was insecure before, imagine how I feel/felt after your "Joelle is the love of my life" e-mail. Your e-mail was pretty clear about who is most important to you. I do not think I can live with being second-best and knowing that you will always choose her over me. Who is going to choose me? I know you love me! I was there, I felt it! Help me Jake … I don't know what to do or what is true or real or how I am to exist within your relationship with Joelle. If you still want me, then why did we just go through this?

Oh fuck, Jake! I love you so much! I don't know what to do! This is so crazy. I wish I could see you. I wish I could just tell you to fuck off and leave me alone. I wish I could just walk away but I fucking can't! Am I weak, a fucking idiot? Or just a girl in love?

I am okay, Jake, just confused and scared. I just want you to love me and for us to be happy.
Love, Elysia xoxo

* * *

SURPRISE

Well, I certainly can't claim our relationship was functional. Believe it or not, after many phone calls and e-mails the three of us decided we didn't want to give up on 'us.' The dust settled again, so to speak. Jake called me several times to make a big blanket apology for changing his mind so much, for being unsure, and for being unclear as to how he really felt about me. He really was sorry. I knew Joelle understood and we grew very close through our many discussions. I trusted her. We supported each other. Really, whatever disharmony existed was between Jake and me. I decided to visit them again.

Jake didn't know I was coming. It was to be a complete surprise. Joelle and I cooked up a plan and she promised to keep it a secret, which was normally difficult for her to do. About an hour before I was to arrive, she blindfolded him and tied him to the bed with handcuffs. She then proceeded to cook dinner, with plans for candlelight, soft music, and a whole night of fooling around. The only thing she told him was that someone was coming. Unfortunately for Jake, my plane was three hours late. He was going crazy waiting, cuffed to the bed all that time.

Well, he deserved it. Joelle tantalized him with kisses of wine, from her mouth to his. He eagerly sucked it in. Of course he was starving too. To her credit, she still didn't tell him.

I arrived and secretly put on lacy scarlet lingerie. I tiptoed to him and immediately began giving him a blow job. When my hair fell on his leg, he knew, though he didn't say anything. I crawled up and kissed him. I knew as soon as I kissed him, he would know. I started to giggle. We were all bubbling with happiness. We experienced a sense of relief. He insisted I uncuff him and take off his blindfold, which I took my time doing. A little bit of torture was good! From then on it was all ebb and flow with everyone taking a turn in the middle. We were limited sexually only by our imaginations. We laughed lots as Jake directed us to try to different positions in every combination of upside down, in the middle, or all around positions and to try and turn at the same time. There were no limits. We tied each other up. There was lots of stuff going on and it was fun, really fun. Dinner became breakfast. Sex had never been a problem. Sex had always been deliciously pleasurable. We concentrated on that.

We make jokes about equipment maintenance because Jake has a very high libido. He's a nympho. He has stamina and control too. It's kind of like everybody gets a turn with Jake finishing last. That's usually how it goes. We laughed that Jake was a walking horn dog. He admitted it. No bones about it! He just accepted that's the way he was and if he didn't get Joelle or me to help him, he'd take care of it himself.

Joelle expressed to me that she thought perhaps I wanted sex more than she did. And I said to her, "That's only because you're together all the time. The buffet is always open. It isn't for me. So when I'm with you guys, I'm always wanting it, whereas if I was constantly with you, I probably wouldn't want it as much either. I only get a limited amount of time."

E-mail:
From: Joelle
To: Elysia
Subject: Visit
Hey Sweetie,
I just wanted to let you know again how wonderful it was to have you here. It was/is really important to me that we were able to spend some time and get to re-know each other. As I said the other day I truly do cherish you and our time together. I don't know how you have managed to do it, because there is little in your life experience that says you should, but you have

managed to remain one of the sweetest, most generous people I know. I love
you and will talk to you soon. Joelle.

So we recovered but with a new perspective. Maybe. My mind
expected less though my heart didn't. Really, the distance in our
relationship was a killer of sorts. When I was home in Toronto, so many
things came up where I should have been included in the discussions,
the compromises, and whatever happened around the issues. Whatever
the topic, it was all handled without me. I got the done deal. I got the
edited version and I didn't like that. We talked about it. Our
compromise was to continue to communicate by phone, e-mail, and an
Internet chat site everyday.

Even with our renewed commitment, with time our relationship
evolved into the growing pains of reality, just like all relationships.
Things I had overlooked in the excitement of discovery, I began to
notice. I wished we could have continued forever as in those first
months of falling in love. I yearned to still believe in life-everlasting in
our home-style Hollywood video lives.

At some point I became aware of a silent uneasiness. I realized I was
naïve in thinking that love would easily blend me into their fifteen-year-
old relationship. I guess I chose to ignore that reality for months, and I
needed to remind myself I was still the 'new' guy in this relationship. I
didn't have the history.

Now when we were together, I began to notice they were whispering.
I could feel my breathing tighten with concern. I was always aware when
they were together in another room, or in bed together without me.
When I was alone in the bath, I couldn't help but wonder. I could hear
them whispering or kissing. I would think, 'What are they talking
about? Are they talking about me?' I felt really left out and it bothered
me, though I never said anything to them about it. I just let them have
their time but I was always very aware of any space between us.

I started to realize the whispering happened with all of us. Jake said
things to me that Joelle didn't hear, she said things to me that he didn't
hear, and I said things to both of them the other didn't hear. I told
myself it was okay. I reassured myself they're not talking about me, and
if they are, they should have the right to do that, just like I should be
able to do with each of them. As much as I knew it was unrealistic to
believe we could be equal in openness and sharing, my head and heart
still rebelled.

I never concentrated on having sex with only one of them when we were together in bed. But now they sometimes forgot about me when they were making love, even though I was in bed beside them. I don't think it was a conscious thing. They had sex together in a way that has taken fifteen years to develop. I call it the J & J zone, when they are totally lost in each other. It's very intense. It's as if a wall goes up. All of a sudden I would hit it, see it, and feel it and I could see how totally they were into each other. When that happened I would retreat emotionally. I ran away. I've actually gotten up out of the bed and left them there. They have no clue. It made me feel really insecure and jealous and slightly shameful, like 'Oh my God, I can't believe it.' I thought it was me, my fault, my problem. They don't know how much it hurts me. They can't help it, maybe. They think that it should be okay.

But of course it wasn't okay to me. They should have done that when I was not lying there. They should have gone into the zone when it was just the two of them. Otherwise, someone was going to be excluded. Me, I was excluded. I felt I needed to roll over and wait until they were done.

I remember one time when I got up and walked away. It was snowing. It was cold outside and cold in the bed because they were in their J & J zone. I got up and dressed and left the house in the snow. All I had on was leggings, boots and a winter fur coat. I was nude under the coat. I was miserable and I had nowhere to go. It was awful. I walked and walked. When I returned, Jake was really pissed off. He said, "I don't understand why you do that, why you got up and walked away like that." He accused me of being jealous when he's having sex with his wife. But it wasn't that, the three of us were in bed and I was not included. I felt like an intruder. I would never zone them out but they would me, and I thought it rude. I couldn't help it. It was this "Joelle is my whole life" shit that had started to creep again between the sheets of our relationship. I told him I didn't need to lie there and watch him fuck his wife in their zone. I said it was important when we're all together and making love to include each of us, all at the same time.

We talked, I tried to make them aware of this J & J wall. Jake didn't understand, even though I carefully explained it to him. He claimed they always tried to include me, to make me feel loved and wanted. Joelle understood. I had seen her do the same thing, turn away when Jake and I were in sexual 'La la Land' but I didn't let it happen. I always reached for her. Jake explained they were used to watching each other have sex with other people. Jake had no problem watching Joelle and I make love without him. He'd been watching her have sex with other women for years. It was comfortable for them but not for me.

I questioned myself. Was I being excluded or was I being too sensitive? I remember we were sitting together in the living room when Jake's band partner called. Jake and I were sitting together on the couch and Joelle was sitting in a chair across the room. She answered the phone and had a heated conversation with him. He must have called her a loser or something, because she told him to fuck off and hung up on him. Jake and Joelle started a conversation about it. He got up off the couch and sat down on the floor at her feet, looking up at her while discussing what was going on with him and his partner. I thought, 'Am I invisible? Is there some reason why you can't have this conversation with both of us? Is there a reason for excluding me? Could you not say, hey you guys, this is what I'm thinking. What am I? Fucking chopped liver here?' I got up and left the room. I immediately kicked myself for allowing my first reaction to affect me SO MUCH. I thought 'Now, okay wait. Maybe I need to give them the space to do this, to be able to talk to just each other.' But I couldn't get the image of Jake physically removing himself from the couch to isolate himself in conversation with only her. He'd dropped to his knees to talk to her about his feelings! Doubts were creeping in and I couldn't help it.

At one point I asked them if they felt our relationship was changing. I asked Jake specifically if he felt it was different, if he still felt happy about us. He rolled his eyes and said, "You know, you think too much" and blew me away with dismissal. I thought, 'Here I am trying to have a relationship, trying to communicate my feelings and I am invalidated by being told not to feel that way.' I didn't get 'Gees, I can see something is bothering you. You seem upset. What is it? Let's talk about it.'

Upon returning to Toronto and, as fate would time it, the jeweler called Joelle to say my ring was finished. The third wedding/bonding ring. They decided to fly to Toronto to bring it to me. I rented a private cabin on a lake in the woods, complete with an outdoor hot tub. I filled the car with food, extra blankets, champagne, and fruit juices for Joelle. She was obviously pregnant now and I wanted to do whatever I could to make our retreat enjoyable. We walked in the woods, luxuriated in the hot tub and went rowing on the lake. One night, near the end of our week and our last night on the lake, the three of us were sitting on the deck under the stars having dinner. Joelle said to Jake, "It's in the outside pocket. Why don't you get it?" I knew it was the ring since she had told me they were going to bring it. I had wondered if they had

181

forgotten but decided they were probably waiting to do something special, to make it an event. After all, this was my ring to signify our dedication to each other. Jake walked to their suitcase, which was behind me. I felt excited but apprehensive. He walked back around the table and stood beside Joelle seated across from me.

From across the table, Jake literally threw the ring box in front of me. Thwack. I was shocked. He said, "Here, I think this is yours." It was still in the plain brown box from the jeweler. It wasn't wrapped. I opened it, after I realized they would not do it for me. I was nervous and anxious to see what was inside. There it was. I turned it over in my hands, noticing the candlelight flicker tiny sparkles off three heads entwined in a vine of hearts. I hesitated looking at them, wondering what would happen next. I waited. Finally Joelle said, "Now you're stuck." She was kind of cute, in her own way. That was it. No sweetness or romance. I knew then they wouldn't place the ring on my finger, so I did it myself. Joelle kissed the ring and smiled at me. Jake did the same and that was it. Nothing more. Could it be any less? I had a ring now. To me it represented the love that we shared, the love that brought us together and kept me 'stuck' for almost a year. It was supposed to remind me there were two people far away who loved me. It was meant to represent a unique relationship, our circle of love and caring.

I waited. I needed to hear what it meant to them. No more words were said. I realized no one was going to say anything else. I said, "Oh, there it is." I looked at it and tried to see the three shiny figures surrounded with hearts through my controlled tears.

Am I married? NO. Am I a wife? NO. Are they committed to me? Will I always just be "the girlfriend?" Am I just a girlfriend? What is my title anyway? Mistress, concubine, soul mate, partner, playmate, stuckee? What am I to them? How do I define myself in terms of us so that I feel such a belonging that I can thumb my nose at the world of judgment? Yet here I am with a copy of their wedding ring on my finger. We are still chasing after happiness. We are still trying to find a place in a world that looks at us as 'sinners' and me a 'fool.' It's not the ring I wanted. It was the emotions that solicited the giving that mattered…

Joelle's comment kept ringing in my ears. "Now you're stuck." I think I laughed. I know I was stunned. I thought, 'I guess that's what I'll tell people when they ask me about my ring.' I'll say, "Oh, yeah, I got stuck." I was disappointed. Maybe they had already done their 'ring ceremony' thing when they got married. Maybe they had forgotten that in the beginning of a new relationship you make things special. You buy flowers and court that person and when you propose to somebody or give them a ring, you make a big deal of it.

I didn't make a big deal out of their not doing anything more. I let it go. I didn't want negativity to hang around the ring. Perhaps we all knew something had been lost. Jake was not really there. Something had been lost along the way in transition and I had refused to accept it.

Later when we were alone, I asked Joelle if something had happened with Jake. She said, "I sense it, but I don't really know either." She surmised that perhaps it was because when she became pregnant his friends started giving him a hard time about me. "You're married. You have a baby on the way. What are you doing with a girlfriend?"

I figured that was what drove him to write the letter to me where he said Joelle was the love of his life and to basically dump me. After that he realized it wasn't over. What his friends had tried to get him to believe was not how he felt. Joelle was the glue that held us together, and she expressed that they had come to a place where they wanted me, accepted me as a part of their relationship. She said they wanted me to come for the baby's birth and to stay for an extended period of time. This was an acceptance I had not experienced nor seen. I had not heard the words. I had not been reassured and I wanted more than being "stuck." I thought, 'Oh, wait a minute. I'm not trusting this relationship. I'm not so sure.' I was not part of the process. They were leaving again for Boston. I was still expected to stay in Toronto. I needed Jake to prove he really wanted me. I knew Joelle did. For me, the ring giving had left a whirlpool of doubt. Jake needed to know that I no longer trusted him and he needed to work at changing that.

This was my first time in a ménage à trois. This was not their first time, but they told me I was different. Now it didn't feel like I was any different. I felt like another pair of shoes they tried on and decided didn't fit but weren't ready to toss out. That's what it felt like. The shoes are just a little too tight, not quite enough room, but still desirable enough to keep. He thought he was a big man. He thought he could handle it and he couldn't. He couldn't even handle her. She handled him. If she hadn't wanted me, it would never have happened. In the end, he would do anything to please her.

No matter what I was feeling, I hid it from them. I tried to go back to a life without them. I kept reminding myself what Jake had said in the beginning, "I can't be your boyfriend. I'm married. I can't be with you." Without them, I felt so empty and lonely. I realized I couldn't be committed to a relationship that was half with them and half without. I couldn't have it casual anymore. It was not just a booty call. I couldn't live that way. I had to be either in it or completely out of it. It's too hard to love and be loved long-distance.

We backed off, which was mostly my own doing because I decided I was no longer going to chase them. They were going to have to prove to me they wanted me by making some kind of effort because it was always me who phoned, me who wrote, me who e-mailed. I hit the brakes. I said to myself, "That's it. I'm not doing that anymore."

Weeks passed. The three of us hardly exchanged e-mails. We never phoned. We never wrote. Nothing. Our communication had pretty much dwindled away. I was painfully alone.

I decided that I needed to get on with my life. A client gave me a guitar and I took lessons. I joined a yoga class and began working out in the local gym. I tried to make new friends with the people I met in those classes. I kept my life as busy as I could. I pushed the desire to wallow in the pain right out of my mind. I had to find a way out. I applied for a nursing job. I was seriously trying to get over them and get past us.

Then one day I got a phone call from Jake. He told me he had just returned from a gig in Ohio where he had been thinking about me a lot. He told me he really missed me and wanted me to come to Boston for his birthday, which was less than two weeks away. He totally threw me off. I tried not to respond. I said things like, "Well maybe, okay, well you know, we'll see." I wasn't going to go crazy over the idea. So I hung up the phone and, of course, I immediately started getting excited, really happy and thinking I should go. My brain was buzzing, 'This is going to be great.'

I considered this might be an opportunity for me to try out my new perspective. So, I thought, 'Okay, fine. Obviously, they're always going to be married. They're always going to be J & J. Now there's going to be the baby. Our relationship is not going to be what I had hoped. And that's okay.' I was getting to the point of just accepting it.

I wanted to believe that everything we had experienced couldn't have been for nothing. I hoped, at the very least, we could be friends. I remembered when Ian and I broke up, it seemed so sad to have all that anger and to walk away from a three-year relationship without being friends. I wanted there to be some way, as adults, that we could come to some kind of friendship, without the punishing unkindness of dissolving it in anger. I guess I was trying to be a mature person. I told myself I could be okay with the fact that they're married and I'm not part of it. I told myself that it didn't take away from the value I had in their life or theirs in mine. It just wasn't going to be that three-way-marriage couple thing that we had agreed to. Who was I kidding? I still couldn't get the "couple" out of my "three-way-marriage" vocabulary. Go figure.

I phoned an airline and realized that the ticket would be around $1500, since it was less than two weeks. I was devastated. It would be absurd to spend that kind of money. I went from guarded on the phone call, to ecstasy, to devastation in a matter of an hour. My emotions were out of control. I tried to come to grips with my wanting to go after the last rejection. Then I wondered how he could have invited me at the last minute, knowing I needed more time to book a plane reservation. I realized the invitation was on the spur of the moment. I figured he had called to talk and it had occurred to him then. I decided he was going to have to prove to me he really wanted me by asking me at least one more time to come. And he did. He phoned several times a day for three or four days. If I was out, he left a message. I could hear in his voice that he really wanted me to come. All of a sudden the wheels changed again. He wanted me. But I didn't book it right away. I waited. I was worried because I might be setting myself up again for pain. I thought, 'This is not okay. I need to get a grip.' I sat on it for two days and then booked the ticket.

I went with the intention not to re-start, not to re-build, and not to fix what was broken. I wanted to take the next step in my life: to heal and restore my emotional sanity. I wanted to forgive him because I blamed him for everything. He started it. He came after me. I blamed it all on him. At the time, that's how I saw it.

When I first arrived, Jake was at a gig. Joelle welcomed me with open arms but we were walking on eggshells, so to speak. We were both guarded. Joelle later told me that she and Jake had agreed it was either going to be really great or bomb. I mostly thought myself an idiot to even continue to consider a relationship with them as a possibility. But I was drawn to them like dust being sucked up in a vacuum. I kept coming back to wondering why I was there, why I needed to see them. I told myself it was because they were important to me, because I loved them both. Even so, I knew things were going to be different. I knew I was asking too much.

When Jake returned that night, the magnetic sexual attraction settled all my questions for a while at least. That hadn't changed. It started in the kitchen when he put his arm around me and kissed me. He was such a good kisser. Soon all three of us were in bed and all thoughts of any problems were immaterial. At some point, after we had satisfied ourselves, Joelle went to the kitchen for some food. Jake turned to me and told me how happy he was that I was there. He said he really did love me and missed me in his life. He apologized for changing his mind so much. He thanked me for forgiving him. I wanted to blurt out 'What makes you think I forgave you?' but didn't. I was completely on guard the whole time. He assumed because I came to Boston I had forgiven him.

We did all the same things as in other visits. We hung out in the apartment. We drank coffee, watched movies, and went for walks. It was always more than just the sex. I think the caring was the thing that kept pulling us back together. We still felt it, especially between Joelle and me.

The night before Jake's party, we discussed doing some ecstasy, which a friend was bringing to the party. I had done it before at 'rave' parties in Toronto and told Jake to include me. His birthday party was Saturday night at a local club. The place was packed with his friends. An old friend of theirs, named Cybil, was there too. The week before my arrival, she had been staying with them. She was attending a drug rehab program and was in recovery from drugs and alcohol. Joelle told me that Jake had told Cybil she had to leave because I was expected. Apparently she asked Jake what the big deal was with me and asked him if he was going to get laid. He had said, "No, no. It's not about that. I could fuck you if I wanted to." Those were his exact words. When I heard that, it made me feel good because sometimes I felt I was just his fuck toy. That night at the party Cybil gave 'Ice Princess' a new meaning. She gave me major shade. And I thought I was the mistress of the cold shoulder! Everyone else was warm and friendly and happy to meet me. Cybil could barely look at me. Not that I cared.

We were all hanging around listening to the music when Jake announced he had the ecstasy. He looked over at Cybil and offered her some. Actually he had to make an effort to turn away from me and lean over to offer her some. She took the ecstasy. So much for rehab. She said, "Don't tell Joelle." She was in recovery from drugs and alcohol and all of a sudden Jake's giving her 'E' and she's asking us to not tell anybody.

I didn't give a shit about Cybil and her drugs but I did give a shit that Jake didn't offer me any. I thought, 'OK, FINE.' It pissed me off.

Maybe he wasn't paying attention to me the day before when I said I wanted some. I tried to calm myself. It wasn't about not getting the drug. I thought, 'They're high, whatever. It's his birthday and he can do whatever he wants.' I tried not to care. I purposely stayed fairly sober and just smoked pot and had a couple of drinks. Cybil circled Jake like a cheetah hunting prey. More need not be said of my amusement level.

Later that evening we were downstairs partying after the music ended. It was a recreation room in the club where everybody sits and parties. Jake, Joelle and I were sitting on a sofa when the girlfriend of one of Jake's friends walked in. Jake yelled at the top of his lungs in front of everybody, "Hey, Sarah, I want you to meet my wife, Joelle." He didn't introduce me. Didn't even think of introducing me. I had to get up and go over to the woman and say, "Hi, my name's Elysia. I'm a friend of Jake and Joelle's."

As we were outside the club preparing to leave, Cybil started walking towards me, looked at me, turned around and went right back to Jake and started kissing him. She planted one on, tongue and everything. And he responded. I saw it as premeditated, hell, she could have come and peed on my clothes for how I felt. He was kissing her with his eyes open while he was watching Joelle and me flag down a cab. At that moment, if I could have blinked myself back into Toronto, I would have. My brain screamed, 'You fucking prick. You fucking selfish mother fucker.' I was furious. He didn't get it. He still had no clue how I felt about kissing.

Joelle and I got into a cab while this was going on. Joelle didn't see it and I didn't tell her. Cybil finished kissing him and walked over to say good night to Joelle. She gave her a hug and a kiss goodbye. She didn't even acknowledge me. I played Miss Control. She was nothing to me.

The next morning Joelle and I were talking about Cybil giving me shade. Jake was there and said, "Really? She did? Every time Cybil and I ran into each other, we would start necking." The look on Joelle's face was shock and surprise. Jake continued, "She wasn't doing it because she liked me or loved me or because I'm her best friend." I got the impression they hadn't gotten along before. Cybil was playing some kind of fucked-up game. I didn't care what she was up to. But I sure as hell cared what Jake was thinking. Then Jake looked over his shoulder at me and he said, "Please don't be mad at me for kissing another girl."

I tried not to show my heartache. To me, our relationship had transformed into accepting reality, and the reality was that Jake didn't honor my feelings enough to NOT kiss other girls, or at the very least to not kiss girls in front of me. I didn't care how stoned he was, I didn't care if it was his birthday, and I didn't care who the woman was, but I sure as hell cared about his lack of respect for me. He added insult to injury when he asked me not to get mad at him, to just blow it off that he was necking with another girl. To me, that said he knew he was wrong and did it anyway.

It hurt and disgusted me. Before I came, I knew I was not choosing the best emotional path for myself. Now, there was no question. I talked to Joelle about it. She wanted our marriage/relationship to work as she had envisioned it in the first place. She said she felt at the mercy of Jake and me. I told her I was not willing to invest myself emotionally while standing on such unstable ground. We agreed we were at a really shitty place to be.

Joelle was better able to deal with our relationship than Jake. She was able to be his wife and my girlfriend at the same time without letting either one of us feel she was taking away from the other. I never questioned her intentions with me, or my place with her. The trouble was always Jake. I think he felt if he was giving to me, he was taking something away from Joelle, that somehow he wasn't being loyal to her. He never said that to me. That's just my gut feeling.

I was to leave on Friday. Jake took Thursday off so we could be alone together that last day. I ended up covered in hickeys and rug burn. I mean, the sex was great, as always. We were extremely passionate. We didn't really talk about anything of significance.

I want to believe we communicate in other ways besides lovemaking. But honestly, that's how we communicated. We showed we loved each other through sex. Direct communication was never easy. But then, I guess, direct communication for me with any man has never been easy. It was easier for both of us to express our connection through sex than to talk about what we wanted our non-sexual relationship to be. Perhaps other than sex and Joelle, we never really had anything in common. We had a connection of sorts but his heart was already taken, his life already full.

Friday Jake came home around 7:30 PM. Since my flight left later that night, we had a very short time to say a final good-bye. The three of us laid around on the bed, holding each other. There really wasn't much to say because we were all on the same page in that we had all realized we weren't there to rebuild. I think we were there to be friends.

I think we wanted to feel the love that was left, rather than all the hurt.

After awhile Joelle said, "Okay, well, I'm going to take the dog out." I knew she didn't need to take the dog out. She did it so Jake and I could be together and say a final goodbye. When she left, nothing happened. We just kind of clung to each other. He thanked me for the gifts I had given him for his birthday; the CD's, the liquor, and the music equipment. He thanked me for loving him and said it meant a lot to him that I had come for his birthday. He was sincere.

* * *

When we first met and fell in love in Club Erotica we were all living in dreamland, a fairytale land where we based our relationship on fantasy. I will say we really believed it would work and believed we wanted the same things. Each of us was trying to please another, but not equally and not for the same reason. Jake wanted to please Joelle who wanted a woman in her life. I wanted to belong in loving permanent relationship. The sex was so fantastic for all of us that we dreamed we could each have a slice of the pie. To this day I'm not sure what destroyed it. Certainly Jake ended the relationship as it was. He delivered the wake-up call. A 'Look, this is really what's going on here' kind of thing. I lived in another city, he was married to the love of his life, and they were going to have a baby. I guess it boiled down to Jake not being able to share Joelle in that framework, and her commitment to Jake still took precedence over me. I needed to be able to see that and see beyond the rejection.

I guess, all along, I felt threatened by their relationship and their marriage. I didn't feel as important, as validated, or as an equal third. It wasn't balanced. My hope was that my relationship individually with each of them was going to be just as important, just as significant, as theirs was with each other. I hoped our relationship, as a three, would replace their relationship as a two. Instead, I felt like a group of two and a group of one that sometimes came together to make a three. We all acknowledged I couldn't compete with fifteen years of a friendship and six years of marriage. I kept trying to scream from the mountaintop, "Here I am. Me too, me too, me too." I was not willing to give up my life for that.

E-mail:
From: Jake
To: Elysia
Subject: Hey

I miss you very much, I'm about to do something that I've been putting off for at least a month. I'm going to the post office to mail you a box with the rest of your stuff, which I'm sure you'll be happy to get (since it is your stuff) but it's depressing the shit out of me. It feels FINAL. And I don't like it, not one bit. I don't know how we came to this, every couple of days I find myself trying to chart where things went wrong and I can never really seem to figure it out. So the sky is gray here. It's unseasonably warm and yet still really fucking cold, nothing but dirt weed and bad porn. And I miss you and your cucumber on ham sandwiches and you walking around in your pretty pink p.j.'s and rolling doobs. So watch your mail for your stuff cause I swear I'm gonna get to the post office today if it kills me and it just might.
Jake.

I'm trying not to blame either one of them. I believed Joelle honestly struggled with how to make 'us' work. But I knew by then it was their home, their life and that I would be the guest. All our wonderful plans had deteriorated into that. They were just being themselves. We all took a chance. It was great while it lasted. I tried not to think about them with too much emotion. I wanted to be an Ice Princess again who could be very severe, detached, cold, and distance myself from anything. For some reason, with them, I just let it all go and was completely open. I would have done anything to have our relationship work. But clearly, this was the final, painful debilitating rejection. I was like a pendulum, right? I could swing either way but with them I swung too far from the Ice Princess.

I knew I needed to at least try and find somebody else, but emotionally I was not ready to date again. I was a basket case. At that time it occurred to me that I did not want to have sex with another man unless it was a man I loved and who loved me. The thought of another guy touching me, after eighteen years of on and off escorting, well, if I never had to look at another fucking guy's dick, except for the man I love, well, I would have been okay with that. I mean a part of me still needed stimulation, I am human, but I'd had enough sex in my life that I didn't need to go running around dating and screwing guys. I knew I wanted the commitment Jake and Joelle shared. The kind of committed partner that makes life livable and makes the journey meaningful.

I painfully put all our stuff, tokens of memories, the ring, other jewelry, pictures, and all the music into a box. I had to move on.

I suppose the 'lesson' of having them in my life is that I needed to learn how to communicate with a man other than sexually, to start with the non-sexual relationship first. Build on that first. I realized I had a need for reassurance and affirmation of my worth in a relationship: mental and spiritual validation, not the material/physical stuff. In accepting that, I eventually healed, though I will never forget them. In my subconscious, realistic or not, I will continue searching for a mate, male or female, a partner, someone to share in my journey.

So I sleep
To close my eyes
And rest:
To ignore the world,
The screaming cars,
And screaming voices.
So I sleep
To hide away:
Myself

and my desire
And my endless
Lonely hunger.
So I sleep
Heart open,
Eyes closed.

Thirteen

FAMILY FINDING OUT

It's out, it's out.
Locked inside for 17 years
A secret, hidden
Hiding me
A burden, a bag of rocks
An anchor, a base.
Secrets have a way of working themselves out
No matter how buried.

Now everyone knows.
I did not burst into flames
Although I was prepared for it.
17 years of rehearsal
Waiting.

What changes now?
Does the revelation preclude great change?
Metamorphosis?

The weight of it!
I could hardly breathe
The pain and fear
And shame and worthlessness
Look what I have become.

Look what I have become.

It's out, it's out
Like a big fucking splinter!
The agony of release
To give up and be completely
Lost in the moment of
Powerlessness
To float away.

17 years worth of nothing
To come shooting out the other end
Fractured, dreamless
A rolling ball of fire.

Well, we all harbor secrets. Pick up any newspaper and read about all kinds of exposed secrets. Companies defrauding investors, serial killers leading double lives, terrorists taking flying lessons under the pretense of becoming airline pilots. My terrible secret was that I was for hire to give men pleasure. Yet, getting 'caught' by my family probably hurt me more than anything hurt any of the above crime-makers. The thought of losing the respect of the people I loved sent me into an emotional nose-dive that was as close to devastation as I could get. I was heartbroken.

My sister's husband phoned me at 7 o'clock one evening. Chris has never, in all the years I have known him, picked up the phone and called me. Never. I immediately went into nervous flight, "What's going on?" I was thinking a family member had been killed or some other disaster. I could tell he was struggling and felt very uncomfortable telling me his news. He said, "Well, um, people know what's going on." I said, "What are you talking about?" He said something about the stuff on the Internet. I immediately went into total shock. He said a cousin had found my pictures on the Internet and told my sister about it. Apparently, my cousin was playing around looking for hookers and found the site where I advertised. There was no hiding that it was me. It was my face. It was my body. It was my spiel. It also had a link to the footfetish.com site. My first thought, rather my first prayer, was that my cousin had only found the foot fetish site. So I said, "What? What?" Chris said, "Oh, you know, the whole thing. All of it. The prostitution."

A tidal wave of nausea hit me. I kept saying to Chris, " What should I do?" He said, "I don't know. I just wanted to call you and let you know." I asked him if my parents knew and he said he didn't think so but couldn't be sure, but that my sister had told my brother. Chris went on to tell me that he had called me because he got the impression that my brother and sister wanted him to call me.

Nobody in my family ever wants to get involved. I like to think it's not because they don't care. As usual, I guess they didn't want to get involved because it's my family's way of not talking about problems so that they don't exist.

'Oh what a tangled web we weave, when first we practice to deceive!' I felt such a panic. I didn't want them to feel shame.

Shortly after I talked to Chris, Natasha called, quite by chance. She was a good friend from Texas and an escort too. She was the first person I spoke to, if you call it speaking. I could barely talk. She was very, very protective of her secret. She didn't even advertise on the Internet. She would die if her family found out. She could really relate to what happened. She was there for me in those first few moments. I mean, really, what could she say? Right? Not much, other than to empathize.

Then everything became such a blur. The anxiety was exhausting. Also by pure chance a client named Colin called me. At that point I had only spent maybe 8 hours with him and didn't know him very well. Several times, when he was working in Toronto, he had called and we had lunch together and then he paid for sex. He was single and tall, dark and handsome and really smart. He had tons of money and was generous with me. He frequently called and e-mailed me to chat. He had offices in every major city in Canada.

Colin was friends with Cecilia too, my footfetish.com cohort, even before all this happened. He had learned about both of us on the Internet Review Board of Hookers. After the first time I 'turned him,' and before my family found out, he flew to Toronto to take Cecilia and me to lunch. We got bombed on two bottles of champagne and ate raw oysters and had such good time. I was supposed to see a client that night but he said, "No, no, no. Come with me. I'll take care of you. Just come to my hotel." So I did. We had sex because at that point I was still thinking it was professional. There was a lot of gray area because we were becoming friends and it was a bit confusing. So often problems begin when one spends time with clients without a clear understanding about being paid. When I left, he handed me some money and it made both of us feel weird. I didn't ask for the money but he handed me $1,000 US and since I didn't leave until 4 in the morning it wasn't my hourly rate. If I had been on the clock, it would have been much more.

He said, "Here, just take it because I said I'd take care you and I want to help you out." With a wink and a smile I said, "Great, you want to make my car payment. I'll take it. Thanks." I called him later and told him, "If we are going to do this in the future, just put the money in an envelope. Don't even talk about it. Just put it in my purse. Don't even hand it to me. If you want to give me money and help me, don't make me feel like a cheap hooker by handing it to me." Gentlemen, never hand a high class lady money. Don't make her feel cheap. Have some class when you do it. Give it to her in a present, put in her purse, deposit it directly into her bank account or in an envelope on the night-stand.

E-mail:
From: Colin
To: Elysia
Subject: A Gentle Thought
Hi Sweetie, I wanted to let you know that I genuinely like you. The money doesn't/did not cheapen that for me at all. You're an amazing lady. I haven't felt that comfortable with someone in a long time. I would love to see more of your smiling face. You're a good one. Thanks for everything. Colin

From: Elysia
To: Colin
Subject: A Gentleman Guy!
I am glad that the money thing wasn't a problem. Although an unusual aspect, no doubt. The way I see it is ....oh, I don't even know for Pete's sake. (Who's Pete?) I am glad that my 'part-time career' is not a secret from you. How about this ... if we make an arranged date like we did in San Francisco, then it will be as it has been in the past. If we spend time with each other like yesterday, then I do not expect, nor want to be paid just for hanging out with you. If you make a request for my time (or nookie) like last night, of course I appreciate your helping me out with a little purse money :o) Now if only I could find a way to give you a receipt so you could expense it! I consider you a friend and friends help friends whether it's with love, understanding, support, cash, hugs, whatever. How does that sound to you? Your thoughts are always welcome. Talk to you later, Scoobie! Elysia xoxo

Anyway, he called in the middle of my crisis of my family finding out and I couldn't hold it in. It just all flowed out, along with my tears. My heart was breaking and he offered me support, care and understanding. I was on the phone with him for a long time. I told him everything about my family, my fears, and basically my problem with what people think about escorts. He said, "Don't ever feel guilty about what you do. The problem is with how the world perceives you, not what you do."

195

He really calmed me down and took me from a high crisis moment to where I could breathe again. He was really there for me. It was from then on that we became friends.

I told him I would have to quit escorting now and how would I support myself? Whenever I went into the 'I quit' mode, I mentally moved into what I called my 'starvation' mode. I panicked to the point where I honestly believed I would have to give up my car and go on welfare and collect food stamps. I would think, 'That's it. I'm going to starve because there is no other way for me to make money out there.' When I was working at the massage parlor, the Madam peddled paranoia to brainwash the girls into staying with her by claiming we would starve if it weren't for working in her parlor and in the business in general. Unfortunately I bought into it, which seems so crazy in hindsight. But most massage parlor girls are young, not highly educated, lack a sense of self-worth, are impressionable and since they are usually solely responsible for supporting themselves, they are aware that it would be difficult to earn that kind of money elsewhere. My goal was to make a $1,000 a day, usually I made more, when working at the massage parlor. The girls knew they would be unable to make such good money working at a department store or anywhere else and the Madam played on that.

So I was crying to Colin, that I was going to have to change my lifestyle. I said things like: "I'll be paying off my credit cards at fifty bucks a month for the rest of my life." He asked me, "Well, what else do you want to do?" And I was like 'Miss Dreamless in Toronto.' He was so supportive with words like, "You can do anything. You're so smart you can do whatever you want." So I bought into that. But I couldn't figure out any options or choices. It's embarrassing to realize that now. I was moving my brains around in a wheelbarrow from place to place, when I should have been speeding away in a race car. Colin gave me some options. He said, "Okay, I can get you a job in my business. We can figure something out. Come with me. I'll show you around my offices and you can see what interests you." I agreed to meet with him the next morning.

Then I called Cecilia and we talked for hours. She was shocked too, of course. I admit I tend more to the theatrics side, so Cecilia gave me some calming perspective too. Still, that night I phoned the Internet escort service and pulled my ad. I said I had been outed, and to just pull the fucking ad and not to waste a second. At that point I was thinking it was all over. No more working. I was done. I planned to go to the appointments I had set up for the end of the month and then that would be it. I don't think I slept more than an hour that night.

The next morning I met Colin at his office because I didn't know what else to do. I was just doing what I was told. On automatic pilot, you know. I was vaguely there. I regret not paying more attention because he was really good. He was busy working but he was great fun. He was like a distraction, my procrastination, my avoidance, denial and a rest from being who I was and dealing with it.

At some point he said, "Look, we are not going to do business any-more. It's personal now. I can't pay you anymore. We're friends. I care about you." I was fine with that, though I had never welcomed a client into my personal life. Colin became the rare exception. I said, "Fine, but if it isn't business and it's personal, I'm probably not going to be sleeping with you. In my personal life I only sleep with someone when I feel like it, and because of what is going on, I need to take time out and make sure everything is real." I was really thinking, 'I just want to be held and the last thing I want right now is some guy's dick. I'm taking that word right out of my dictionary for now.' Instead I said, "Sex is just not what I want right now." He said he completely understood and for me to take as long as I wanted. After that I believed we were going to spend time together as friends. Later I sent him the following;

E-mail:
From: Elysia
To: Colin
Subject: Just some thoughts.
Hi Colin :o) I am sitting in my room just looking out the window trying not to think about things too much. Just mellow. Good mellow. Those things I said to you this morning about how I feel and stuff … was really how I feel. I am not even sure what I said, it was just from the heart. I hope that my pace is not too frustrating for you. I am nervous and scared. Calm and at peace. A lot is going on and I am carefully trying to get through it all honestly and without being hard on myself or those around me (you). The nature of our relationship (don't get freaked out I said the "R" word) has changed and I am not sure I have processed it all. It's a lot so fast! And yet so comfortable and easy and NOT what I was not looking for! (You read that right) You have been put into my life for a reason and I am willing to travel down this road for awhile with you by my side. Xoxo Elysia

From: Colin
To: Elysia
Subject: Good stuff …
I am in exactly the same headspace. With the right attitude this should be

fun. You're a lovely lady and I am glad this has happened (whatever this turns out to be). Be well. Love, Colin

Meanwhile, after having spent the morning with Colin, I went to Cecilia's apartment. We smoked a joint and then I started to get really upset. It made me feel so vulnerable. She kept trying to distract me by talking to me about anything and everything. She knew the pain in my heart. She made dinner. She just kept things going. She kept talking. She was such a good friend. I sat there, totally empty. Numb, really numb.

I considered talking to my brother and sister, explaining to them that I was an escort, a working girl with a Web site. Then they would have the opportunity to tell me that they knew and we could discuss it. I thought honestly that was a good approach. Then I thought I should let some time pass. I also didn't want them to feel responsible for any gossip or hurt this might cause in the family. Obviously I was confused as to what to do. I decided to just put it off. Well, I do have a way of focusing on the worst case scenario until I'm convinced that something terrible is going to happen.

I was shell-shocked and needed time to recover, so when Colin offered to fly me to join him in Edmonton for a week I decided to go. He had to complete a project and invited me partly to explore a new job situation and partly to get me away from my personal situation. I had no other plans and I thought I'd go and just be open to whatever. I wasn't going with any expectation. I said to him, "You know, I've been through a lot lately. Don't push. I can't go from being an escort one day and having my own life, to giving up everything to be with you in a full-time, full-on love relationship all in the course of a week." I felt he understood that I was happy to share some time with him but that was it.

Well, he was one of those proactive guys that fix it, do it, get it done, deal with it, work on it, nurture it and whatever. I'm certainly fine with that, but I was just going to go with the flow. I was in neutral and I was going wherever the universe wanted to take me for the time being. And I wasn't going to play-act as Elysia-the-escort. There was no point. I needed to be just me. If I was having a personal relationship, it needed to be real. But I had come to a point where a lot of the time I didn't know what was real. I knew what it wasn't. It wasn't rushing a relationship along as in living together. I was worried about spending ten days with him but I decided to go anyway.

E-mail:
From: Colin
To: Elysia
Subject: Limo info. etc.
Here is the Air Canada itinerary and the information for your limousine ride. You will be picked up at the airport by Limo Livery. They will meet you with a sign. In case you have any trouble the phone # for them is ......, Our room number at the hotel is .... Colin

From: Elysia
To: Colin
Subject: Hello
Good morning Colin
Probably more like good evening by the time you get this. You sure sounded bagged last night ; I hope today goes really well for you and everything runs smoothly. The rain is still here... boooo. My friend and I are going to meet again tomorrow morning to talk and get more info for 'the book.' Yesterday when we talked she said I sure was hard on myself. Of course I thought of you and Cecilia having said the same thing! So today is Be Kind to Elysia Day! I am going to go to the gym (I ate almost a whole cake last night) and start to think about packing and getting ready to come see you. Anyway ... enough about me. I hope you are doing okay and that things are going well. See you soon sunshine!
Love, Elysia

Okay, I was hard on myself but I didn't know how to change the pattern or my way of thinking to make my anguish go away. I was vulnerable. I tried to just not think about my family knowing. I just had to let it go. And visit Colin in Edmonton.

E-mail:
From: Colin
To: Elysia
Subject: Hello Lovely Lady....
It is 10:50 PM. I just had one of the most wonderful dinners. Sushi, lots of slimy stuff. Mmmmmm good. Now I am going to try and get some sleep. I can't tell you how much I look forward to seeing you.
You're the Apple of my Eye.
Love, C.

In addition to his supportive e-mails, he began sending me e-mail cards. One had a picture of a sweet stuffed bear with "I miss you" written on it and Colin added, "I'm sooo looking forward to seeing you. I really do care with all my heart." Another had a picture of a rose with

"To the one who is all I ever wanted – And more" written beside it. Colin added, "Soon you will be getting the real thing. Love, Colin."

We started talking for hours on the phone about anything and everything. He was easy to talk to.

E-mail:
From: Elysia
To: Colin
Subject: Some kind words
Hello sweetie! We are about to jump on the broom … and I was thinking of you :o) = smart, funny, caring, loving, strength, passionate, understanding, reverence, kind, soul, friend, laughing.
See you soon!
Love, Elysia

From: Colin
To: Elysia xoxo
Subject: Back at ya ….
Hi Elysia, Yes, I think I love you too …. You're a lovely lady. You should enjoy your every breath. If you don't, I might have to give you a severe spanking! Thank God I met you. I haven't 'felt' at all in a long time. I am patient and have a calm belief in this phase of my life. Most important of all let the sunshine in. You deserve it. I'm not going anywhere. Here are some kind words for you …. Fun, love, safety, warmth, soft, wise, better, good, nice, friend, trust, honesty, happy and you're a Peach. Love, Colin.

He was crazy about me but I wasn't sure of my feelings. I met him as a client. He met me as an escort. Personally, now I really cared about him, enjoyed his company and was comfortable with him. He was certainly very supportive and loving and I really needed that. But honestly, on my personal level, that certain passion was missing. I think I was afraid to let my walls down and open my heart to it. Anytime before when I had that instant chemistry it had gone nowhere. Colin had everything I wanted in a man. Mostly, I loved his energy; his drive.

What's most important to me in a man is that he has some kind of drive or ambition and goals and a strong sense of security and grounding in who he is. I mean he could be the best McDonald's worker on the planet, and if he had ambition and confidence in himself, then I'd be attracted because sometimes I'm like a kite on a string. I need someone I can root to, to feel safe with.

Colin was certainly in the running. It's a shame men don't come in a kit – where you can pick and choose your pieces, like a part for passion and a part for brains, etc. - so you get your perfect fit. I thought, 'Fuck it.' If I was willing to chase that passion-chemistry thing, I should be just as willing to chase someone who's got all the other qualities and give it a chance.

Somewhere in this time frame and my expressing to Colin my worry over making money and paying my student loan debt, he came up with the idea to offer financial help. I remember he said something to the effect, "I have a good life. I have money. I have a home. I have a great career. The only something I'm missing is someone to love and share it with. I'm not multi-mega rich but I'm definitely always going to be very comfortable." Then he offered to take care of my bills, including my student loan, so I would not have to be an escort. He told me to cancel my appointments for the end of the month. He FedExed me a check for $20,000 US.

Colin phoned a few days before I was to fly to see him. I don't know how it came up but he said something about, "Maybe you shouldn't be coming if you really are not wanting to have sex right now. Maybe it's not a good idea for you to be spending ten days in a hotel room with a guy." A red flag shot up in my brain. It totally caught me off guard. It was not what I was expecting to hear from him. I said, "Oh, so you're telling me not to come?" I was thinking, 'What happened to friendship? What happened to take as long as you want?' Now he was basically saying, "Well, you probably shouldn't be coming to Edmonton to spend ten days with me if you're not going to be putting out." I guess that was his expectation. I said something like, "Well then, I'm not really very comfortable accepting the money you sent."

I didn't want someone to own me. If I accepted the money, things could change somewhere down the road and I feared it would come back to haunt me. The price can be very high for $20,000. Now I wondered what strings were attached. Colin insisted, "No, no, no. You don't have to do this anymore. Here. Take this money. I don't want you working. I don't want you worried. I want to give you a chance." He said, "The only thing I ask of you is that you don't work as an escort."

It was hard, you know, because I really wanted out so badly, I wanted to take it … the new life, the money and him. I wanted to just say fuck it and be in love with him. I thought it would be foolish of me not to take this opportunity to let somebody love me, to take away this burden, to give it a try, to just be open, to see where it went. I felt I had to accept the money if I was not going to work and give it a try. I made him promise he'd never make my accepting the money an issue. I told him if sex came up while I was there, "I'll deal with it then." I packed my condoms. I was going to honestly give us a chance, to try to open my heart to it and to see if I had feelings for him. I went with the best of intentions. I was excited.

The limo picked me up at the Edmonton airport and took me to our hotel. I knew the room number so I went up to the room and he was there. I was definitely excited to see him. There was champagne waiting on ice and eventually dinner was delivered to our room. We talked and laughed and hugged and enjoyed each other. He told me he loved me. It started off really great. Even the sex was enjoyable that first night!

His Edmonton office had fifteen female staff workers and I knew he had told them his girlfriend was coming to visit. Of course he would never mention I was an escort to anyone. Well, you can just imagine the 'cats meowing and tails twitching' waiting to meet the new girl. He was handsome and I didn't doubt for a minute that some of the women had a crush on him. I wanted to look like a beautiful sophisticated respectable woman like them. I felt everything I owned was sleazy compared to what women wore in his world. I was embarrassed my clothes were basically escort clothes. I told him they were bugging me and, even though it might be superficial, I should go shopping for new ones. He said, "You know, you have every right to want to have a fresh look, to have new clothes, to be proud to stand up and show off how beautiful you look. No problem, I would love to take you shopping." Then he brought up the *Pretty Woman* movie. The second red flag shot up in my brain. He said, "Remember in the movie?" I was like *awk!* I told him to stop making that fucking comparison. One minute he told me he didn't want me to be an escort and the next minute he was in a client's fantasy movie. He was paying me not to be an escort, just *his* escort. Fuck, who was more twisted? I was so pissed off. I decided we should go shopping anyway and he spent thousands on clothes for me. One of my favorite outfits was a Dolce & Gabbana suit, which cost around $2,000, a matching turtle neck for $500 and a Gucci belt for $250. The only thing I got on sale was Brown's boots for $450.

We began to have fun, actually we had a blast. He was so funny. Even though he was working, we went out for dinner and drank champagne every night and went on a hunt for the best fois gras in the city. We had long intimate conversations. We discussed everything, even my secret that I had Hepatitis C. We had such a good time. At some point along the way, I don't remember if there was a defining time, I realized he thought he was really in love with me. He told me he loved me all the time. I loved spending time with him but I was hanging out. I loved the fact that we liked to do the same things and that we had the same sense of humor but I, sadly, wasn't in love with him and he was definitely falling in love with me.

Colin hinted about what it would be like to be his wife. He'd say something to the effect that his wife wouldn't have to work. He gave me spending money and every time I spent it, he'd give me more. He would open his wallet and hand me four brand new unused $100 dollar bills right across the table in the middle of a restaurant and it really pissed me off. Everyone could see. I was so insulted but what was I going to say? I can only imagine the look on my face. I didn't take it right away. I didn't want to. He insisted. I felt like a welfare case. And he told everybody at his office about buying me expensive clothes, like I was some kind of trophy that he was showing off and who he could afford to dress expensively. I felt embarrassed walking into his office with the women checking me out. I tried to keep an open mind but we were spending so much time together, everything started bugging me. Everything. Even the sound of him walking across the carpet in our hotel room. Sex became a non-issue. And the more he wanted me, the less I wanted him.

I sensed he was feeling the walls closing in too. He was used to travelling alone, eating alone, thinking alone and planning each day alone because of his work. I was used to spending all my time alone too. All of a sudden we were put into a hotel room and compelled to simultaneously adjust to an unnatural dating/courting sort of thing. Instead of evolving slowly and adjusting to a relationship, we had trapped ourselves. Our room became a cage. We were sleeping in the same bed and he felt like shit and I felt like shit. It was awful. He really wanted a lasting romantic loving relationship and I couldn't do it.

One night I asked him for a modeling agent's name in Toronto and his anger snapped. He did one of those calm-anger things, like he was about to blow! I said, "You know what? I just asked you a question. I didn't ask you to bite my head off." He was the one who had suggested I could be a model because he knew an agent. In fact, I already had professional photos taken at his suggestion. But he was always too busy to come up with the agent's name.

That was the night he broke up with me. We both had reached our limit and he told me, "I can't do this anymore. You're so distant. I feel like a loser. You don't want me. You don't love me. I can't live like this. It's over for me. We're not going to be seeing each other anymore after this." He immediately fell asleep and started snoring his head off. He was right. I couldn't live like that either. I laid awake most of the night feeling like shit. I wanted it to happen but the chemistry just wasn't there. As I listened to him snoring, I kept thinking, "I've just been dumped and I'm a thousand miles away from home. What am I going to do?"

The next day he woke up and said, "I'm really sorry. I was really stressed out and I didn't mean it. Oops." I just looked at him and said, "You've got to be fucking kidding. You can't put me through that and then say 'oops' the next day." The Ice Princess had arrived.

I could have played him. I could have given him what he wanted until I suckered him for everything I wanted and then walked. I could have done it for sure. I was a professional. And I chose not to. I knew I was making the right decision to end it then and there. I didn't have the right kind of feelings for him and it wasn't fair to him to pretend. I thought, 'No, this is not what I want in life.' I was really kind of proud of myself because I knew how easy it would have been, at that point, to play him for so much more.

I gave him a kiss goodbye and I left. I flew to meet Cecilia in Mexico. Ten days later when I arrived back home, there were several messages on my answering machine from him. "Are you back yet? Please call. Why haven't I heard from you?" So I phoned him and he told me he had been worried about me and asked when he could come see me. I said, "I thought we weren't going to see each other anymore." He freaked, "What? Oh my God, I feel like the biggest fucking fool. It's over and I didn't even know it. And I just dropped $25,000 on a girl in one month. Thanks for telling me we're finished." I reminded him he had dumped me. I said, "Don't you dare mention the money to me. You insisted I take it." He was furious. And I had an angry tiger on my hands.

He thought a hooker had 'played' him. It wasn't true. If he thought that, he was stupid. He'd been seeing escorts for a long time and he needed to get his game on. If that was true, then what the hell was he doing falling for an escort? He wasn't an innocent lamb. If he got suckered, then he got suckered. He knew better. It was his own fault. He should have been smarter if that's what he thought. If he was going to play the game, then he needed to remember how to play the game. His thinking was convoluted and twisted when he thought I had played him but, because I was an escort, he figured I must have played him for his money instead of rejecting him because the magic wasn't there. His ego was bruised and he was taking it personally and he was a bomb waiting to go off.

You know, men of the world, it just doesn't work falling in love with an escort. Well, it would be very rare if it did. They're falling in love with their own fantasy, which is that the escort really wants them, is attracted to them and is turned on by them. Men forget that prostitution is money for service. It's a game for hire where we each have a role. Doesn't matter how much she says, "Oh, you're the best," or how many times he tells the escort she's the best. It's part of the game. Having said that, it's not always cut and dried, black and white as in a one-time escort experience. As a human, I do care about some clients and develop a respectful friendship, especially with my regulars. Seeing a client for years can't help but develop into a connection on a more human level. But men should remember prostitution is what it is and no more, no matter how much men want it to be otherwise.

Colin fell the very first time I saw him as a client. He fell for Elysia and my game and he wanted to save a hooker from the life of hooker-ness. Fuck that, buddy! He'd brought up the *Pretty Woman* movie a couple of times while we were no longer client and escort, which felt patronizing. I'm not a movie script. He was thinking he would give me everything I needed and I'd fall in love with him and we'd live happily ever after having fantasy sex. In my mind, that's not what was fucking going on. He adored our professional hour and pursued me personally because he thought that the connection that we made as Elysia and Colin was real. And it wasn't. He fell for the act. I was an escort paid to be passionate. Colin offered me an opportunity to get out. I appreciated the chance. I appreciated how kind he was to me. It didn't work because Elysia is not who I really am.

E-mail:
From: Brock
To: Elysia
Subject: What the ...... rumors????
Have you heard that someone posted on the Internet Review Board that you have contracted a STD, (hep C?) and are not telling anyone about it. I hope that this jerk is just out to get you and the info is not true! I get concerned when accusations and lies are abound on the forum board! It's an outrage! Sorry to let you find out this way. Brock

From: Elysia
To: Brock
Subject: Gossip

Hi there :o)
Thank you so much for the e-mail, great to hear from you, even if it is under
these circumstances. I am aware of the rumors about me on the Review
Board. I quit participating and reading it a while ago for this very reason.
I found it to be a forum where people were often mean to each other and
vindictive for no reason. I think that not responding to such wild accusations
is the best approach considering the source. It only adds fuel to the fire. I
thank you for your kindness and warm thoughts. Peace!
Love, Elysia xoxo

I never told any trick that I had Hep C. Not ever. The only person I had told was Colin and I told him in confidence. It was in our personal relationship and that made a huge difference. If I had revealed it to him as one of my clients then he could have posted it to the Board. I was certain it was Colin and he had no right. He came up with some fake e-mail name and address and posted it. The amount of business I lost because of it cost me more than the $20,000 he had given me. I should have never trusted him. He was a trick trying to have a relationship with a hooker. He tried to ruin my career and my name by writing to the Board, "I have to protect the guys." It was bullshit. It was really all about revenge. There was never anything that I did with my clients that would ever put them at risk. Even if the condom broke, there is an extremely low risk of anyone catching anything. I was always absolutely careful of that.

E-mail
From: Colin
To: Elysia
Subject: Hello
Dear Elysia, I was wondering if we could chat sometime. I felt like we never
had a civil conversation after you left for Mexico. Love to hear from you and
have one of those nice conversations we used to have. I'm seeing someone so
it's not that. I really cared for you.
If not, that's OK.
Love, Colin

From: Elysia
To: Colin
Hey you, Thanks so much for e-mailing me! You have been on my mind and
I would love to have one of those nice conversations too!
I am in the middle of moving. yik. My new job....what a disap-
pointment. I won't be going to Central America. As you know I have really
been trying to go the 'straight' route but it seems everything I try ends up in
a flop. I keep trying and trying but when is something going to work?? Two

steps forward, one step back. It is so frustrating and drives me to tears and discouragement. Nevermind......

At this point I am considering going back to work. Things are really shitty right now and I am having a really hard time. I may have to go back to it in April if something doesn't give.

Apparently there is a "frequent poster" on the Internet Review Board who is telling people that I have hep. C. I was wondering if you know anything about this?
Love, Elysia

From: Colin
To: Elysia
Subject: ???????
I have heard nothing.
I am in Calif. on vacation.
Somehow the e-mail got screwed up and my office got your e-mail. It was addressed to ... That is not my e-mail address. It is ... From now on if you want to e-mail me use this one ... My VP called me this morning and asked me about a lady who was trying to live a straight life. Stuff that I'm sure you didn't intend for others to read. It was certainly something I didn't need to explain to my place of business. Sorry you're having a rough time. I tried to call but no luck.
Be well. Maybe we can talk one of these days. Love, Colin

He denied it all. As if I believed it. I already knew the truth. I just wanted to see if he would lie to me. I will always believe he did.

E-mails
From: Colin
To: Elysia
Subject: Request
Dear Elysia,
I have a request of you. I would like to see you in person at a location of your choice. I understand this is over. I would like to say a few words. I hope you choose to extend this courtesy to me. As far as I am concerned I deserve a little consideration. I will wait to hear from you. If I hear nothing in the next two days I will assume you do not wish to be in my presence.
Deepest Sympathy, Colin Smith

From: Elysia
To: Colin
Subject: Re: Request????
What's with the e-mail? One minute you're telling me how much you love me, the next I get this cryptic note. Extend this courtesy?????? As far as you're

concerned???? Deserve a little consideration??? Deepest sympathy???? All of a sudden you feel it necessary to sign with your last name. Don't want to be in your presence???? Come on! If this is how you are going to be then I do not want to see you.
Deepest Sympathy, Elysia

From: Colin
To: Elysia
Subject: Call ya back .....
Hi, At this point I'm guessing that return call isn't coming anytime soon. Hope the new gig is treating you well.
Be well, Love, Colin

From: Elysia
To: Colin
Subject: Re: Call ya back .....
Quit acting so crazy! I have been busy. You are not making this easy. E.

Of course, it was all about survival. And having money means survival to me. My family wasn't heartbroken. I had clients that didn't want me to quit. It was a hard time to go through. I am a survivor but it was just awful how I felt and so much energy lost. I decided to stay in the business until I earned enough money to buy an apartment of my own. Once I had it paid for, I would be free. Then I would support myself as a nurse.

E-mail:
From: Elysia
To: Colin
Subject: Letting you know.
Hey you, it's me! :o)
I think you might be off to Halifax to work and I wanted to drop you a note before you get all crazy-busy. As some letters go, there is good news and bad news. The good news is I may have solved my car situation. Yeah! I am also thinking that I want to purchase my very own first home so I will no longer be paying rent. What I am really trying to tell you is that you may see my ad on the Internet site some time soon. I really would like it if you can understand that if I have a reasonable down payment, I will not be stuck with large monthly payments. I know we had an understanding and my only other option is a cash advance on a credit card for the car. I do not believe that I am going to have a husband/ partner in my life who is going to provide a home for me. Although I will make a good wage as a nurse, I will never be able to save up enough to buy, so I am able to make it another way and have security and something of my own in the end. I really want a home

of my own. I am not in a relationship now, and if I have to work on the side to get a down payment to purchase, then I am willing to choose to do that. I asked myself why I felt the need to tell you and I guess what you think still matters to me and I feel like I have let you down. I hope your big heart understands and doesn't think less of me for this decision.
Love, Elysia

From: Colin
To: Elysia
Subject: Not like that at all ....
Hi Elysia, Don't worry about that at all. I don't think that we had a binding agreement once the dating part had ended. I can't control what you do. I am extremely sad that you have to go back to work. I am even sadder that things didn't work out between us. If it had you wouldn't be stuck in this spot. The reason I gave you the dough was to give us a chance at a relationship. It just failed more quickly than I had expected. I absolutely don't think any less of you at all. The reason I wanted you to stop working was because I had fallen in love with you and didn't want to share. You're still in my thoughts often.

You have not let me down at all. You have to make a living. That is an honorable thing. Society is the one with the silly label crap. Ok, I found out the only thing that bugs me when you work. I am concerned for your safety. I know, I know: You're a big girl and can handle yourself. Please be careful and keep in touch. Thank you so much for telling me. I really appreciate it.
Much love, Colin

As for my family, to this day, years later now, none of my family has ever talked to me about it. Nor have I brought it up with them. It became silent, a non-event. Secretly, I hoped it didn't matter to them and that is what seemed to happen and I was fine with that.

Fourteen

LONELINESS AND SEARCHING

I want someone
Who will fight for me,
Protect me
And hold me through the storm.
Someone who would give
Anything,
To be by my side,
Who will listen to my dreams,
And ease my fears.
I want courage and strength,
Arms around me,
Gentle words,
A kind touch.
One who will love
ME
Forever.

Of course you don't ever get something for nothing. Would you believe I'm lonely?

I just want a relationship with a man or a woman that is meaningful. Well, you know, something like everyone wants: commitment to each other as we hold hands and experience the journey of life together, adoring each other always in unconditional love. Ha! Well, it's not any easier for me to find than it is for most women in any profession. I was lucky enough to be given a classic look, I'm educated, can hold an intelligent conversation, bring orgasmic flashes from heaven to men's dicks in bed and still can't find Mr. Ideal, or at least one that wants to commit solely to me. No home, hearth and children for me. Maybe it's my fault, maybe it's not, but I gotta' say I get dumped and cheated on just like everyone else. Whether they know I'm an escort or not.

I know I'm happier when I have someone in my private life, someone I can care about, fuss over and share experiences with. I figure the biggest part of the meaning of life is to 'love and be loved' and in seeking it, along with the incumbent approval, my life unfolded as it has. That's why I do what I do. To this day I'm still searching for it and the illusive peace it brings. But I remain single. I can't maintain a permanent relationship. Committed love? Do you think I can find it? It's always been the one puzzle piece missing.

There's the saga of Dan. He was not a client and didn't know I was an escort. I met him one hot summer's day at a boat race in younger, more innocent times. He was good looking and it was his sexiness that drove me to accidentally bump into him, pressing my scantily clothed tanned breasts against his arm. I had that slightly oiled summer hot body smell about me and I got his attention and we became lovers. He told me, up front, he was not interested in having a relationship. I said, "Fine, but if you are going to tell me that, you must promise if someone comes along that you are interested in dating, then you'll be honest with me and tell me." That was the condition. For months we wined and dined, had fantastic sex, went scuba diving, water skiing, and eventually in the winter we went snow skiing because he was a ski instructor. On one particular outing we were waiting for the chair lift when Dan noticed a woman ski into the line. I knew instantly when I saw them look at each other that something was going on. I just knew. I asked him and he claimed he had taught her to ski. He even went so far as to sarcastically say, "How dare you accuse me! This is a teacher/student relationship. Can't I just have a friend without you being all jealous and insecure?" He gave me the works man, the fucking works. A few days later when I went to his office, I noticed the pictures of me were positioned on his desk so that he couldn't see them. The only one he could see was a picture of his "student," the girl in the chair lift line up. I questioned him about it and again he said, "It's just a picture." I thought, 'Okay, fine, fine, fine, fine, no problem. Whatever.' When he left his office to do something else I got her number out of his book. Then I packed up my pictures and just left. Problem was, I had forgotten my cell phone so the next day I had to go back. He begged me to stay and placated me with, "Don't worry, it was nothing." He convinced me enough that I agreed to go for a walk with him. We drank hot chocolate and ate chocolate chip cookies while sitting on a snow-covered rock wall while he insisted I was his only love. I fell for it.

Then one day Dan phoned me from her place. I had call display and since I already had her phone number I checked it and knew he was lying. Again I called him on it and he said, "What! I can't even meet someone for coffee?" Well, I called her and left a message on her answering machine telling her we needed to talk. She called me back and said, "Thank God you called. This has been going on for months and I kept telling him to tell you." She asked me to come over, which I did, and she told me everything. Apparently she had recently dumped him for being a big loser. She showed me a love letter he had written to her (on stationery that I had given him). She told me he had called her from Mexico while Dan and I were there on vacation to tell her he loved her and that he wished she was with him and not me. He *told me he had called his sister.* To add insult to injury *I* had paid for his airplane ticket and all his expenses while we were in Mexico.

A day later I calmly called Dan to come over to my place. Calm: as in a tigress about to jump her prey. I was shaking I was so angry. I asked two friends to hide in the bedroom because I didn't know what was going to happen. It was a Sunday morning and I didn't start work at Madame Anita's massage parlor until noon. When Dan arrived, I just snapped. I screamed at him and I booted a door so hard that the handle popped right through the wall. I had to pull hard on the door to get the door handle out and I was left with a hole in my wall. To make things worse, after he ran out the door I phoned work and said I couldn't come in that day. I was just bawling. I was so upset. Anita, the witch from hell who is the owner, said, "You know, I know you're lying. I know it's a sunny day and you just don't want to come to work. Consider yourself suspended for two weeks." There was no convincing her. I had no work. It was horrible and I was a mess for a long time. It took months before I finally got over Dan-the-lying-man. God forbid the thought of some poor woman married to him someday!

* * *

It's difficult for lots of women to meet eligible single 'normal' men who aren't afraid of commitment, even for women who are eye candy. So I do what lots of single people do: look for a date on the Internet. I visit a "Web Personal" site and of course I never tell anyone that I'm an escort. I'm already way too high maintenance for most of the men on the Web. I did meet a single man who told me flat out that he was not good with commitment and was married to his job. He was the only cute looking guy of the fifty I found on the Web and he was the only one who called me for a date. So how do I say no to the only guy who calls me? He picked me up in his Porsche. He was successful, handsome and seemed to have lots of money. As expected, it basically turned into a booty call, all about sex. The whole time I kept thinking, 'This is not what I want in my life. I do not need to get fucked. The last thing I need is a booty call. I've got an hourly rate for this.' Yep, the one guy I find who I'm attracted to is emotionally unavailable.

However I must admit, since I am manless, that I do fall for the occasional booty call. It's hell to be human sometimes, well, a lot of the time. I had fun with a boy toy who had his penis pierced. That's unusual. I met him at a private party and we exchanged numbers. He came over one night and we talked for hours but I was the only one who got naked because, in his words, it was all about me, which was a pleasant change. I did manage to pull out his cock because I had heard it was pierced and it was my first pierced throbbing member. I wasn't sure what to do with it. It felt weird in my mouth, but it was brief and I sent him home with a hard-on and wanting more. Unfortunately his technique on me needed some work. I didn't tell him that but decided to see if he was trainable. Eventually he was out the door.

I know I come across as independent, strong, very confident and powerful. Most men are initially drawn to it like the moth to the flame. They're attracted to all those things in a woman and find it exciting, and it's kind of like they want to own it or have it. I believe once they've experienced such power, it intimidates them and they want the woman to be that way when they want it that way. They need the 'little woman homemaker' too so they can still feel number one, and I'm not the wifey-wife type. I know men are attracted to that strong side of me, but I guess it doesn't really fit into their view of a long-term relationship. Perhaps it proves to be too challenging. In the end they run from it, well, at least so it seems to me. That's my take on it. Soon I'm going to sound like an Anthony Robbins self-help tape dude.

So who am I going to have a relationship with? There's the problem in being honest about being an escort. Sooner or later, I would have to tell him if it is to be a real relationship. Who's going to want to marry the girl that used to be an escort? There are women men will date, women they'll fuck and women they'll marry. I'm telling you, there are few who will say, "Aw, it doesn't bother me," because really it does. It's no big secret that men don't want to be with the girl that's been with lots of guys. All men want a nymphomaniac virgin. They all want to be the first one. Even when I'm working I sometimes tell my clients, "You're the first one I've seen today," because they don't want to know they're the fifth guy. I've definitely learned that from boyfriends over the years.

Perhaps men who try to love an escort are the men who want to believe a prostitute's 'act' for hire is how she really is all the time. My regular clients, especially those who took me on trips, eventually told me that our relationship had nothing to do with my being a prostitute. They expressed that it had grown into so much more. But it wasn't real. They fell in love with Elysia, the escort. They were still paying me, which meant I was still working. That's the difference. I was the escape from their normal lives because I certainly never expressed my exhaustion or frustration with everyday life when I was with a client. They never saw me washing the kitchen floor on my hands and knees or nursing a baby or irritated by co-workers at the office or in a grumpy exhausted mood. I was the accommodating sweet dream that energized them and made them feel like kings - but it wasn't real.

For example, one memory is Harold. He owned a manufacturing company in the U.S. I went on a fishing expedition to Alaska with him, amongst other fun trips. Mostly he would fly me to meet him in different cities while he was selling his products. He always rented a posh suite for me while he stayed in an adjacent room.

Well, the earth moved I guess, and he felt there was some kind of connection between us. He wanted to pursue it further on a personal level. As I always tell my clients, I am not interested in a relationship. However, Harold and I kept talking and somewhere along the line we decided he should come to my apartment to see me for the weekend, since he was coming to my city for business anyway. Then I got an offer to work in San Francisco, so I changed his visit to the middle of the week. I was fairly relaxed, though it was a little bit weird having him in my space. I don't have people over to my house very often, let alone clients or whatever the hell he was. While he was there, my phone was ringing off the wall because I was booking appointments for my trip. I was trying to ignore the calls to be with him. He knew it was business and said, "Go ahead and answer the phone. If you need to work, no problem, no big deal." And I said, "Are you sure because I don't need to work while you're here?" He said, "Oh, no problem. I totally understand about your work. Don't worry about it. I know you can separate the two and differentiate your personal life from work." I figured he got it. Accepting that, I took a couple of calls while he was in the room, so he clearly heard me doing business with clients. I didn't think any more of it.

Well, my head nearly popped off when, after he left, he sent me an e-mail about how we should just be friends, and that my work was something he had to cope with but that he would try to deal with it. He accused me of giving more of myself to my clients than I gave to him during his stay. Silly me! I figured I'd just spent two days of quality time with a friend. We didn't have sex, which I thought was a non-issue, because he'd already said in an e-mail before coming, "Don't worry about sex. I'm not coming expecting to get laid. If it happens, great. If it doesn't, no big deal. We're just going to be friends, right?" He'd changed his tune in the e-mail. He said he was extremely disappointed that sparks didn't fly when we were together and he was upset we didn't have sex. He said he now knew some of my tricks' names and that it had become an issue because he had heard me working. I thought, 'Fuck him.' He had told me explicitly it was okay to not have sex, to talk to clients and now he had a problem. I flipped out and e-mailed back, "If that's what you really wanted, the kind of attention I give to my clients, all you had to do was pay me, mother fucker." I said more, but you get the drift. I was angry. So he e-mailed a poem he wrote about me losing control and my "smoldering" anger and whatever the hell!

E-mail:
From: Harold
To: Elysia xoxo
Subject: A poem I wrote for you.

She's got a thing about losing control,
Commands each mile just to see how far she'll go.
She brushes up her hair as she tries to fake a smile
A friend indeed but what I need is her to stay awhile.

She drops hints but won't tell you what's really on her mind
But I know if I look that it's easy to find.
And she's got a way with her anger and the way she lets it show:
Like the smoldering smoke when the fire's left the coals.

My door is always open and I've always got the time
To give a little something even though I get behind.
And your trips become mine as our lives intertwine
Like the shadows in the darkness it's all in my mind.

I came along and you showed me your home,
Not the place you live but where a cold heart roams.
You can bend my ear; we can talk all day
But my dream's been crushed, is all I can say.

After these harsh e-mails, we still occasionally e-mailed each other. I'm not sure why he wanted further contact. I decided to just let it all dwindle away to nothing. I suppose I should have just dealt with it and nipped it in the bud, right? Be proactive, responsible, right? Since I encouraged nothing, we eventually became silent and he didn't hire me again. It doesn't pay to let anything ruin the illusion I create while working. Men buy into it. Business should always stay business. I regretted losing him. He was a lucrative client.

Sometimes I think that you get back what you put out into the universe, or so one would think. I spend lots of time thinking about the ying and the yang of life. I realized as long as I was working, it was probably impossible to get commitment because the only energy that I put out towards men was *I'm unavailable*. You can have me for an hour, a day, a week, but that's it.'

Near the end of my relationship with Jake and Joelle, I met a wonderful man named Norm on the beach one day. I was there by myself, wearing a little flame-colored bikini and sitting reading with my back leaning against a log. It was hot and I had bought an ice cream cone and of course it was melting. I was sitting there, trying to eat it as fast as I could but it kept dripping on my body. A dog came by and, try as I might to keep him away, the dog started licking the ice cream off me. A guy on the other side of the log was watching and made the comment, "Oh to be a dog," which was funny. He was quite charming and wasn't intrusive or rude in any way and we started chatting. We must have talked for two hours and eventually he said, "Well, I don't know what you're doing tonight, but if you feel like joining some friends and me for a casual BBQ, let me give you my number and if you want to come, just give me a call." He wrote his name on the inside of the book I was reading. Somewhat later, while I was driving home, I thought, 'Where am I going? Home? To do nothing by myself?' So I called him. I found out later that he was totally blown away that I did. That was our beginning.

Norm was super-intelligent. He knew about the world, electronics, Fords, and big words. He was funny and made me laugh and told me I was his dream girl. He was big with a great body and strawberry blonde hair. He was sweet too. He called me his 'shiny girl.' Girls who are shiny are high maintenance pretty girls who look sexy and wear jewelry and lots of make-up. We were together every day for 2½ weeks. Of course I didn't tell him I was an escort. I told him I was a nurse. Things went well with us. He came over to my home and saw pictures of of Jake, Joelle and me. I told him the three of us were lovers. He had a lot of questions about it and I answered them honestly. He was completely blown away by my honesty and was respectful to me.

Then Norm basically dumped me. I like to think it was because he didn't want to share me. I know he really liked me but certainly didn't want to join our ménage à trois either. He said, "What am I supposed to do when they're here? Go away for a week while you run off and have sex with this other couple. You're with them emotionally even if you're not with them physically." When I accused him of callously dumping me, he said, "I didn't dump you. You're not available." It hurt like hell, but I understood it totally. Part of me was hoping that someone would come along I would care enough about to make me forget Jake and Joelle. A part of me thought that I could have both.

What was I thinking! I knew perfectly well that nobody in their right mind was going to have a relationship with me while I was involved with someone else, and a married couple at that. Not exactly conducive to catching a committed man.

A week after Norm and I broke up, we chatted on the Internet. The following is a part of our conversation:

Norm: Hey, how was your day?
Elysia: Not too bad, I guess, went to the gym, working, boring day.
Norm: My brain is working overtime. What about you? Am I intruding?
Elysia: Intruding? Not at all. No, didn't go to the b-be-q, just stayed home, shaved my legs, washed my hair and laid naked around the house.
Norm: Where's my web cam when I need it?
Elysia: I'm sad.
Norm: Yes, sad … me ….you ….us ….sad.
Elysia: Yes, yes, yes.
Norm: Me too.
Elysia: But I understand how you feel.
Norm: Life is full of surprises and ups and downs.
Elysia; I miss you. I did not expect that.
Norm: I miss u but I don't understand your relationship with Jake and Joelle.
Elysia: You make me think and to have more respect for myself.
Norm: GOOD, U DESERVE IT!!!!!!!!!!!
Elysia: I don't really understand it either. None of us do.
Norm: Love???? is strange and certainly not logical.
Elysia: Shit, no kidding!!!!
Norm: Since you told Jake about me, does this mean he is going to "kick my ass" or is he happy?
Elysia: Hmmm, I'm not sure what you are asking but I don't think so on either accounts but he is/was jealous of you.
Norm: Just curious, maybe my ego is involved there as well. Fuck him, be

more demanding of others for yourself.

*Elysia: because I was spending time with you. Always ego involved. Hmm...
which to choose. You make me think.*

*Norm: Good, the only person who should have multiple lovers is Hugh
Hefner ....just kidding.*

Elysia: How can someone so gross get so many chicks?

*Norm: Because he is Hugh! Jake, famous, powerful....etc...sounds like a
good retirement thing he has for himself.*

*Elysia: You are absolutely right!! I have been through a lot of emotional
bullshit. But I believe we all have, and it was not meant to be reckless,
however selfish on their part.*

*Norm: Me too. I told you about the married girl who led me on for a long
time.*

Elysia: Yes, and I sure know about wanting more!!! It feels like such a rip off!

Norm: I don't think u r being reckless, just selling YOURSELF short.

*Elysia: I think you are right babe! Just my insecurities revealed!!! Sshhh...
don't tell*

Norm: Ok, I won't, I will go with the hot sexy shiny babe from the beach!

*Elysia: Who knew! ...shiny boy and shiny girl. I feel like I disappointed you.
I let you down.*

*Norm: If everyone was as honest and up front as you, life would be much
simpler. Thanks.*

*Elysia: I know I feel disappointed. My honesty and up-frontedness is almost
a self-sabotage.*

Norm: NO! U r 100% wrong.

*Elysia: I feel like I am so 'irregular' with all of my stuff and that I am
undesirable because of it.*

*Norm: Most women go a long time before you get all their info. You are to
be commended for being honest.*

*Elysia: Well, I am who I am and I am becoming very aware of my bad choi-
ces. Sorry I was just thinking, you make me think.*

*Norm: Bad...good....just depends on what you are looking for at certain
times in your life.*

Elysia: I am sorry about all of this Norm.

*Norm: Don't, u r wonderful and I have no regrets. I learned a little about
me as well. Thx!*

Elysia: Maybe one day when I get my shit together you'll want me back!

*Norm: Sure, at my rate I am not going anywhere fast. Elysia; You'll see my
picture in muscle media ...hubba hubba! And you still owe me doggie
style.*

Elysia: Oyeeee! You are going to love it....

Norm: I know.

*Elysia: LOLOL!!!!! Hey, you can't dump me and still want sex...! Woof,
woof.*

Norm: Hey, I didn't dump you! You are already involved with others and I can't compete with that.

Elysia: I knoooooow, I guess we will just drive each other nuts with naughty thoughts. That's just your hormones and dick talking!

Norm: So my dick and hormones like your hormones and pussy ... nothing wrong with that!

Elysia: natural normal occurrence. But I'm glad you are not pissed at me over my relationship with Jake and Joelle.

Norm: I am not pissed off at you at all. If anything I am very appreciative of your honesty. How do you think most guys would react? Maybe a question to think about.

Elysia: Well, when I met you I wasn't looking or expecting a relationship and then it was there. I trusted you right away. So then I wanted to be honest with you. And now it feels like I have lost so much.

Norm: Lost what? Not me! I'm just some guy with a bad golf swing!

Elysia: Nope you are wrong there. You were so cute when you asked me out. You know, guys do NOT ask me out!

Norm: Maybe they are just scared of the hot babe in that sexy yellow bikini! I was nervous.

Elysia: I didn't know you were nervous. I thought you were a player.

Norm: just trying to be oh soooooo cool. Thx.

Elysia: Well, I'm glad to be talking to you. It means a lot to me. I need to go and take care of some patients.

Norm: Are you at WORK?

Elysia: Yes.

Norm: Yikes, I did not know that. I hope nobody is pushing the button!

Elysia: No, no the patients are ok so far. They are asleep. I have medicated them but want to check on them. Ok baby, good night. Kiss me!!!

Norm: I put that one on your pussy.

Elysia: Sweet kisses only for you, my prince.

Norm: Well done, you blond Xantippe!

Elysia: !!!!!! ?????

Norm: A female goddess who torments men!

Fifteen

COMFORT ZONE

SEE, I DIDN'T MAKE IT.
I DIDN'T MAKE IT OUT.
I TRIED THE TRY.
I TALKED THE TALK.
AND IN THE END,
I GAVE IN.

IF I CAN'T HAVE LOVE,
I WILL HAVE MONEY.
I WILL COUNT IT.
I WILL SPEND IT.
PAY THIS, PAY THAT.

IF I GO THERE
AND THERE,
I AM NOT HERE
AND HERE.
TO SEE DISAPPOINTED FACES.
TO HEAR THEIR TISK, TISK, TISK,
TIMELESS BIGOTRY.

I WILL MOVE FORWARD
SHADOWING NO ONE.
TOMORROW IS ANOTHER DAY.

I had been trying to quit escorting for years and years and years but it was really hard to give up all that power and all that money. Of course, then it came back to my question, my never-ending question, of why I felt I needed to do something else. I mean, sometimes I was completely okay with escorting and questioned if I really needed another job. Certainly I made enough money to live really well. Was I really only pretending to think I wanted another job because I was supposed to or because that's what people expected of me? Does society say it's so wrong to be a prostitute, so go be a dog catcher? It's more respectable? And be miserably poor, like everyone else!

Women have worked as prostitutes forever and in every kind of civilization and within every religion. If prostitution was such a bad business not that many women would continue to do it. Yet, unfortunately, prostitution remains a big shameful deal. Ever heard a man tell his wife he visits a hooker twice a month? Or a guy tell his girlfriend that while he is away on business he'll take care of his sexual needs with an escort? Yet it happens every day in every city and in every country of the world. If the perception of prostitution was positive, I certainly would have chosen to be open about it. I would have liked to have just been me: a professional escort. I mean, that's what I did. That's the way my life evolved. I have no regrets.

The general public believes prostitutes are victims, or drug addicts, or dirty, unintelligent, dysfunctional, self-destructive women with no other choices. Some are. But the escorts I know treat it as a business. Most escorts will agree that women are exotic creatures to the forever horny male. Men cannot resist the goddess in the woman that brings them sexual gratification. It's a power most women never learn to use. I use that power to make money and provide a valuable release for men's fantasies and desires. But I still can't add 'Escort' to my portfolio. I still can't proudly tell the women of a golf club's women's auxiliary that I'm a professional escort. That is why I choose to remain anonymous in this book. There are some things people do not need to know, and the stereotype the job escort incurs is not something I'm prepared to be branded with forever.

It's always been steps to go and be and try and maybe one day I'm going to get there. It's going to be peace, satisfaction, peace of mind, comfort, to be okay in my own skin where I don't need to have money. Where I don't need to have a boyfriend or a husband. I don't need to have all this stuff. I want to feel okay sitting by myself, no matter what profession or what situation. I'd like that.

With time I began to realize my need for drama and excitement in my life. I am not one of those women who is going to get married, settle down, live in the suburbs and have 2.5 children. The thought of that bores me to death even though the innocent little girl in me still sometimes wishes to make life simple by meeting the man of my dreams, becoming the little bride, having that baby and living happily ever after. The usual fairy tale. But I know it's an unrealistic old tape I have somewhere in my head. When I was a child, marriage, kids and the white picket fence was the acceptable expectation for growing up. I have struggled with that concept and now I know I'm not meant for that role. I have not made the choices I have, or that were made for me, or the universe has given me, to be led down that path.

I like travel, meeting new people, having different experiences and challenges. I accept that the stuff I attract in my life just comes. Sometimes I have a choice and sometimes it chooses me. I choose no other choice than to follow. I listen to my heart. I like life exciting. Perhaps my spontaneous side needs to ask myself more often: "Are you friggin' nuts?"

Realistically, since I was approaching age forty, I needed to think about my options. Like lots of people in any job, escorts are not particularly good at saving money, despite earning tons of it. They generally just spend it all. I freely admit I spent it all. It's like running sand through one's hands. Working girls have an addiction for money because it becomes the security that buys them a vacation, new clothes, the spa scene, a rental penthouse apartment, a sexy car, that new $1,500 purse, or whatever makes them feel acceptable. Most of the time, working girls are single or in dysfunctional relationships and they don't get what they need emotionally so they spend their money to get it. Having material stuff and looking good substitutes for love. Having said that, I know only one working girl who bought her own house, and the only other successful ex-escorts I know now own their own massage parlor businesses.

I was feeling a need for security. I wanted to buy an apartment of my own in a swanky part of the city. I wanted the stability of my own place. I decided I would quit escorting when I owned my own car and home and had a steady job. It was time to give nursing another try, but in the meantime I had to keep working where the money was. I needed a down payment. Eventually I planned to walk away from escorting and into the sunset sort of thing. Someday I would go back to university, work as a full-time nurse or maybe become a bookkeeper. I had options. I could live quite nicely, quite comfortably.

I had to have a job to get a mortgage. Once again I applied for a nursing job. The woman who interviewed me complimented me by saying that mine was the best interview she'd had in a long time. I felt hopeful. I was delighted when I got the job. I began working in a local hospital, part-time, and this time I liked my job. I was proud being a nurse, though it was shocking what I made as a nurse considering what I could make as an escort.

After working in the hospital for a year, the head nurse took me aside and said, "All the feedback I'm getting is really great. Everybody likes working with you. They think you're doing a great job. It's all really positive stuff. There are two full-time jobs available. One's yours, if you want it." I asked, "What's going to happen if I don't take one, if I just want to stay casual? Is that going to be a problem?" She said, "No, no problem at all. Stay casual or you can work full time. It's up to you."

I could do this, happily…

Except, it's really hard to give up all that power and all that money.

Eventually, I bought my own apartment in an up-scale part of town. I remodelled it to my specifications. My car is paid for. I have a closet full of beautiful clothes and accessories women would drool over. And I have money in the bank.

I am grateful for today.
I am grateful for my grandmother, my mother, my child somewhere.
I am grateful for the driving range with a friend today.
I am grateful that I am able to golf and move my body.
I am grateful for the chance to talk to someone new.
I am grateful he didn't hit on me.
I am grateful for choice and the freedom to choose.
I am grateful for opportunity to grow, learn and appreciate.
I am grateful for tomorrow and a chance to try again.

E-mail:
To: myself
The warmth of the hot afternoon sun feels good on my skin. The sound of the rolling ocean, quiet, peaceful, rocking me into sedation. At last I feel at peace and exactly where I want to be. Finally, happy to be me. With the setting sun glowing red and orange, the night brings to me an offering. Challenged to have patience, strength, and courage. I accept and am instantly swept away by the depths of emotion. A blessing. A curse. I know that I am changing. Growing as a woman, a person, a soul. Warm crystal water

washes over me. Cooling the fire inside ever so slightly. The feel of the night, the wind, the hand of God and inside my mind, my heart. Part of everything I am and everything I have ever dreamed to love.

*   *   *

Tom kept calling. I guess he was still in love with his image of me as his escort. So I provide him with a service and he still enjoys it enough to continue paying for my company. But then, we enjoy each other's company. He recently flew me down to attend a live play with him. We were sitting in our seats reading the program when, suddenly, I noticed a gold ring on his fourth finger on his left hand. Seeing a ring was a shock. I said, *"Oh my God, have you re-married?"* "Yes," he said. He hadn't bothered to tell me. After all the years we had been seeing each other, how could he treat getting married like a trip to the grocery store? Obviously we still don't really know each other. We still need to keep secrets *for* each other and *from* each other to protect the illusion.

About the Author

Ellen Thomsen was born and raised in California. After attending the University of British Columbia in Vancouver, Canada, she stayed in Canada choosing to raise a family while building a property rental company and writing short stories and poems for children.

Surprised when asked by Elysia to write this biography, Ellen informed her that she knew little about the lives of prostitutes, let alone the secret world of a high class one and was therefore not qualified. Despite this hesitancy, Elysia won her over.

Ellen turned that lack of knowledge into an advantage as she discovered this intriguing profession from the eyes of an outsider and asked the fundamentally curious questions we have all wanted to know about women - and men - in the sex trade business.

book blog site: www.illusionsbook.com

ISBN 142516966-X